OUR

LOST

NATIONAL

IDENTITY

To VAlenae

Good Luck

OUR
LOST
NATIONAL
IDENTITY

Tracing the Lineage of Israel's Lost Ten Tribes

JOHN PINKSTON

TATE PUBLISHING *& Enterprises*

This title is also available as a Tate Out Loud product. Visit www.tatepublishing.com for more information.

Scripture quotations are taken from the *Holy Bible, King James Version,* Cambridge, 1769. Used by permission. All rights reserved.

The opinions expressed by the author are not necessarily those of Tate Publishing, LLC.

Published by Tate Publishing & Enterprises, LLC
127 E. Trade Center Terrace | Mustang, Oklahoma 73064 USA
1.888.361.9473 | www.tatepublishing.com

Tate Publishing is committed to excellence in the publishing industry. The company reflects the philosophy established by the founders, based on Psalms 68:11,
"The Lord gave the word and great was the company of those who published it."

ISBN: 978-1-5988698-1-1
1. Biblical Studies: Commentaries: New   2. Biblical Studies: General Studies:
07.10.30

ACKNOWLEDGEMENTS

I would like to express my profound gratitude to those who helped in the research and development of this book. Specifically, I would like to recognize the long, hard labor my wife, Anita, contributed from the initial typing of manuscripts to the finalization of this work. Also, I would like to thank Rick Allen for the extensive research material he provided in this book's development. I would like to thank Kelli Carter, Ben Pellom and Jennifer Weyman for their proofing and editorial assistance.

TABLE OF CONTENTS

INTRODUCTION

For centuries, historians and theologians alike have mused over the question of whatever happened to the Ten Tribes of Israel that appeared to vanish from the scene in about 721 BC. The last recorded evidence of the existence of Israel as a nation in Bible history can be found in II Kings 17:22–24.

> For the children of Israel walked in all the sins of Jeroboam which he did; they departed not from them; Until the LORD removed Israel out of his sight, as he had said by all his servants the prophets. So was Israel carried away out of their own land to Assyria unto this day. And the king of Assyria brought men from Babylon, and from Cuthah, and from Ava, and from Hamath, and from Sepharvaim, and placed them in the cities of Samaria instead of the children of Israel: and they possessed Samaria, and dwelt in the cities thereof.

These three verses show the conclusion and end of the great empire of Israel which had enjoyed many of the blessings and successes originally promised to its father, Abraham. You will notice that God said He brought the nation to the end and took it captive because it continued in the sins of the first king of the Northern

Tribes of Israel, Jeroboam. The question might be asked, what did Jeroboam do that caused God to punish the nation in such a drastic way? A quick review of history, which led up to the events causing a separation between the ten Northern Tribes and the three Southern Tribes, can be found in I Kings 11:1–13.

> But King Solomon loved many foreign women, as well as the daughter of Pharaoh: women of the Moabites, Ammonites, Edomites, Sidonians, and Hittites—from the nations of whom the LORD had said to the children of Israel, You shall not intermarry with them, nor they with you. Surely they will turn away your hearts after their gods. Solomon clung to these in love. And he had seven hundred wives, princesses, and three hundred concubines; and his wives turned away his heart. For it was so, when Solomon was old, that his wives turned his heart after other gods; and his heart was not loyal to the LORD his God, as was the heart of his father David. For Solomon went after Ashtoreth the goddess of the Sidonians, and after Milcom the abomination of the Ammonites. Solomon did evil in the sight of the LORD, and did not fully follow the LORD, as did his father David. Then Solomon built a high place for Chemosh the abomination of Moab, on the hill that is east of Jerusalem, and for Molech the abomination of the people of Ammon. And he did likewise for all his foreign wives, who burned incense and sacrificed to their gods. So the LORD became angry with Solomon, because his heart had turned from the LORD God of Israel, who had appeared to him twice, and had commanded him concerning this thing, that he should not go after other gods; but he did not keep what the LORD had commanded. Therefore the LORD said to Solomon, Because you have done this, and have not kept My covenant and My statutes, which I have commanded you, I will surely tear the kingdom away from

you and give it to your servant. Nevertheless I will not do it in your days, for the sake of your father David; I will tear it out of the hand of your son. However I will not tear away the whole kingdom; I will give one tribe to your son for the sake of my servant David, and for the sake of Jerusalem which I have chosen.

You will notice that Solomon allowed himself to be swayed by his many wives to commit idolatry against God which resulted in God dividing the kingdom into two parts. However, God decided that He would not completely eliminate David's throne and chose to separate out one of the tribes, Judah, which would carry on David's throne.

And he said to Jeroboam, Take for yourself ten pieces, for thus says the LORD, the God of Israel: Behold, I will tear the kingdom out of the hand of Solomon and will give ten tribes to you but he shall have one tribe for the sake of My servant David, and for the sake of Jerusalem, the city which I have chosen out of all the tribes of Israel. (I Kings 11:31–32)

The city of Jerusalem was located within the territory of Benjamin since the settling of the Promised Land (Joshua 18:21, 28) so Benjamin stayed with Judah. After the split-up of Israel and Judah, it quickly became apparent that King Jeroboam was not going to continue using the Levites in their priestly roles. (I Kings 12:31) As a result of Jeroboam rejecting the Levites, they returned to Rehoboam and their service to the people in the Kingdom of Judah. This resulted in the Kingdom of Judah being made up of three tribes: Judah, Levi and Benjamin. Ten tribes remained with Jeroboam which made up the Northern Kingdom of Israel. The southern three tribes were known as the Kingdom of Judah.

The tribes of Benjamin and Levi aligned themselves with Judah and became national and religious Jews; they were commonly referred to as "Jews" from the nation of Judah. Just as today, people who live in the small nation of Israel are not all of the Jewish bloodline; they are considered national Jews when they become citizens of that nation. In fact, there are many different religious people living in the state of Israel today who would consider themselves Israelites, but who are not direct descendants of the father of the Jews, Judah, nor do they practice Judaism as their religion. This was also true when God split up the nation into the Northern Ten Tribes which He called Israel and the Southern Tribes which were later referred to as Judah; the tribes of the Northern Kingdom became known as Israel and the tribes of the Southern Kingdom became known as Judah.

After God anointed Jeroboam to be king over Israel, it wasn't long before Jeroboam turned away from God and caused the people to worship in a form of idolatry when he set up two golden calves in the area of Dan and Bethel.

> And Jeroboam said in his heart, Now shall the kingdom return to the house of David: If this people go up to do sacrifice in the house of the LORD at Jerusalem, then shall the heart of this people turn again unto their lord, even unto Rehoboam king of Judah, and they shall kill me, and go again to Rehoboam king of Judah. Whereupon the king took counsel, and made two calves of gold, and said unto them, It is too much for you to go up to Jerusalem: behold thy gods, O Israel, which brought thee up out of the land of Egypt. And he set the one in Bethel, and the other put he in Dan. And this thing became a sin: for the people went to worship before the one, even unto Dan. (I Kings 12:26–30)

With Jeroboam's idolatrous act, the seeds of Israel's national destruction that came 200 years later were sown. Unfortunately, as you study the scriptures of I and II Kings, you will find that the nation of Israel continued the idolatrous sin that was set up by Jeroboam until their sins were so horrible before God that the people caused their sons and daughters to be sacrificed upon the alter of idols.

> And they left all the commandments of the LORD their God, and made them molten images, even two calves, and made a grove, and worshipped all the host of heaven, and served Baal. And they caused their sons and their daughters to pass through the fire, and used divination and enchantments, and sold themselves to do evil in the sight of the LORD, to provoke him to anger. Therefore the LORD was very angry with Israel, and removed them out of his sight: there was none left but the tribe of Judah only. (II Kings 17:16–18)

Since the nation of Israel, under King Jeroboam, perverted the worship of the true God, the stage was set for a later introduction of Baal worship by King Ahab and his wife, Jezebel.

The signs God established between Israel and Himself were the Sabbath Day and physical circumcision of all the male children.

The fact is Israel turned away from God and embraced the god of the Sun, Baal, because they rejected the two identifying religious marks which were (1) the Sabbath Day, replacing it with the mark of the sun god, Sunday, and (2) circumcision. Stop and consider: one of the identifying marks of modern-day Jews is the fact that they continue to observe the Sabbath Day. The other identifier is the ritual of circumcision which has helped them maintain their identity, even though they were dispersed throughout all nations of the world on several occasions. Those of you who know Jews will think of them as those who worship on Saturday, the Sabbath Day, and those who circumcise their male children on the eighth day. A third identifying mark is the observing of clean and unclean meat/food laws of the Bible. All of these are signs that help to identify that particular group of people.

Over the history of the ten Northern Tribes of Israel, they slowly rejected all of these identifying marks, and as a result, when they were taken into captivity and dispersed throughout the tribes of the world, they lost the knowledge of their identity.

In this book, you will see the astonishing proof of the true identity of those people God calls "Israel." Religion, essentially Catholicism, in its effort to stamp out knowledge almost completely succeeded in destroying any trace of those people whom God calls *Israel*. Even today, most Christian religious leaders reject, without any foundation, the knowledge that clearly identifies Israel. The church, throughout the Dark Ages and over the years, has been so successful at hiding the evidence indicating where the Children of Israel went, that even those Israelites themselves no longer know who they are and, in fact, think they are "Gentiles." This perversion of knowledge has been so complete that even the Jews think they make up the totality of the nation of Israel. The Bible clearly shows that there were two nations, one called "Judah" made up of Jews, Levites and Benjaminites, and the other made up of the ten tribes God called "Israel."

To disclose their true identity, we will start at the beginning and show who the true Israelites are. Biblical prophecies are still to be fulfilled regarding these modern-day Israelites, even though they do not know who they are. A study of prophecy reveals that most prophecies in the Bible deal with the nations of Israel and Judah; the only time other nations are mentioned is in their relationship to Israel or Judah. The lack of knowledge that most Christians have regarding the true identity of Israel prevents them from ever understanding the true meaning of Biblical prophecy.

To understand prophecy, you must have the *key* to know about whom the prophecy is speaking. This book will give you that key and, as a result, you will be able to have a much better understanding of the prophecies found in the Old and New Testaments.

Most people have been taught erroneously that most of the prophecies of the Old Testament have been fulfilled and that this information was simply preserved to enhance the faith of devout men. We have also been led to suppose that the unfulfilled prophecies of "Moses and the Prophets" were of no special concern to

Christianity after that great momentous event—the Coming of the Savior. Consequently, when Christian scholars come across some prophetic utterance which they are forced to admit has not yet become an historical fact, they invent all sorts of scenarios to explain away the discrepancy.

The Bible is approximately one-third prophecy, most of which has not yet been fulfilled.

ABRAHAM, THE PATRIARCH

Most people who read the Bible read it very casually and pay little attention to the content of the material being presented. However, the Bible is filled with facts and vital information which, if read with understanding, provides all of the answers to the meaning of life and what the future holds for mankind, as well as holding many clues to the location of the Lost Tribes of Israel.

Since this literary work is about the peoples of Israel, we will therefore begin with the father of all of the Israelites, Abraham.

Most people do not know that God made two covenants with Abraham; one while he was still named Abram and the other after his name was changed. God changed the name of Abram to Abraham, meaning "a father of many nations." The name also symbolized the new character and a better, unconditional covenant that God intended to carry out with the descendants of Abraham through Jacob, whose name was changed to *Israel*. The fact that this covenant became unconditional plays a major role in helping us to understand who the Israelites are.

The first covenant is found in Genesis 13:14–17.

> And the LORD said unto Abram, after that Lot was separated from him, Lift up now thine eyes, and look from the place where thou art northward, and southward, and eastward, and westward: For all the land which thou seest, to thee will I give it, and to thy seed for ever. And I will make thy seed as the dust of the earth: so that if a man can number the dust of the

earth, then shall thy seed also be numbered. Arise, walk through the land in the length of it and in the breadth of it; for I will give it unto thee.

Notice God was promising Abraham that his descendants would be like the stars of the sky and the dust of the earth; this means that these people would not be a few, but would literally be billions of people over the ages. Again, God repeated this first covenant in Genesis 15:5–6, "And he brought him forth abroad, and said, Look now toward heaven, and tell the stars, if thou be able to number them: and he said unto him, So shall thy seed be. And he believed in the LORD; and he counted it to him for righteousness."

Abram believed God and it was counted as "righteousness" for him. "For if Abraham were justified by works, he hath whereof to glory; but not before God. For what saith the scripture? Abraham believed God, and it was counted unto him for righteousness." (Romans 4:2–3)

What this means is that Abram had faith that God would, in fact, do what He said. Again, God restates this first covenant in Genesis 17:1, "And when Abram was ninety years old and nine, the LORD appeared to Abram, and said unto him, I am the Almighty God; walk before me, and be thou perfect."

UNCONDITIONAL PROMISE

But God said that this promise was conditional upon Abraham walking in the way that God would instruct him. Therefore, God told Abram that, if he would obey and follow Him, then God would do all of these marvelous things He stated in the covenant. Again, we see the covenant restated in Genesis 17: 2–5.

And I will make my covenant between me and thee, and will multiply thee exceedingly. And Abram fell on his face: and God talked with him, saying, As for me, behold, my covenant is with thee, and thou shalt be a father of many nations. Neither shall thy name any more be called Abram, but thy name shall be Abraham; for a father of many nations have I made thee.

As the story goes, Abram had two sons. The first son, Ishmael, was not the son that God intended to raise up as the nation of Israel, but it was to be the son, Isaac, whom Sarah, the wife and love of Abram's life, bore. As Isaac grew, God put Abram to one final test to see if, in fact, he would follow God's instructions. In Genesis 22, God instructed Abram to sacrifice his son, Isaac. Abram obediently followed God's instructions and only at the last moment did God intervene to stop Abram from killing his only son of promise, Isaac. Once God saw that Abram was totally committed to Him, God changed the conditions of the covenant as we find stated in Genesis 22:16–18.

> And said, By myself have I sworn, saith the LORD, for because thou hast done this thing, and hast not withheld thy son, thine only son: That in blessing I will bless thee, and in multiplying I will multiply thy seed as the stars of the heaven, and as the sand which is upon the sea shore; and thy seed shall possess the gate of his enemies; And in thy seed shall all the nations of the earth be blessed; because thou hast obeyed my voice.

At this point, God made His promise of national greatness to the descendants of Abram unconditional because of Abram's obedience. It was at this point that Abram's name was changed to *Abraham.*

Did you get that? Unconditional! Now God would do what He promised with Abraham's descendants no matter what Abraham's descendants did regarding obedience. God cannot lie and He gave His Word that He would bless Abraham's descendants no matter what. This is a key factor in understanding who the Israelites are.

The great majority of Bible students and schools of Biblical thought totally overlook the fact that God, when making this covenant with Abraham, promised that he should become the father of more than one nation. The general trend of teaching is that, of all the people who dwelt upon the face of the earth, the Jewish people are distinctly those people, the one nation, which composes all the descendants of Abraham. Of course, the world also recognizes that the Arabs are the descendants of Abraham through Ishmael, but they are not Israelites. The fact that people overlook the statement that God said, "You will be the father of many nations," causes colossal confusion in most Biblical students' understanding regarding the difference between the Jews and the Israelites.

For emphasis, let me restate that the second covenant was given to Abraham as totally unconditional. That is, the Lord has promised, irrespective of the moral or spiritual character of the people themselves, to increase the prosperity of Abraham's descendants through Jacob. Because his name was later changed to Israel, his descendants are known to this day as the "children of Israel."

God restated this unconditional promise and covenant to the next generation when the statement was made to Rebekah, the wife of Isaac. Genesis 24:60, "And they blessed Rebekah, and said unto her, Thou art our sister, be thou the mother of thousands of millions, and let thy seed possess the gate of those which hate them." Just as before, God promises that Isaac and Rebekah's descendants would possess the gates, or the entrances, to the nations who hate Israel.

In the next generation following Isaac, we find that this blessing and covenant promise that God made to Abraham and Isaac was passed on to Jacob, Isaac's son.

> And God Almighty bless thee, and make thee fruitful, and multiply thee, that thou mayest be a multitude of people; And give thee the blessing of Abraham, to thee, and to thy seed with thee; that thou mayest inherit the land wherein thou art a stranger, which God gave unto Abraham. (Genesis 28:3–4)

You will notice that this blessing and promise given to Abraham was passed to the third generation, Jacob.

JACOB'S FAMILY

The fulfillment of the promise made to Abraham could not possibly have been through the Jews or the Arabs. Remember, the Arabs descended from Abraham through his son Ishmael whose mother was Hagar, Sarah's handmaiden. In fact, Hagar's son, Ishmael, did become a great nation because he was Abraham's seed. Twelve sons were born to Ishmael and today we know them as the Arabs. But, they were not to receive the blessings. (Genesis 25)

It was not until the Twentieth Century that God finally fulfilled His promise to Ishmael when oil was discovered under the Arab lands. Since World War II, the princes who lead the various Arab nations have become exceedingly rich and powerful on the world scene. But God plainly shows in the scripture that Ishmael was not to receive the more abundant blessing that was reserved for Abraham's son, Isaac. (Genesis 17:21)

God's promise that Abraham's descendants would be as numerous as the sand of the sea or the stars in the sky would eliminate any possibility that this promise was fulfilled in only the Jews or the Arabs. Neither of these groups of people has grown into a great nation or an overwhelming multitude of people. Therefore, we must consider the totality of this promise and look beyond the Jews and Arabs for the fulfillment of this prophecy. "And he brought him forth abroad, and said, Look now toward heaven, and tell the stars, if thou be able to number them: and he said unto him, So shall thy seed be." (Genesis 15:5)

God also promised Abraham that his descendants would possess the gates of their enemies. "That in blessing I will bless thee, and in multiplying I will multiply thy seed as the stars of the heavens, and as the sand which is upon the sea shore; and thy seed shall possess the gate of his enemies." (Genesis 22:17)

If you understand the meaning of this blessing, it will further help you identify where the modern-day descendants of the ancient Israelites reside. This statement concerning "possessing the gates of their enemies" has been fulfilled in a multitude of ways. The phrase "gates of their enemies" refers to controlling the land and sea access to nations with whom they engage in commerce or warfare. The British colonized and developed their holdings around the globe, finally attaining the status of a major empire. A study of any pre-World War II map of the world shows that the British controlled land masses all across the globe. It was said, when I was a child in school, that the "sun never set on the British Empire." Of course, the meaning of this phrase was that the empire extended around the globe; therefore, the sun was shining on some part of the empire twenty-four hours per day. Victorian furniture even carried the theme. Tables, couches, and even bathtubs were created with "ball and claw feet" or "ball and lion feet," indicating that England ruled the world; the ball representing the world and the claw or lion's paw representing England.

The British Isles, lying offshore of the continent of Europe, were able to secure the waterway known as the English Channel between Europe and Britain. As a result, they controlled the gateway into Europe through the ports of Holland, France, Spain and the Scandinavian countries. The physical location of the British Isles has played an important and decisive part in the course of history throughout both of the World Wars!

When you also consider the vast territory under British control which produced many of the natural resources necessary for an industrialized country to operate, it provides an awesome array of controlling factors over their enemies. Take, for instance, the natural resources of Canada, Australia, New Zealand and South Africa, and their rich deposits of minerals and other natural resources.

The British Century truly was the Nineteenth Century, as can be seen by Britain controlling many other nations such as India, Egypt, the Anglo-Egyptian Sudan area, and many of the nations including those of eastern Africa. In addition, Britain had control of the Palestinian area, the Trans-Jordan area, Malta, Crete, the Suez Canal, the Khyber Pass, Singapore, the straits of Malacca, Hong Kong, and the Gilbert and Solomon Islands. In the Atlantic, Britain controlled the Hebrides, Falklands, Bermuda, Bahamas, and Cayman Islands.

The Twentieth Century is said to be the American Century. Where Britain left off controlling the world, the Americas picked up. Under President Teddy Roosevelt's slogan of "speak softly, but carry a big stick," America gained control of several of the Caribbean Islands, including Cuba; she also constructed the Panama Canal, controlling all sea trade between the Atlantic and Pacific Oceans, through the tiny isthmus of Panama.

During the Twentieth Century, two allied nations were able to influence the outcome of World War II because of their ability to control the flow of raw material resources, thereby preventing their enemies from gaining the upper hand during the war. Oil, iron, and other essential raw materials that the Axis powers needed in order to successfully fight their battles were greatly restricted because of Britain and America controlling most of the sea lanes and overland routes leading to Germany and Japan. The Suez Canal, the Rock of Gibraltar, the Panama Canal, and the domination of the Far East by Britain, America, Australia and New Zealand severely interrupted the flow of raw materials to the Axis powers during World War II.

The power of the United States of America proves that our nation has become the greatest nation in all history. The American economic system today is essentially in control of all the economies of all the nations of the entire world. If the American economy is booming, the rest of the world can also be prosperous. Conversely, if the American economy is suffering, the entire world will be suffering.

The strategic location of the United States itself plays an important role in controlling the gates of our enemies. During the Twentieth Century, America has virtually controlled every important sea gate and strategic island defense in the western hemisphere, as well as the Far East. The Pacific has been protected due to the stepping stone islands of Midway, Guam and Wake, and our fiftieth state, Hawaii. Also included are the Aleutian Islands which have served to alert us to the movements of the former Soviet Navy.

In addition to our economic prowess, America also possesses some of the largest deposits of mineral wealth and natural resources in the world.

One might well point to the Roman Empire as being the greatest empire ever known. However, you must remember the Roman Empire only affected the regions immediately surrounding the Mediterranean Sea and parts of Britain. Even though the Roman Empire exerted great influence over central Europe, it had no effect on any part of the western hemisphere, separated by the Atlantic Ocean or the far eastern empires of China, Japan, and India. Its power could never approach the power that Britain exerted in the Nineteenth Century and now a power even greater, as seen by the American Empire of the Twentieth Century. America today has the ability to affect and control the world through its economic and military power.

According to *Jane's Encyclopedia of Aviation,* the American aviation industry is a good example of our dominance over all other world powers. Most countries, including our former and present enemies, fly commercial planes built in American manufacturing plants. Over 90% of all aircraft avionics essential for safe operations are built either by American companies or their subsidiaries for the world's aircraft. English is the international language of aviation. No matter what country you fly into, the international language of the pilots and ground controllers is English and no other. The American political, economic and social structures are the dominant factors in the world today. Immigrants from around the world consider America the "land of opportunity." Third world immigrants do everything in their power to reach the American shores for a new life. Communism failed simply because the people under communism came to see how much better life was in America than in the communist countries. The "information revolution" rang out the "death knell" of communism in the Old Soviet Union. Television and computers based in America became the vehicle by which the citizens of the Soviet Empire demanded a change. America controlled the gates of their enemies and the result was that the Berlin Wall fell and the *communist empire* crumbled!

God promised Abraham and his descendants that they would control the gates of their enemies. We can now look back on history and see that God continues to fulfill this promise to Abraham's descendants—Great Britain and the United States.

When, throughout all recorded history, have the Jews or the Arabs ever possessed the "gates" or "entrances" to the nations of their enemies? The answer is never! Furthermore, God also said that, through Abraham's descendants, all the nations of the earth would be blessed. (Genesis 22:18)

God not only made these promises to Abraham and Sarah, but He also passed the same promise down to Isaac and his wife Rebekah. In Genesis 24, Rebekah was blessed by her kinfolk and they were inspired to deliver a blessing from God. This blessing indicated that she would be the mother of thousands of millions, and that her descendants would possess the gates of those who hate them. (Genesis 24:60) These verses prove that God passed the same blessings from Abraham down to his son, Isaac, and his wife, Rebekah. Abraham gave all of his possessions, which was the *birthright,* to his son, Isaac. "Abraham gave all that he had unto Isaac." (Genesis 25:5)

TWO SONS

Isaac and Rebekah had two sons, Jacob and Esau. The oldest son, Esau, had a different lifestyle from that of Jacob. Esau was a huntsman and a man who liked living in the wild. Jacob, on the other hand, was a young man who devoted himself to learning trades concerning farming and animal husbandry. In time, Isaac grew old and Jacob's mother, Rebekah, became concerned about his inheritance. Rebekah devised a plan by which Jacob would receive the birthright in place of his older brother Esau.

The birthright was an extremely important blessing; Rebekah wanted it for her son, Jacob, even though he was not the eligible child. The birthright implies that which comes by "right of birth," or an inheritance a father passes down to his firstborn son. Rebekah understood that the promises God had made to Abraham and Isaac would pass with the birthright to the next son. That birthright included God's promise, "I will make thee exceedingly fruitful, and I will make nations of thee;" The birthright also included the promise from God which said He would make a royal line out of Abraham's descendants, "Kings shall come out of thee." Therefore, these promises God made to Abraham would also be part of the birthright passed down from generation to generation.

Esau was next in line of succession to receive the birthright from Isaac. Jacob was actually Esau's twin, but he was born after Esau. Even today, the law recognizes the firstborn son, in many cases, as the rightful heir to his father's possessions. This tradition of passing from father to eldest son, called *primogeniture,* has been upheld throughout the history of Israel and its descendants.

Esau had the right to dispose of his birthright in any way he pleased. He was an impetuous young man and did not consider the birthright an important possession. The scripture tells of a day when Esau was extremely hungry. At that time, Jacob was preparing a meal which Esau greatly desired. As a result, Esau was willing to sell his birthright to Jacob for the instant gratification of a "hot" meal. (Genesis 25:27–34) This certainly indicates Esau's lack of understanding of the birthright, and the lack of importance he attached to it.

As Isaac grew older, Rebekah conspired with Jacob to make sure that he would receive the birthright blessing. Genesis 27 records that Rebekah took full responsibility for deceiving Isaac. (Verse 13) Jacob went along with the plan and Rebekah prepared a meal for his father; while serving this meal, Jacob claimed that he was Esau, the firstborn son. Isaac suspected something was wrong and he asked Jacob directly if he was Esau. (Verse 24) However, this did not fully convince Isaac, because he noticed some differences in the voice claiming to be Esau. At this point in Isaac's life, he was blind and unable to distinguish by sight with whom he was speaking. Isaac asked that Jacob come closer to him so that he might feel him and smell him to make sure he was speaking to his son, Esau.

The trick worked and Jacob supplanted Esau and received Isaac's birthright blessing. (Genesis 27:27–29) Later, Esau came to receive his birthright blessing from Isaac only to find that Jacob had beaten him to the punch. (Genesis 27:35–36)

The birthright blessing had now passed to Jacob, but don't forget, Esau had already sold that blessing to Jacob for a mere bowl of soup. As a result, God honored that transfer of the birthright blessing from Esau to Jacob and it was confirmed by Isaac bestowing upon Jacob the birthright blessing. Isaac also blessed Esau, but his blessing could not come close to the birthright blessing that Jacob had received.

The birthright included the blessings and the promises God had made to Abraham and Isaac alike. Now, Jacob received the birthright with all of the blessings and promises God had made to his grandfather and father. As a result of this deception, Jacob was forced to leave home, and Rebekah and Jacob never saw each other again.

JACOB'S DREAM

Jacob traveled far from home to Rebekah's relatives in Padanaram.

He was on his way to the home of his Uncle Laban, the brother of Rebekah. (Genesis 28:5) As night came, he stopped for the night, sleeping under the stars. There he found a rock which he used for a pillow. That night he had a dream of a ladder reaching all the way to heaven, with angels moving up and down the ladder. Then God spoke to him in the dream.

> And, behold, the LORD stood above it, and said, I am the LORD God of Abraham thy father, and the God of Isaac: the land whereon thou liest, to thee will I give it, and to thy seed; And thy seed shall be as the dust of the earth, and thou shalt spread abroad to the west, and to the east, and to the north, and to the south: and in thee and in thy seed shall all the families of the earth be blessed. And, behold, I am with thee, and will keep thee in all places whither thou goest, and will bring thee again into this land; for I will not leave thee, until I have done that which I have spoken to thee of. (Genesis 28:13–15)

After Jacob received this tremendous promise concerning his descendants, he awoke and realized that God had been there while he slept reaffirming the promise. As a result, Jacob took the stone he had been using as a pillow, and set it up as a pillar, a memorial to this great blessing God had extended to him. Jacob anointed the stone with oil and made a vow to God that, if God would take care of him and provide for his needs, he would honor God with a tenth of all of his earnings—a tithe. Jacob called the place Bethel, which means God's House. Believe it or not, this stone Jacob anointed plays a very important part in our being able to identify the modern-day descendants of the ancient Israelites. This pillar, known as Jacob's Pillar, will appear over and over in the history of ancient Israel and, even today, in the descendants of those ancient Israelites.

JACOB IS DECEIVED

Laban welcomed Jacob into his family. After Jacob had worked for a month with no wages, Laban asked what kind of wages Jacob would like to receive for his labor. Rachel, the younger daughter of Laban, caught Jacob's eye, and he fell in love with this beautiful, "well-favored" young woman. Jacob said he would work for Laban seven years for the hand of Rachel and Laban agreed. Genesis 29:18, "And Jacob loved Rachel; and said, I will serve thee seven years for Rachel thy younger daughter."

After seven years of toil, "which seemed unto him as a few days for the love he had for Rachel," a great wedding feast was held and Jacob thought he now had the love of his life! Later, after the wedding night, Jacob found that Laban had *deceived* him and he had, in fact, married Leah, the older daughter. Verse 25, "And it came to pass, that in the morning, behold, it was Leah: and he said to Laban, What is this thou hast done unto me? did not I serve with thee for Rachel? wherefore then hast thou beguiled me?"

No doubt, Jacob was irate over this deception; perhaps he thought about how he had deceived his father, Isaac, seven or eight years before. Laban told Jacob that, in their country, it was customary for the oldest daughter to marry before the younger.

Jacob had prospered while working for Laban and, therefore, Laban too had prospered. Jacob bargained once again for the hand of Rachel. Laban agreed to give him Rachel if Jacob would commit to another seven years of labor. Laban first insisted that Jacob spend a week with Leah before giving Rachel to Jacob. Jacob, loving Rachel, quickly agreed to these terms. And now, Jacob had two wives. But Jacob loved Rachel.

Because God saw that Jacob did not love Leah, He opened Leah's womb to conceive a child for Jacob and they named that child Reuben. (Genesis 29:32) Soon, Leah bore another son, Simeon. (Verse 33) In a period of time, she conceived again and bore him another son named Levi. (Verse34) After an appropriate time, she again conceived and gave Jacob a fourth child named Judah. (Verse 35) Leah had four sons, but Rachel did not have a single child.

In those days, a woman felt great shame and became very down-hearted if she was barren. As a result, Rachel, while seeing her sister bearing these children, began to envy her, even though Rachel was the one Jacob loved. Rachel devised a plan to send her handmaiden, Bilhah, to Jacob that she might bear a child in Rachel's stead. It worked and Bilhah bore Jacob's fifth son who was named Dan. (Genesis 30:6) Bilhah, once again, was sent to Jacob by Rachel and she conceived another son whose name became Naphtali. (Verse 8)

As a result of Rachel sending her handmaiden to Jacob to bear sons, Leah then became jealous and also gave her handmaiden, Zilpah, to Jacob to conceive a child. Sure enough, Zilpah bore a child and his name was Gad. (Verse 11) After a while, Zilpah again conceived a son for Jacob and his name was called Asher. (Verse 13) Later on, Leah, who had been very fruitful, bore her fifth son, whose name was Issachar; later, she bore her sixth son and called him Zebulun; then a daughter, Dinah. (Verses 17–21)

By now, Rachel felt extremely down-hearted over the fact that she had witnessed Leah, Bilhah, and Zilpah bear Jacob ten sons. No doubt, Rachel was very discouraged over these births and she prayed that God would remember her and give her sons for Jacob. God did not forget and, after a time, Jacob and Rachel bore a son whose name was Joseph. (Genesis 30:22–24)

After the birth of Joseph, Jacob asked Laban to let him go to his own country and find his own place. (Genesis 30:25) Laban did not want him to go because Jacob's blessings had spilled over onto Laban and he very well knew it. He had become rich during the years Jacob worked for him. Jacob agreed to stay and work for a herd of cattle and finally, when God told him to leave that country and return to the land of his father, Isaac, he felt he had to leave secretly. (Genesis 31:13) Jacob told his wives to prepare to leave. Rachel stole some of the family treasures. (Genesis 31:19) After three days, Laban became aware that Jacob had left with Rachel, Leah and all of Laban's grandsons and granddaughter. Laban chased Jacob in hot pursuit; when he reached him, he accused him of leaving secretly and stealing some of his family treasures. Jacob said that whoever had stolen the treasures would not live. He never would have said this had he known it was his beloved Rachel. (Genesis 31:32)

JACOB'S NAME IS CHANGED

God told Jacob to go back to his own land, perhaps to see Isaac before he died. He heard that Esau was in the area and Jacob felt he should send Esau gifts in hopes of seeking Esau's forgiveness for past trespasses against him. The night before he met Esau, Jacob had an encounter with someone which resulted in his name being changed from *Jacob,* meaning "the supplanter." Perhaps Jacob was having a restless night, knowing Esau would meet him tomorrow, but when Jacob was left alone, he encountered an individual who wrestled with him for an entire night. When his wrestling partner determined that the bout was about over and decided to end it, Jacob would not let him go until this individual blessed him before departing. (Genesis 32:24–28) The blessing is as follows: Verse 28, "And he said, Thy name shall be called no more Jacob, but *Israel:* for as a prince hast thou power with God and with men, and hast prevailed."

From this point on, Jacob had a new name, Israel, which actually is translated as "a prince of God." God repeated this name change to Jacob when He appeared to him as he came again to Bethel. "And God said unto him, Thy name is Jacob: thy name shall not be called any more Jacob, but Israel shall be thy name: and he called his name *Israel.*" (Genesis 35:10)

Not only did God change his name from Jacob to Israel, but He restated the promise He had made to Abraham and Isaac— that Jacob's descendants would become great nations and, out of his loins, kings would be produced throughout all the generations. (Genesis 35:11–12) In Bethel, Jacob again anointed the pillar, the same stone he had anointed many years ago.

Later during this journey, when Rachel was ready to bear her second son, Jacob's beloved wife lost her life because of the vow Jacob made to Laban concerning the articles Rachel had taken. Rachel was truly the first and great love that Jacob had. As a result, these two sons of Rachel, Joseph and Benjamin, became his favorite among all of his children. Jacob buried his beloved Rachel in the place we now call Bethlehem. (Genesis 35:19)

Shortly thereafter, Jacob lost his father, Isaac, who died at the age of 180 years in Mamre, the city of Arba, later becoming known as Hebron. Sarah and Abraham were also buried in Mamre.

Now, Jacob/Israel set the stage for the twelve tribes of Israel. They are, in order of their birth, as follows: Reuben, Simeon, Levi, Judah, Dan, Naphtali, Gad, Asher, Issachar, Zebulun, Joseph, Benjamin. These are the twelve sons of Israel, for whom the twelve tribes are named!

Though Jacob's name was *changed to Israel,* this book will continue to use *Jacob* and *Israel* interchangeably and sometimes Jacob/Israel for emphasis.

JACOB'S NIGHTMARE

Joseph and Benjamin were much younger than the rest of the brothers and Jacob paid special attention and showed extra love to these two boys out of memory for his beloved Rachel. Because Jacob showed favoritism toward Joseph, his other brothers became intensely jealous of this special young man whom Jacob loved above the rest.

Jacob and his sons became extremely prosperous, possessing many animals and riches. However, Jacob's family was not without problems which caused embarrassment to his family and great heartache to him.

Jacob's family lived and prospered in the land of Canaan for several years. When Joseph was seventeen years old, Jacob had a beautiful coat of many colors made for him. This coat would have looked something like the plaid colors of the highlands of Scotland.

Jacob loved Joseph because he was the firstborn of Rachel, born during his old age. When Jacob gave this beautiful coat to Joseph, it incensed his brothers because evidently they did not receive this special treatment. To add to their misgivings about Joseph, he related a dream to his brothers that further incensed them, causing their jealousy to turn to hate. These dreams Joseph told indicated that his brothers, and even his father, would at some time bow down to him. (Genesis 37:5–11)

Another reason Jacob loved Joseph was because he could depend on him. Joseph was a willing helper. His father made him an overseer, even at his young age. (Genesis 37:13–14) One day, when Joseph was sent out to check on his brothers, he was unable to find them while they were tending their flocks. Unknown to Joseph, his brothers conspired to kill him, but Reuben, the oldest brother, proposed that they throw Joseph into a pit. Hoping to prevent the rest from killing Joseph, Reuben thought he would return later, rescue the lad and reunite Joseph with his father. After searching for them, Joseph found his brothers and he appeared wearing that beautiful coat of many colors that Jacob had made for him. Seeing the colorful coat which symbolized to them the status which Joseph had and realizing that he was there to check up on them made them even more jealous. They did as Reuben suggested and threw Joseph into a dry pit.

As they looked in the distance, they saw a caravan of merchants going to Egypt. Judah said it might be better to sell Joseph into slavery rather than kill their brother.

So, Joseph was sold to a traveling caravan headed for Egypt. The other ten brothers concocted a story that Joseph had been slain by a wild animal. They had smeared blood on Joseph's coat to offer proof that he had been slain by a wild animal. They brought this coat with the blood all over it to their aged father, with the awful tale that Joseph had been killed.

When Jacob heard the news, he tore his clothes and put on sackcloth as he mourned for his beloved son. In fact, the scripture says that all of his sons and daughters rose up to comfort him, but he could not be comforted. He believed that he would die in mourning over his beloved lost son.

It was necessary for Joseph to go into Egypt for the salvation of his father and his brothers. In the beginning, Joseph was subjected to the life of a slave for many years.

Meanwhile, the family continued to prosper, and Israel's sons sired children, increasing the family to a sizeable number of people.

THE SCARLET THREAD

Before we pick up the story of Joseph, we should pause to introduce the story of one of Israel's other sons, Judah. The story will help trace the lineage of the tribe of Judah.

According to Genesis 38, Judah married a Canaanite woman by the name of Shuah, who bore him three sons—Er, Onan and Shelah. (Genesis 38:1–5) Finally, the first son, Er, grew up and Judah chose a wife for Er named Tamar. (Verse 6) Er was a very wicked young man in the sight of God and God slew him because of his wickedness. According to the custom of the time, Judah's second son was to take Tamar for his wife and raise up a child so that Er's posterity would not end. However, Onan chose not to father a child with Tamar. As a result, God was actually displeased with this situation and slew Onan. (Verses 8–10)

Judah spoke to Tamar and promised her his youngest son once he grew of age to be her husband. While Tamar was waiting for Shelah to grow of age, she returned to her father's house to live.

After many years, Judah's wife, Shuah, also died. Judah went with the sheepshearers to Timnath. Tamar learned of Judah coming to her area to shear sheep. Tamar, unhappy because she did not have a child, decided to take matters into her own hands. She pretended to be a harlot to entice Judah.

> When Judah saw her, he thought her to be a harlot; because she had covered her face. And he turned unto her by the way, and said, "Go to, I pray thee, let me come in unto thee;" (for he knew not that she was his daughter in law.) And she said, "What wilt thou give me, that thou mayest come in unto me?" And he said, "I will send thee a kid from the flock." And she said, "Wilt thou give me a pledge, till thou send it?" (Genesis 38:15–17)

However, Tamar was not happy. Since Judah did not have the price for her with him, he agreed to give Tamar a pledge until her price was paid. "And he said, What pledge shall I give thee? And she said, Thy signet, and thy bracelets, and thy staff that is in thine hand. And he gave it her, and came in unto her, and she conceived by him." (Genesis 38:18–20)

When Judah sent his men with the goat to pay Tamar for her services, Judah's men could not find her and returned home.

After three months, Judah was told that Tamar, his daughter-in-law, had played the harlot and now she was pregnant as a result of the whoredom. She was brought to Judah so that he could determine what should be done with her. When Tamar was presented to Judah, she produced the signet and bracelets Judah had given her as a pledge. Judah acknowledged his sin realizing that Tamar had done this thing because Judah's sons had not fulfilled their duty of providing an heir for the sake of her dead husband.

Here, the plot thickens. In verse 27, it shows that, at the end of her nine months, she was about to give birth to twins. Apparently, the hand of one of the twins protruded as if that child would be the firstborn. The midwife tied a scarlet thread around the hand which protruded first. (Verse 28) However, it turned out that the other baby was born first. His name was called *Pharez*. (Verse 29) The midwife said this would cause a breach between the two brothers. Immediately after Pharez was born, *Zarah* was born with the thread around his wrist. (Verse 30) This red thread around the wrist of Zarah is extremely important because we will see it become one of the identifying marks upon this branch of Judah's descendants.

Notice that these two sons then became Judah's descendants. Pharez and Zarah will play an important part in helping to identify Judah's modern-day descendants and where the Israelites ultimately migrated.

JOSEPH IN EGYPT

Joseph's ten brothers sold Joseph to a caravan of Midianite traders for twenty pieces of silver rather than kill him. The Midianites took Joseph to Egypt and there they sold him to Potiphar, an officer of Pharaoh's army and captain of the guard.

GOD'S PLAN SPRINGS INTO ACTION

Even though Joseph had been sold into slavery in Egypt, God was with him and Joseph prospered in the house of his Egyptian master, Potiphar. It wasn't long until Potiphar began to recognize that whatever Joseph set his hand to do, God prospered him. As a result, Joseph found much favor in Potiphar's sight to the point that Joseph was made overseer of Potiphar's house and all that he had. God continued to bless the Egyptian's house because Joseph was part of it.

As Joseph became more familiar with Potiphar's affairs, he was to face his first major challenge which came from an unexpected source. The wife of Potiphar began to lust for Joseph and she began to throw herself at him in order to entice him into an illicit love affair. Joseph displayed incredible character that must have greatly pleased God because he was able to say "No" to the advances of Potiphar's wife. However, she was a persistent woman and time and again, she tried to entice Joseph through every wile available to her to enter into an illicit sexual affair while her husband was away.

There is an old saying that "there is no wrath like that of a woman spurned." Unfortunately, the wrath of this woman almost proved to be his undoing, even though he was totally innocent. When Potiphar's wife realized that Joseph would not become sexually involved with her, her rage was so great that she tore at his garment and he fled, leaving the garment in her hand. In her rage, she called for the men of the house and accused Joseph of attacking her with the intention of rape. Potiphar, who could have Joseph killed, decided to put him in prison and strip him of all his worldly goods and personal prestige. "And Joseph's master took him, and put him into the prison, a place where the king's prisoners were bound: and he was there in the prison." (Genesis 39:20)

Even in prison, Joseph's lifestyle and his exceptional character were noticed by the keeper of the prison and soon he became a trustee of the prison and all the prisoners were committed to his care.

GOD TURNS A BAD SITUATION INTO A BLESSING

While Joseph was in prison, the king's baker and butler had offended Pharaoh and had also been cast into prison. The captain of the guard put Joseph in charge of the baker and butler while they were there. As time went by, the baker and the butler each had a dream. Each man dreamed about his own situation, causing concern and puzzlement. Joseph observed their countenances and recognized that these men were depressed. Then Joseph asked Pharaoh's officers what their problems were. They related the dreams, but did not understand what they meant. "Do not interpretations belong to God? Tell me them, I pray you." (Genesis 40:8) The butler had a dream about a grapevine from which a cup of wine was made which the butler gave to Pharaoh. Joseph explained that the dream actually meant that in three days the butler would be restored to his former position as a wine taster and butler to the Pharaoh. (Genesis 40:9–13)

Joseph asked the butler to remember him when he was restored to his position of authority in Pharaoh's court. The dream came true, the butler was restored to his former position, but he forgot all about Joseph when he went about his courtly duties.

Observing this was the chief baker who saw that the interpretation of this dream by Joseph was good. Therefore, he, too, related his dream to Joseph for an interpretation. Joseph told him that in three days his dream would also come true; the dream resulted in his being hanged for treachery against Pharaoh.

After two years, the Pharaoh had a dream which troubled him. (Genesis 41:1–7) He called for all the magicians and wise men of Egypt, recounted his dream to all of them, but none of them could interpret it. After a time, the chief butler remembered the young man in prison who was an interpreter of dreams. The butler told Pharaoh about the young Hebrew who had interpreted his dream and that of the baker, and that both had occurred just as this young Hebrew prisoner had said.

Pharaoh sent for Joseph to interpret his dream. After hearing the dream, Joseph explained what Pharaoh's dream meant.

> And Joseph said unto Pharaoh, The dream of Pharaoh is one: God hath shewed Pharaoh what he is about to do. The seven good kine are seven years; and the seven good ears are seven years: the dream is one. And the seven thin and ill favoured kine that came up after them are seven years; and the seven empty ears blasted with the east wind shall be seven years of famine. This is the thing which I have spoken unto Pharaoh: What God is about to do he sheweth unto Pharaoh. Behold, there come seven years of great plenty throughout all the land of Egypt: And there shall arise after them seven years of famine; and all the plenty shall be forgotten in the land of Egypt; and the famine shall consume the land. (Genesis 41:25–30)

Joseph recommended that Pharaoh select a wise and discreet man whom he should put in charge to prepare for the coming lean years. He recommended that they store twenty percent of all the production of the land during the good years so that food would be available during the famine. Pharaoh believed Joseph, released him from prison and placed him in charge of Egypt's farm supplies. Joseph oversaw the building of storage facilities to hold all the extra food in preparation for the coming seven-year famine. It is interesting that dreams got Joseph into trouble with his brothers, but a dream also raised his prestige from a slave to second in command in Egypt. In so doing, Joseph gained great favor in the sight of Pharaoh and all of the Egyptians. Joseph was methodical about this project and, eventually, became a ruler over all of Egypt, second only to Pharaoh. "And Pharaoh said unto Joseph, I am Pharaoh, and without thee shall no man lift up his hand or foot in all the land of Egypt." (Genesis 41:44)

At the end of the seven years of plenty, Joseph was 30 years old. Pharaoh had even given him a wife, Asenath, the daughter of Potipherah, prince of On. So, Joseph was given a princess as a wife because of his important position as second in command.

He had two sons; Manasseh was the firstborn and the second son was Ephraim.

At the end of the seven years of plenty came the seven years of drought and famine, just as Joseph has predicted through the dream of Pharaoh. When the famine was causing hardship among the Egyptians, the people cried out to Pharaoh who instructed them to go to Joseph and he would tell them what to do. The famine was all over the face of the earth and Joseph opened the storehouses and sold grain to the Egyptians and others who needed food.

The fame of Pharaoh's second in command spread throughout the land, even to the land of Canaan where Israel and Joseph's brothers lived. They, too, were now being affected by this famine.

Israel sent Joseph's brothers to Egypt to purchase grain to stave off the famine. (Genesis 42) However, he did not allow Benjamin, his youngest son, to travel with them for fear that harm might fall upon the one remaining son of his beloved wife, Rachel.

GOD FULFILLS JOSEPH'S DREAMS

Israel sent his sons to Egypt to purchase grain. Of course they did not realize Joseph was the governor over all the land and who was in charge of selling and distributing the grain to whomever he chose.

When Joseph met his ten brothers coming to purchase grain, they did not recognize him; they were coming humbly before this governor of Egypt. Remember, it had been many years since his brothers had sold their young teenage brother into slavery. Now we see the fulfillment of the first of Joseph's dreams when his brothers came in and, as custom dictated, they bowed their faces to the earth before this great Egyptian ruler.

Joseph recognized them and remembered his dreams as a young man. Of course, the early years of his vanity had long since passed due to the testing and trials to which he was exposed in his early years in Egypt. I am sure he was awed when he realized how God had worked out the interpretation of his dream of long ago.

Joseph disguised himself so that his brothers would not recognize him, questioned them and accused them of being spies. They told him about their father and younger brother and Joseph asked their father's condition. He demanded proof that they were not spies; the proof was that they should bring the younger brother, Benjamin, when they came back to Egypt. As security, Simeon was left in Egypt.

The nine brothers went back to Canaan and related the story to their father, Israel. When the grain supplies which the brothers had purchased in Egypt ran out, Israel instructed his sons to return to Egypt and purchase more grain. They remembered that the governor of Egypt had told to bring their youngest brother with them on their next trip. Jacob hesitated, but because their food was running out, he had no choice but to send him; Judah promised to act as security for Benjamin.

They returned and were invited to Joseph's home where they were united with Simeon who had stayed as a prisoner. Joseph put them through some trials and tests before he revealed himself to them. It was such rigorous testing that the brothers thought back on and discussed what they had done to their brother, Joseph, many years before. Finally he revealed that he was Joseph.

> Now therefore be not grieved, nor angry with your-selves, that ye sold me hither: for God did send me before you to preserve life. For these two years hath the famine been in the land: and yet there are five years, in the which there shall neither be earing nor harvest. And God sent me before you to preserve you a posterity in the earth, and to save your lives by a great deliverance. So now it was not you that sent me hither, but God: and he hath made me a father to Pharaoh, and lord of all his house, and a ruler throughout all the land of Egypt. Haste ye, and go up to my father, and say unto him, Thus saith thy son Joseph, God hath made me lord of all Egypt: come down unto me, tarry not: (Genesis 45:5–9)

The brothers went back to their father, Israel, and told him all about Joseph and Egypt. It was a joyous occasion to now realize that his son Joseph was not only alive, but that he had ascended to a position of great prosperity and prestige as governor over all of Egypt, second only to Pharaoh.

Joseph had invited them to come to Egypt to live. On the way, Israel stopped in Beersheba to offer sacrifices unto the God of his father Isaac. God spoke to him there.

> I am God, the God of thy father: fear not to go down into Egypt; for I will there make of thee a great nation: I will go down with thee into Egypt; and I will also surely bring thee up again: and Joseph shall surely put his hand upon thine eyes. (Genesis 46:3–4)

Israel and his sons moved their entire families to the land of Egypt. There were a total of seventy in the house of Israel who came to Egypt. This included Joseph, Ephraim and Manasseh, but excluded the women. At that time, Israel was 130 years old.

Even though Joseph befriended his brothers, they were concerned that Joseph would seek revenge upon them after the death of their father, Israel. The eleven brothers sent a message to Joseph asking for his forgiveness. Joseph now understood that it had been God's will all the time for Joseph and the rest of his family to reside in Egypt and he forgave his brothers for the evil deed they perpetrated upon him. (Genesis 50:15–21)

After living in the land of Egypt for seventeen years, Israel came to the end of his life and the *birthright* and the *blessings* were to be passed on to the next generation.

ISRAEL ADOPTS JOSEPH'S TWO SONS

A significant event occurs which ultimately helps us determine who the modern-day descendants of Israel are.

Israel departed from the tradition established by Abraham and Isaac in passing the birthright blessings to the next generation. In this case, Jacob skipped the generation of his own children to pass the birthright down to his two grandsons, Joseph's sons Ephraim and Manasseh. From this point this forward Ephraim and Manasseh would be known as *Israel*. Israel adopts Joseph's two sons, Ephraim and Manasseh, as his own sons just as the other twelve children. "And now thy two sons, Ephraim and Manasseh, which were born unto thee in the land of Egypt before I came unto thee into Egypt, are mine; as Reuben and Simeon, they shall be mine." (Genesis 48:5)

What follows is a very curious occurrence as Israel begins to bless his two grandchildren and pass the birthright down to Joseph's children, rather than to his first son Reuben.

The next legal inheritor of the birthright was Reuben, since he was the firstborn son of Jacob by his first wife, Leah. But, Reuben, like Esau, lost his birthright and Joseph, the eleventh son of Jacob and the firstborn of Rachel, actually received it through his two sons.

> Now the sons of Reuben the firstborn of Israel, (for he was the firstborn; but, forasmuch as he defiled his father's bed, his birthright was given unto the sons of Joseph the son of Israel: and the genealogy is not to be reckoned after the birthright. (I Chronicles 5:1–2)

Notice in these two verses that Reuben lost his birthright position because he defiled Jacob's bed. "And it came to pass, when Israel dwelt in that land, that Reuben went and lay with Bilhah his father's concubine: and Israel heard it. Now the sons of Jacob [Israel] were twelve:" (Genesis 35:22)

However, one might question why he chose to pass the birthright blessings to his two grandsons, rather than to Joseph. The answer can only be that God intended to build two great peoples, rather than a single great nation which would have been the case had Israel passed the birthright to Joseph. "Moreover I have given to thee one portion above thy brethren..." (Genesis 48:22) Israel determined in his mind to give his favorite son a double portion of the inheritance because he felt through God's inspiration that he deserved. it.

THE CROSSED HANDS

Joseph, knowing it was near Israel's death, took his two sons, Ephraim and Manasseh to be blessed. Manasseh was the eldest and, therefore, Joseph placed Manasseh under the right hand of Israel and he placed Ephraim under the left hand of Jacob/Israel. However, under the guidance of God, Israel, even though he was blind, chose to place his right hand on the head of the younger brother, Ephraim, and his left hand on the head of the older brother, Manasseh. Israel had to cross his hands to achieve this position. (Genesis 48:13–14)

Jacob restated the point that his name, Israel, would only be applied to the two sons of Joseph whom he had adopted.

And he blessed Joseph, and said, God, before whom my fathers Abraham and Isaac did walk, the God which fed me all my life long unto this day, The Angel which redeemed me from all evil, bless the lads; and let my name be named on them, and the name of my fathers Abraham and Isaac; and let them grow into a multitude in the midst of the earth. (Genesis 48:15–16)

Obviously, Joseph noticed that his father had placed his right hand upon the head of the younger son and his left hand upon the head of the older son, which meant the birthright blessings would be passed to the younger son. At this point, Joseph tried to intervene and place Israel's right hand on the head of Manasseh and his left hand upon the head of Ephraim, but Israel indicated that he knew exactly what he was doing.

And when Joseph saw that his father laid his right hand upon the head of Ephraim, it displeased him: and he held up his father's hand, to remove it from Ephraim's head unto Manasseh's head. And Joseph said unto his father, Not so, my father: for this is the firstborn; put thy right hand upon his head. (Genesis 48:17–18)

ISRAEL'S BIRTHRIGHT BLESSING FOR THE LAST DAYS

Notice that Israel gave an overall blessing to Joseph, but specifically he showed that Ephraim would grow into a large multitude in the midst of the earth. Another significant point concerning Ephraim's blessing was that he would become not only a large number of people on the face of the earth, but that he would ultimately be a conglomeration of nation states as the single most powerful government the world has ever seen. (Genesis 48:19) "... and his seed shall become a multitude of nations." During the course of the same blessing, Jacob-Israel also blessed Manasseh and said that he too would become a great nation, but that his younger brother would far surpass the older in the course of human history. This crossing of the hands and these birthright blessings given to these two sons of Joseph also will provide valuable information in our quest to determine the final outcome of this birthright blessing given to the young men, Ephraim and Manasseh.

The birthright involved material and national greatness. It was the assurance that a multitude of people with great national and material prosperity would have dominance over all the other nations including the other sons of Israel.

Notice, the birthright was not to be inherited by all the tribes of Israel, nor was the name of Israel to be used by all the other sons, only the name of *Israel* was to be applied to the sons of Joseph, *Ephraim* and *Manasseh*.

These material promises included a prominence among nations of the world like no other nation could ever hope to achieve.

THE NAME OF ISRAEL GIVEN ONLY TO JOSEPH'S SONS

Even though Israel was blind, God made sure that he passed the blessings down to the two sons of Joseph, Ephraim and Manasseh, according to his design. Notice that Israel did not just confer the blessing on one of the two sons, but to both of the lads as he blessed them jointly. One can only come to the conclusion that the name *Israel* was only to be applied to the two sons of Joseph whom Israel adopted. Only Ephraim and Manasseh could carry the name Israel.

The other sons would use the name of their fathers, i.e. Reuben, Levi, Simeon, Judah, Dan, etc.

ISRAEL PROPHESIES ABOUT
HIS REMAINING SONS

At the end of his life, Israel called all of his twelve sons together to tell them what their posterity would become "in the last days."

These prophecies about the twelve sons (tribes) will greatly assist us in identifying the descendants of Jacob's children today. "And Jacob called unto his sons, and said, Gather yourselves together, that I may tell you that which shall befall you in the last days." (Genesis 49:1)

Notice that these sons of Jacob/Israel had different mothers.

LEAH, JACOB'S FIRST WIFE HAD SIX SONS

Reuben

> Reuben, thou art my firstborn, my might, and the beginning of my strength, the excellency of dignity, and the excellency of power: Unstable as water, thou shalt not excel; because thou wentest up to thy father's bed; then defiledst thou it: he went up to my couch." (Genesis 49:3–4)

In this prophecy, Reuben was also to be a nation of strength and power. Yet, it was prophesied that their people and their government would be as unstable as water in the latter days.

Simeon and Levi

> Simeon and Levi are brethren; instruments of cruelty are in their habitations. O my soul, come not thou into their secret; unto their assembly, mine honour, be not thou united: for in their anger they slew a man, and in their selfwill they digged down a wall. Cursed be their anger, for it was fierce; and their wrath, for it was cruel:

I will divide them in Jacob, and scatter them in Israel.
(Genesis 49:5–7)

Simeon and Levi were not promised nations of their own, but they were to be scattered throughout Israel. A tell-tale sign about these people is that they have a short temper and, due to their self-willed ways, they are brawlers.

Judah

Judah, thou art he whom thy brethren shall praise: thy hand shall be in the neck of thine enemies; thy father's children shall bow down before thee. Judah is a lion's whelp: from the prey, my son, thou art gone up: he stooped down, he couched as a lion, and as an old lion; who shall rouse him up? The *sceptre shall not depart from Judah,* nor a lawgiver from between his feet, until Shiloh come; and unto him shall the gathering of the people be. Binding his foal unto the vine, and his ass's colt unto the choice vine; he washed his garments in wine, and his clothes in the blood of grapes: His eyes shall be red with wine, and his teeth white with milk. (Genesis 49: 8–12)

It was promised that Judah would be the progenitor of many kings who would rule throughout the world. This is what is meant by "the scepter will not pass from Judah." As we know today, there is no king ruling the Jews, so this prophecy is for the end-time. Therefore, we must look elsewhere to find out where a Jewish king might be ruling in the world. This is also a major point in helping us to identify where Jacob's sons will be residing at this end time.

The scripture also indicates that Shiloh (Jesus Christ) would come from the descendants of Judah.

Zebulun

"Zebulun shall dwell at the haven of the sea; and he shall be for a haven of ships; and his border shall be unto Zidon" (Genesis 49:13).

Zebulun was to be a seafaring nation and their nation would be located in an area where ships could easily navigate.

Issachar

"Issachar is a strong ass couching down between two burdens: And he saw that rest was good, and the land that it was pleasant; and bowed his shoulder to bear, and became a servant unto tribute" (Genesis 49: 14–15).

This scripture indicates that Issachar will be a nation that tries to be independent, but throughout the world wars, and especially in this latter time, they will be forced to serve their enemies.

BILHAH, RACHEL'S HANDMAIDEN HAD TWO SONS

Dan

"Dan shall judge his people, as one of the tribes of Israel. Dan shall be a serpent by the way, an adder in the path, that biteth the horse heels, so that his rider shall fall backward" (Genesis 49:16–18).

Dan is especially important in helping us to understand where the children of Israel traveled. These two verses indicate that, wherever Dan travels, his descendants will leave markers following the tracks of the ancient Israelites. Dan's descendants will hold positions of judges and enforcers of the law. The name *Dan* will probably appear somewhere in the lands, rivers and mountains through which they travel.

Naphtali

"Naphtali is a hind let loose: he giveth goodly words" (Genesis 49:21).

There will be a land where traditional values have been let down, and yet, he has been able to obtain his independence by appeasing his neighbors.

ZILPAH, LEAH'S HANDMAIDEN HAD TWO SONS

Gad

"Gad, a troop shall overcome him: but he shall overcome at the last" (Genesis 49:19).

Gad was to be a very small country, but in the end, he will maintain his independence from those who have tried to climb the high mountains to take him captive.

Asher

"Out of Asher his bread shall be fat, and he shall yield royal dainties" (Genesis 49:20).

Asher is to be a land where food, dainties and pastries are in abundance.

RACHEL, JACOB'S BELOVED WIFE, HAD TWO SONS

Joseph

Joseph is a fruitful bough, even a fruitful bough by a well; whose branches run over the wall: The archers have sorely grieved him, and shot at him, and hated him: But his bow abode in strength, and the arms of his hands were made strong by the hands of the mighty God of Jacob; (from thence is the shepherd, the stone of Israel:) Even by the God of thy father, who shall help thee; and by the Almighty, who shall bless thee with blessings of heaven above, blessings of the deep that lieth under, blessings of the breasts, and of the womb: The blessings of thy father have pre-vailed above the blessings of my progenitors unto the utmost bound of the everlasting hills: they shall be on the head of Joseph, and on the crown of the head of him that was separate from his brethren. (Genesis 49:22–36)

Joseph's sons, in the latter days, will combine to be the most powerful two nations the world has ever known. They received these blessings because they were the two sons of Joseph, through Israel, Isaac and Abraham; those blessings will continue up until just before the Return of Christ.

Benjamin

"Benjamin shall ravin as a wolf: in the morning he shall devour the prey, and at night he shall divide the spoil."

Benjamin will be like a wolf constantly looking to spring upon his prey and divide the land among his tribe. Benjaminites are also to be scattered through many parts of the land of Israel. The Apostle Paul tells us that, even though he embraced Judaism, he was actu-ally of the tribe of Benjamin. Romans 11:1, "I say then, Hath God cast away his people? God forbid. For I also am an Israelite, of the seed of Abraham, of the tribe of Benjamin." Notice that Paul was not born in Judea and he, in fact, was from the tribe of Benjamin, but that he embraced Judaism as his religion. Therefore, Paul con-sidered himself a Jew because he was of the Jewish religion and an Israelite, descended from Benjamin, the twelfth son of Israel.

Israel was 130 years old when he and his sons came into Egypt. He died at the age of 147 years. The children of Israel were left to sojourn in Egypt for approximately 350 more years before they were led to the Promised Land by God's servant, Moses. (Exodus 12:40)

ISRAEL ENSLAVED
AND DELIVERED

Joseph's father, Israel, and his eleven brothers left the land of Canaan to take up residence in the land of Egypt, just as God had prophesied to Abraham.

> And he said unto Abram, Know of a surety that thy seed shall be a stranger in a land that is not theirs, and shall serve them; and they shall afflict them four hundred years; And also that nation, whom they shall serve, will I judge: and afterward shall they come out with great substance." (Genesis 15:13–14)

This scripture shows that from the beginning, God intended to take the descendants of Abraham into the land of Egypt for at least 400 years. This prophecy had its fulfillment when Israel and his eleven sons joined his beloved son, Joseph, in the land of Egypt. (Genesis 15:13)

As the number two man in Egypt, Joseph ruled for many years. In fact, Joseph died at 110 years. Before his death, he asked the Israelites to pledge that, when they left the land of Egypt, his body would be taken along with the departing multitude. Joseph lay in his coffin in Egypt until the Israelites departed Egypt. During that time, the Israelites increased to several million people and they continued to live in the lush Nile Delta area. (Exodus 1:6–7) Unfortunately for the Israelites, the memory of the great ruler Joseph soon faded from the minds of the Egyptians.

After the sons of Israel and their families had been in Egypt for several centuries, a new Pharaoh came to the throne who did not know of Joseph. He greatly disliked the Israelites living in his country and planned to prevent them from increasing in numbers by giving them hard labor and enslaving them.

The Egyptian leaders promised good wages to the Israelites to draw them from their farms and pastures to construction jobs in the cities. When it was too late, the Israelites realized they had been maneuvered into slave labor conditions. The Egyptians supposed that, in these miserable circumstances, the Israelites would decrease. But, surprisingly, they increased even more. Pharaoh was so outraged that he ordered them to be worked harder. The Egyptian taskmasters were told to work the Israelites until they dropped, using whips and sticks on them to break their spirit and their ability to reproduce. These taskmasters were told to divide the Israelites into different groups to keep them under control; total control led to slavery. The Israelites were herded over the land to dig canals, line the banks of the Nile with stone and build fortresses and pyramids. Most of the Israelites slaved long hours, seven days a week, making bricks from clay and straw. (Exodus 1:9–14)

Even after all of this hard labor, the Israelites continued to increase. This cruel new Pharaoh, therefore, decreed that all Hebrew midwives would be expected to kill all newborn Israelite baby boys. Failure to obey this direct command from the Pharaoh was punishable by death. (Exodus 1:15–16) The midwives had no intention of committing murder. When Pharaoh heard that the midwives refused to murder the babies, Pharaoh angrily called them to come and explain why. The midwives gave this answer, "The Israelite women are stronger than Egyptian ones. They so seldom need our help that we never know about many of the births." As a result of this, Pharaoh intended to punish the midwives for their disobedience; because the midwives obeyed God, God caused Pharaoh to change his mind. (Verses 17–21)

Pharaoh decided upon a new tactic to control the ever-growing Israelite population. He instructed his soldiers to watch and seize all new-born Israelite males and throw them into the Nile. (Verse 22)

Many babies probably escaped this inhumane fate, but many were drowned in the River Nile. This incited the Israelites and they longed to flee Egypt. The Israelites could only see a dismal future as slaves to the Egyptians; ultimately, they could visualize the extinction of all Hebrews.

GOD CHOOSES A DELIVERER

When the future was looking bleak for Israel, God looked down upon these twelve tribes of Israel and decided to set into motion a plan by which He would rescue the Israelites from their Egyptian taskmasters as well as serve to punish this idolatrous land. His plan started with the birth of an Israelite baby of the tribe of Levi living near Pharaoh's palace on the Nile. The baby's parents managed to hide him from Pharaoh's soldiers for three months. However, they knew that eventually the Egyptian authorities would become suspicious as the child grew. They developed a plan to save their infant son. The parents placed him in a small basket, covered with water-repellant pitch, and hid him in the reeds along the Nile River. The parents hoped that the baby would be found and kept safe.

The parents were actually fulfilling God's will unknowingly. Soon Pharaoh's daughter came to the river to bathe and found the basket among the reeds. (Genesis 2:5–6) Pharaoh's daughter was so impressed by the appearance of the infant, which she recognized as one of the Israelites, she decided to keep the baby under her own protection. As if by accident, a little girl surprisingly appeared and told the Egyptian princess that she knew of an Israelite nurse who would help care for the baby. The girl was Moses' sister, Miriam. (Verse 7)

Pharaoh's daughter approved and the little girl raced off to her nearby home and gave her mother the good news about her little brother. Of course, the mother of Moses was relieved at this turn of events. She quickly returned to the Princess with her daughter. Not knowing that this was the infant's mother, the Princess asked her to nurse the baby and care for it for an indefinite time. The Egyptian princess told the baby's mother Pharaoh's authorities would not harm the child.

God allowed the child's mother to raise the child as his nurse. Some time after he was weaned, the child's mother took the child to Pharaoh's daughter and he then became her son. It was sad to give up her beloved child, but at least she had been able to see him grow to two or three years old and she could be assured that he would not be killed. Shortly after receiving this young boy, Pharaoh's daughter adopted him and named him Moses. (Exodus 2:10) The princess saw to it that her adopted son was educated by the best instructors in all of Egypt. He then became the grandson of the Pharaoh in training to become a Prince.

Moses lived as an Egyptian prince for the first forty years of his life. He rose to great prominence as a high ranking Egyptian. Moses was considered a possible heir to the Egyptian throne because he was now the legal son of Pharaoh's daughter. Moses was extremely accomplished as a General in the Egyptian army. He engaged in major battles, leading the Egyptians to victory over the Ethiopians and other countries attempting to annex Egyptian land and wealth into their own.

As Moses grew, he also noticed the cruelty Egyptian taskmasters exercised upon these captive people, the Israelites. For some strange reason, Moses felt a strong affinity to the Israelites which would later cause him to turn against his adopted family, when he was forty years old. The story of Moses intervening on behalf of an Israelite and killing an Egyptian guard can be found in Exodus 2:11–15.

MOSES NEEDS MORE TRAINING

After he killed an Egyptian guard who was mistreating an Israelite, Moses managed to flee Egypt and escape to a mountain range located in the land of Midian, east of Egypt. The first people he came across who befriended him were seven young shepherdesses waiting to obtain water for their sheep. Moses intervened on behalf of the young women because other shepherds were trying to prevent them from obtaining water. To show their appreciation, the young women took him to their father, an important man in the land of Midian. The Midianites were also descended from Abraham through Ketura, his wife after Sarah died. The father invited Moses to eat with them. As evidenced by his clothing, manners and bearing, it was apparent that this Egyptian stranger was both intelligent and well-educated. Their father offered Moses work as a shepherd.

While Moses was tending the sheep in many out of the way pastures, he had the opportunity to think and put his thoughts into words. Actually, he liked the solitude and perhaps started writing a journal to record his amazing past. He could never imagine that his writings would ultimately be part of the world's most famous book, the Bible.

As time passed, Moses married one of the Midianite daughters whose name was Zipporah. Moses and Zipporah had two sons.

Meanwhile, back in Egypt, conditions were becoming worse for the Israelites. Finally, the Pharaoh died. The next king to come to the throne in Egypt showed even more cruelty than previous ones. The suffering Israelites cried out to God to free them. Soon, God would act!

Moses had spent his first forty years in the courts of Pharaoh, learning the arts of diplomacy, civil leadership and, as a military leader, learning military skills and how to deal with large numbers of people. As a Prince, he received his formal education from the educated elite of Egypt. The peasantry did not have the opportunity for formal education. Moses studied the reading, writings and mathematics of Egypt. He had a very high position and most likely had a high opinion of himself, as well. However, God wants his leaders to be well and broadly educated and then He will take care of the humbling process needed for a true servant of God.

God chose to train and humble Moses for forty years as a lowly sheep herder, working for his father-in-law, in the desert region east of Egypt. Moses became very familiar with living in the desert and learned how to survive the harsh conditions of the region. When Moses was eighty years old, he came to the end of his forty years of desert training. At this point, he was ready for the next great adventure he would face.

MOSES' MISSION REVEALED

At the end of Moses' forty-year desert training, when he was herding the sheep, he saw a bush, glowing as brightly as a torch, yet not being consumed by the fire. Obviously, this was a strange spectacle to Moses, so he approached the bush to investigate. As Moses approached, a strong voice was heard coming from the bush, "Don't come any closer. You are standing on holy ground. Remove your shoes and listen to what I, your God, have to tell you." (Exodus 3:5–6) Moses was awed and frightened. The voice in the bush said, "I am going to deliver the suffering Israelites from the Egyptians. I want you to go to Egypt and tell Pharaoh to let my people leave his country!" Moses was totally overwhelmed and asked, "Why me?" Also, Moses asked, "Why would Pharaoh listen to a stranger like me?" God revealed to Moses what He intended to do. He could hardly believe God would give him the job of saving the nation. After all, he had fled Egypt forty years ago as a fugitive. Moses argued with God about this task by protesting that the king of Egypt would not allow it, nor would the leaders of Israel have any reason to follow him. However, God told him not to worry about the people leaving Egypt and following him. God said, "I will cause the Egyptians to contribute liberally to Israel at their departure." (Exodus 3:21–22)

In spite of the fact that Moses did not feel he was qualified to do the job, God performed several miracles that convinced Moses he was the one chosen to deliver the Israelites from Egyptian slavery. To give Moses help, God revealed that Aaron, Moses' brother, would be the spokesman to Pharaoh and the Israelites.

Moses told his father-in-law, Jethro, that he was going back to Egypt to bring the Israelites out of bondage. Traveling on donkeys, Moses and his family set out for Egypt northward along the eastern side of the Red Sea. Before they had gone very far, Zipporah became angry with Moses and was sent home with their two sons. This was probably the best idea, because this job he had ahead of him was not conducive to having his wife and children with him.

Aaron was sent by God to meet Moses near the Red Sea; they had not seen each other for forty years. Moses told Aaron what God expected them to do. Together they went to Goshen in Egypt where the Israelites lived. Aaron gathered the leaders together to explain how God intended to deliver the Israelites from the Egyptian bondage.

GOD SETS UP EGYPT FOR THE EXODUS

Obviously, the Egyptian and some of the Israelite leaders did not believe Moses was sent by God to deliver the Israelites. Some of the leaders asked for proof that God sent him. Aaron stood before the people and said, "God expected some of you to fail to recognize that Moses was His servant and, as a result, He has given my brother, Moses, the ability to do many unusual things for proof that God is working through him."

Aaron asked Moses to perform one of the miracles God had previously instructed him to convince the Israelites and the Egyptians that he was truly sent by God. Moses stepped up before the leaders and held out his shepherd's rod, tossing it to the ground. It immediately turned into a snake. The people were astonished. Then Moses walked up to the snake and seized it by its tail; it once again became the lifeless shepherd's staff.

To further convince his Israelite brothers, Moses held up his right hand for all to see that it was a normal hand. Thrusting it inside his robe, he withdrew it to display a white, leprous, decayed hand. There was horror and dismay among the people. Moses again concealed his hand in his robe and then pulled it out to reveal that it had instantaneously returned to normal. The people knew that no one could have done these things without the power of God backing him up. However, some still believed that Moses was some clever magician sent to trick the Israelites by Pharaoh. Therefore, Moses would perform an additional miracle in the sight of the Israelites. Moses motioned for some Israelites to tip over a large jar of water. Many gallons of clear water were emptied to the ground; then, Moses waved his shepherd's rod over the water. The water immediately turned into a curdling mass of blood! This was the final straw for the doubters and now the people began to recognize that Moses was God's man on the scene. (Exodus 4:31) As God had told Moses in the desert, the miracles were so "that they may believe that the Lord God of their fathers, the God of Abraham, the God of Isaac, and the God of Jacob hath appeared unto thee." (Exodus 4:5)

MOSES GOES TO PHARAOH

Moses and Aaron sought an audience with Pharaoh, who was quite indignant that Israelite slaves would be coming to ask a favor of him. However, he allowed them to come forth and Moses and Aaron announced that they came to Pharaoh in the name of the God of Israel. They told Pharaoh to let the Israelites go into the desert to worship the God of Abraham, Isaac and Jacob, per God's orders. Pharaoh said, "I don't know your God. Whoever he is, he isn't going to cause me to let the Israelites go!" (Exodus 5:2) Aaron responded to Pharaoh with, "We must obey our God. All that He wants us to do is to go into the desert three days to sacrifice and worship Him." Pharaoh believed this was a scheme for the Israelites to escape out of Egypt, and issued orders to oppress the people even more because one of their own dared to come before the Pharaoh and make such a ridiculous request.

Thinking that he had failed this task that God had given him, Moses began to complain to God for allowing the Israelites to fall into greater misery. God said that He would deal with Pharaoh; in time, Pharaoh would be anxious to let the Israelites go. God reminded Moses that He was the Creator and that it was He who made promises to Abraham, Isaac and Jacob concerning the great lands and fortunes that lay ahead.

In Exodus 7, the Bible tells how God began to execute miracles and plagues which would result in the Egyptians thrusting the Israelites out of their land.

From the very beginning, God knew Pharaoh would not willingly give up his Israelite slaves until he was convinced that it was in the best interest of his life and the life of his nation.

THE PLAGUES

The plagues were used by God not only to destroy much of the Egyptian economy and the land, but also to destroy the credibility of the Egyptian gods. The first miracle which Moses showed Pharaoh was the changing of his staff into a snake. When the Egyptian magicians did the same trick, Moses' staff/snake consumed the magicians' snake. The serpent in Egyptian folklore represented one of the many Egyptian gods. In this way, God showed that He was the master of all and that humanly designed gods were no gods at all.

Water into blood

The Egyptians literally worshipped the Nile River as if it were a god because of its life-giving sustenance to the plant and animal life of Egypt. The first plague was to destroy the credibility of the Nile River god in the eyes of the Egyptians and Israelites by converting the life-giving water into death-producing blood. (Exodus 7:20)

This was also in retribution for the many little Israelite male infants who had been murdered when they were thrown into the Nile River over eighty years before. God never forgets and vengeance is His.

Frogs

The next plague from God was the curse of millions of frogs throughout the land. (Exodus 8:6) The Egyptians worshipped the amphibians they didn't understand because of their miraculous transition from a tadpole to a frog.

Lice, gnats, mosquitoes and flies

The next plagues would cause lice, gnats and mosquitoes to become as numerous as dust in the land. (Exodus 8:16, 24) Many times, when the Egyptians did not understand certain aspects of insect life, their only conclusion was that they must be representations of some mystical god. Flies were especially curious to the Egyptian mind simply because they did not understand the metamorphosis of the fly egg becoming a maggot and later emerging as a fly.

There was something different from this plague forward. The Israelites had to deal with all the plagues before this, but from this point forward, the plagues did not affect the Israelites. God placed a division between Egypt and Israel.

Murrain

In Exodus 9:3, the Bible records that God inflicted a grievous pestilence which only afflicted the camels, oxen, and other beasts of burden necessary in the Egyptian economy.

Boils

The next grievous plague was boils breaking out upon men and beasts causing great pain among all Egyptians and their animals. (Exodus 9:10)

Even through all of these plagues, Pharaoh refused to allow the Israelites to leave his land. Therefore, God still had even worse plagues which would ultimately result in the ejection of the Israelites from the land.

Hail

The next plague was large hail stones falling from the sky upon men and beasts in Egypt. These hail stones were accompanied by thunder and lightning. (Exodus 9:23) After this plague, Pharaoh's heart began to change and he called for Moses and Aaron and acknowledged that he and his people were wicked. Pharaoh requested Moses to entreat God to remove the plague. Moses did so and the hail storm came to an end. Then, Pharaoh reneged in his heart and it became necessary for God to bring three more plagues.

Locusts

Since Pharaoh reneged on his promise to let the Israelites go, God sent locusts that covered the ground so that the people were unable to see the dirt. (Exodus 10:13) As locusts will do, they ate everything in their path, thus destroying the grain in the field and the foodstuffs of the Egyptians. Still Pharaoh refused to let the Israelites leave.

Darkness over the land

God brought darkness upon the land of Egypt, while at the same time the Israelites had light at their dwelling places. (Exodus 10:21) Three days and three nights of darkness set the pattern for the time when Jesus Christ of Nazareth would be in the grave for three days and three nights, as it were, leaving the whole world in darkness because of the death of our Savior.

DEATH OF ALL THE FIRSTBORN OF EGYPT

Since the return of Moses, God had subjected Egypt to many plagues as recounted in the book of Exodus. In spite of all the devastating plagues, Pharaoh was still unwilling to release the Israelites. God had yet one final plague to guarantee that Pharaoh would thrust the Israelites from his country. Moses told the people of God's intention to inflict one gigantic plague upon the Egyptians which would touch every household, including that of Pharaoh.

But, before this final plague was to occur, Moses instructed the people as to what they should do.

> And the LORD said unto Moses, Yet will I bring one plague more upon Pharaoh, and upon Egypt; afterwards he will let you go hence: when he shall let you go, he shall surely thrust you out hence altogether. Speak now in the ears of the people, and let every man borrow of his neighbour, and every woman of her neighbour, jewels of silver, and jewels of gold. And the LORD gave the people favour in the sight of the Egyptians. Moreover the man Moses was very great in the land of Egypt, in the sight of Pharaoh's servants, and in the sight of the people. And Moses said, Thus saith the LORD, About midnight will I go out into the midst of Egypt: And all the firstborn in the land of Egypt shall die, from the firstborn of Pharaoh that sitteth upon his throne, even unto the firstborn of the maidservant that is behind the mill; and all the firstborn of beasts. (Exodus 11:1–5)

As stated in the scriptures, the Israelites were to spoil the Egyptians and receive from them treasures of gold and silver which they would have upon their departure.

This event, described in Exodus 11, happened during the daytime portion of the fourteenth day of the First Month. This is also the preparation day in which the Israelites were to kill a small lamb and place its blood upon their doorposts in preparation for the climactic event that would occur after the fourteenth ended. During the night time of the fifteenth, around midnight, according to verse 4, God would make His final move against the Egyptians.

> "And Moses said, Thus saith the LORD, About midnight will I go out into the midst of Egypt: And all the firstborn in the land of Egypt shall die, from the firstborn of Pharaoh that sitteth upon his throne, even unto the firstborn of the maidservant that is behind the mill; and all the firstborn of beasts. And there shall be a great cry throughout all the land of Egypt, such as there was none like it, nor shall be like it any more." (Exodus 11:4–6)

This last plague became known as the *Passover*. In Exodus 12, God instructed Moses to tell the people that, at the spring time of the year, God would begin His calendar with a new month called Abib. God instructed the Israelites to set aside a small unblemished lamb or goat of the first year to be offered as a sacrifice, which later became known as the sacrifice of the Passover. Each Israelite family selected a lamb which was to be kept up, beginning on the tenth and until the afternoon of the fourteenth day of the first month, Abib, at which time all of the households of the Israelites slaughtered their lambs. Then, the blood of the lamb was to be painted on the doorposts before the sunset ending the fourteenth day of Abib. After killing the lamb and painting the blood on the doorposts, the Israelites were instructed to eat the lamb with unleavened bread and bitter herbs. In Exodus 11:4, God said that He would go through the land about midnight (it was now the fifteenth day of Abib—remember God's day starts at sunset) and all of the firstborn of the Egyptians would be killed. The only households that would be protected were those households who had painted the blood of the lamb on their doorposts just before sunset. Sure enough, God fulfilled His word (Exodus 12:29) when at midnight all of the firstborn of the Egyptians were killed. Because the Israelites had painted the blood of the slaughtered lambs on their doorposts, no firstborn Israelite was killed that night. (Exodus 12:13)

After the death of the Egyptians' firstborn, while it was yet dark, Pharaoh called for Moses and Aaron and demanded that they take all of the families and all of the herds and leave Egypt in haste. (Exodus 12:31–33) While it was still dark, in the early hours of the fifteenth day of the first month, the children of Israel began their departure from the land of Egypt. And so it was that the children of Israel departed Egypt after sojourning there for 430 years. (Verse 40)

ISRAEL IN THE
WILDERNESS

As the Israelites assembled themselves to leave the land of Egypt on the fifteenth day of the first month (Abib), Moses and the Israelites remembered the promise that had been made to Joseph hundreds of years before to take his bones with them when they departed the land of Egypt. "And Moses took the bones of Joseph with him: for he had straitly sworn the children of Israel, saying, God will surely visit you; and ye shall carry up my bones away hence with you." (Exodus 13:19)

As the Israelites marched, God was their guide by means of a huge vertical cloud which all could see by day and which miraculously glowed at night. (Exodus 13:21–22)

As the people marched, many noticed that the cloud was not leading the people in a direct route toward the land of Canaan. No doubt, many of the people wondered about the wisdom of going in this direction because they were marching into an area of extremely high peaks and giant mountains on one side and water on the other. Naturally, some of the leaders thought they were moving into a position which could not be easily defended, and could in fact become a gigantic entrapment for all of the people in the event that something went wrong.

Sure enough, trouble was brewing for the Israelites as Pharaoh hardened his heart when he realized he had allowed the exodus of his entire work force. He was now being driven by revenge and a desire to recover much of the spoils with which the Israelites had departed Egypt. In fact, God intended to extract one more punishment upon the Egyptians and He was using the Israelites as bait.

> And I will harden Pharaoh's heart, that he shall follow after them; and I will be honoured upon Pharaoh, and upon all his host; that the Egyptians may know that I am the LORD. And they did so. And it was told the king of Egypt that the people fled: and the heart of Pharaoh and of his servants was turned against the people, and they said, Why have we done this, that we have let Israel go from serving us? (Exodus 14:4–5)

Pharaoh, seeing the possibility of victory over the Israelites and reclaiming these slaves, pursued the Israelites into a gigantic trap that God had set for Pharaoh and his mighty army. As a matter of fact, Pharaoh took 600 chosen chariots and his top military leaders to pursue the Israelites with the intention of exacting revenge and recovering the booty from the departing Israelites.

As the Egyptians came nearer, fear swept over the entire multitude of the Israelites because of their present predicament. They were facing the Red Sea in front, mountains at their side and Pharaoh pursuing them from the rear. To many of the Israelites, it seemed as if that they had been brought out into the desert by Moses only to be slaughtered by Pharaoh's great army.

As the people began to murmur and speak against Moses, Moses addressed the Israelites in an effort to calm their fears.

> "And Moses said unto the people, Fear ye not, stand still, and see the salvation of the LORD, which he will shew to you to day: for the Egyptians whom ye have seen to day, ye shall see them again no more for ever." (Exodus 14:13)

Yes, God intended to ultimately destroy the Egyptian power with this final act. According to the scriptures, God instructed Moses to stretch out his hands over the Red Sea and the waters miraculously split open approximately fifteen miles wide to allow the entire Israelite nation to cross on dry land. As soon as the last Israelite set foot on the opposite bank, God lifted the fiery cloud from the front of the Egyptians to allow them to pursue the Israelites into the Red Sea bed. Once the entire Egyptian army was completely inside the dry bed passage way, God closed the sea, totally destroying all of Pharaoh's armies by drowning.

Several years ago, an archaeologist, the late Ron Wyatt, actually found the remains of some of Pharaoh's chariots at the bottom of the Red Sea where the children of Israel made their crossing. These artifacts have been identified as belonging to the Pharaoh and the Egyptians dating back to the time this event occurred. There is now archaeological proof that this Biblical event, as described in Exodus 13, really took place.

Without a shadow of a doubt, all of the Israelites were now convinced of God's great power.

THE DESERT MARCH

It did not become totally clear to the Israelites how God had completely destroyed the Egyptians until they saw the dead bodies, animals, and Egyptian armaments being washed upon the shore of the Red Sea. God had used the waters of the Red Sea to save Israel, while at the same time these waters were used to destroy the armies of Pharaoh. In the New Testament, Paul made this connection showing that the Israelites received a type of baptism when they walked through the Red Sea just as a Christian is baptized in the baptismal pool to escape the penalty of sin. (Romans 6:3–7)

Sin, which was represented by the Egyptian armies, was destroyed in the Red Sea baptismal waters, just as the past sins of a Christian are destroyed in the baptismal waters at conversion.

God chose to lead the millions of Israelites in a non-direct route toward the land of Canaan because of the many unfriendly nations between Egypt and the Promised Land. He chose to lead the Israelites away from many of these war-like people to prevent the Israelites from becoming discouraged and fearful.

BITTER WATERS

As the Israelites moved into the arid desert, water became a premium as it is today among desert dwellers. Soon, the Israelites and their flocks were very thirsty. Just when the people were becoming unruly and discouraged about their trek, they spotted a small oasis at a place named *Marah*. Unfortunately, as the people rushed to the oasis and began to drink the water, they discovered that the water was bitter and undrinkable. (Exodus 15:23–24) As a result of this turn of events, the people again murmured against Moses and blamed him for their predicament.

Moses set the example for all of us in our time of need. He cried out to God for help with this terrible problem the Israelites faced. God heard him and instructed Moses to cut down a particular tree and to cast it into the water. Even this showed the great faith of Moses in following God's instruction precisely. The tree was cut down and thrown into the water. The people may have been surprised at this action, but they tried the water and found that it was now sweet. This tree is symbolic of the *tree of life* that was in the Garden of Eden. (Genesis 2:9) The Bible speaks of another special tree, also called the *tree of life*, which will be in the Kingdom of God, having the power to heal the nations. (Revelation 22:2)

Once again, God used a water miracle to deliver the Israelites from impending disaster. God used this occasion to issue a proclamation.

> And said, If thou wilt diligently hearken to the voice of the LORD thy God, and wilt do that which is right in his sight, and wilt give ear to his commandments, and keep all his statutes, I will put none of these diseases

upon thee, which I have brought upon the Egyptians:
for I am the LORD that healeth thee." (Exodus 15:26)

If we follow these instructions today, God will honor His commitment. For those who are willing to obey God and diligently live by the precepts and standards set forth in the Bible, God promises to deliver them from the terrible diseases which many in our society face today: cancer, tuberculosis, heart disease, AIDS and many of the dreaded diseases that stalk our society.

Soon, the Israelites were on the march again heading toward the Promised Land; they came to *Elim* where twelve wells of water and sixty-three palm trees made up an oasis for the Israelites to set up camp. (Verse 27) After being replenished with water and nourished with fruit from the palm trees, the journey continued on from Elim toward the Wilderness of Sin, between Elim and *Sinai;* this was on the fifteenth day of the second month after their departure from Egypt. (Exodus 16:1) As they marched out through the desert, life became harder as the desert winds and scorching hot days made life very unpleasant. Soon, the ungrateful Israelites murmured against Moses and Aaron for bringing them out of the land of Egypt. In fact, some people said that it was better when they were able to sit at the fleshpots in Egypt and have plenty to eat.

Those ancient Israelites were so much like people today. When I was in the Air Force, I found that people agreed on the two most wonderful locations relating to their assigned duty stations or bases —their previous base assignment and the next base to be assigned. People are seldom satisfied with the status quo and, as a result, they are constantly looking for something better.

The ancient Israelites were no different, as they complained against Moses, forgetting that God had heard their cries and delivered them from slavery in Egypt. He had saved them. Saved them for what? He was saving them for His purpose. That purpose was to call out a nation that He would train and teach so that these people would become beacons for the whole world to see, learn from and follow.

MURMURING

As we follow the travels of the Israelites through the desert years, we find that, whenever things seemed to get a little rough, they murmured against Moses and God. God does not take kindly to His people murmuring against Him, just as parents can become upset with their children who are always complaining. Too many times, we fail to stop and count the many blessings God gives us; instead we focus our attention on our own personal discomforts or problems which we allow to overwhelm us. Many forget that God hears our murmurings as well as our praises. The Israelites displayed carnal human nature by their constant bellyaching against God and His chosen leaders.

Even though the Israelites were murmuring, God rained food from heaven called *manna*. God used this manna from heaven to teach the Israelites about the weekly Sabbath Day. During their enslavement in the land of Egypt and because their taskmasters required them to work every day, the Israelites lost the knowledge of the Sabbath Day. God used the manna to introduce this generation of Israelites to the weekly Sabbath Day.

> Then said the LORD unto Moses, Behold, I will rain bread from heaven for you; and the people shall go out and gather a certain rate every day, that I may prove them, whether they will walk in my law, or no. And it shall come to pass, that on the sixth day they shall prepare that which they bring in; and it shall be twice as much as they gather daily. (Exodus 16:4–5)

Moses called all the people together and explained to them how God would supply all their needs in their travels through the desert. He told them to gather only what they would eat in one day; some did not believe Moses and hoarded manna during the week only to find that it took on a horrible smell and was crawling with worms. Moses told them to gather twice as much on the sixth day of the week (our Friday) because God would not send the manna on the

Sabbath Day. There were those who did not gather twice as much on Friday as they did the other days; those people expected to go out on the Sabbath morning and find manna falling from heaven. Some people just don't follow the rules. To their astonishment, God did not rain down manna on the Sabbath Day. (Exodus 16:27–30)

ON THE MARCH AGAIN

Once again, God instructed Moses to lead the people from the Wilderness of Sin to a new area called *Rephidim*. When the people arrived and set up their camps, they were surprised that no water was available. As before, the Israelites began to murmur and complain against Moses and God for taking them into the wilderness which they thought was not fit for human life; it was hot and dry, no water could be found and the people were thirsty. The situation grew so tense that Moses feared for his life because the people threatened to kill him. At this point, Moses went to God on his knees and cried out for help. God answered Moses by instructing him to stand before a particular rock in Horeb and to smite the rock and water would come from the rock for the people to drink. (Exodus 17:6)

SNEAK ATTACK

After being refreshed with plenty of water and food, the Israelites were oblivious to the fact that there was an enemy nearby. After several days, the Amalekites intended to ambush the Israelites thinking Israel had an ill-prepared army. The Israelites were attacked at night by the Amalekites, descendants of Esau, the twin brother of Jacob. The Amalekites hated the Israelites because of the rift that had lasted between Jacob and Esau over the many generations.

The Amalekites attacked and then withdrew. While they withdrew, preparing for another attack, a young officer named Joshua came to Moses. Joshua was given the responsibility of assembling an army capable of defending the Israelite people. Moses knew that the Amalekites were going to attack again and in greater force the next day. Joshua worked throughout the night preparing the men of Israel for the battle. Sure enough, the next day the battle commenced as fierce hoards of the Amalekites came charging in among the thousands of untrained Israelite defenders who basically had only ordinary knives, clubs and other weapons taken from the drowned Egyptians. Moses took a position upon a high ridge where he could view the battle. With him were Aaron and Hur, his brother-in-law. Soon, Moses became extremely concerned as it appeared the Israelites were facing certain defeat. Moses called out to God for help. As Moses had done at the Red Sea, he held up his shepherd's rod and asked God to intervene. When Moses held up his shepherd's rod, the Israelites gained the upper hand, with the Amalekites falling back in retreat. When Moses thought the battle was under control, he lowered his weary arms. Almost immediately the situation changed and the Amalekites charged back causing the Israelites to retreat. Aaron and Moses soon realized that lowering the rod would affect the outcome of the battle. Moses once again held his rod up and the tide began to turn in favor of Israel. As you might imagine, he became very tired holding his staff above his head; soon, he lowered the rod and, again, the Amalekites began to overcome the Israelites. (Exodus 17:11)

The quick-thinking Aaron and Hur quickly rolled a large rock behind Moses who sank to a sitting position. Each of them held an arm of Moses. Thus, being helped, Moses continued his supplication while grasping his shepherd's rod in an upright position. The three men continued in this position until sundown. (Exodus 17:12) By the end of the day, the Israelites were winning the battle and the Amalekites were beginning to flee for their lives.

GOD'S OWN VOICE

God led Moses and the Israelites into the same area where Moses had fled 40 years earlier when he left Egypt; he knew it well because this was the same location where he had tended Jethro's flocks. That highest mount of rock was *Mount Sinai!*

Since the cloud stopped, the Israelites knew it was time for them to settle down in this location until God chose to have them move out. During this stop, Moses received a divine directive from God to come up to the top of Mount Sinai so that God could speak directly to him.

God told Moses to bring the people out of the camp to meet at the foot of Mt. Sinai. The people must have been very frightened because the ground was shaking, smoke was coming out from the mountain, and lightning was flashing out of the clouds. The situation became more frightening when all of a sudden a majestic, loud voice came forth from the mountain top and the voice grew louder and louder in response to Moses' speaking. This was God answering Moses with His Own Voice. God came down upon the top of Mount Sinai and called Moses up to the top of the mountain. (Exodus 19:17–20)

After Moses ascended into the clouds as he climbed the mountain, God instructed him to charge the people, instructing them not to try to penetrate the cloud or come too close to God, for if they did they would perish. Moses set bounds around the mountain and charged the people that they were, under no circumstances to cross the bounds that God had established.

After Moses returned to the people, God began to speak audibly the words that are written in Exodus 20:3–17. God gave to the Israelites the Ten Commandments by which they were to live.

LET NOT GOD SPEAK WITH US

As God spoke the Ten Commandments to the Israelites, the sound was greater than any man-made speakers could possibly produce. The Israelites, understandably, feared for their lives because they heard the awesome voice of God. As soon as God stopped speaking, after giving the Ten Commandments, the people went to

Moses and said, "Speak you with us, and we will hear: but let not God speak with us, lest we die." (Exodus 20:19)

God heard the people and from that point on, God gave the remainder of His Laws and Statutes and the history of mankind directly to Moses. The first five books of the Bible record the history of man since Adam and Eve. God instructed Moses for the next forty days, while Moses was in God's presence up near the top of Mt. Sinai, what he was to tell the children of Israel. God ended this session with Moses by giving him two tablets of stone on which the Ten Commandments were written with God's very own finger. (Exodus 31:18)

The Ten Commandments and all the *laws and statutes* which God gave to Moses were designed to build a nation, as well as to be an example for all nations to follow. The Ten Commandments, along with the civil laws and statutes were all designed to develop a society in which the Israelites could prosper, with God as their King and His Laws to govern.

ISRAELITES DESIRE TO WORSHIP

The Israelites began to weaken because it seemed Moses would never return from the top of the mountain. They were afraid since their leader had been gone for so long.

As a result, the people felt a need to worship and asked Aaron to make a symbol that represented God. Throughout all human history, man has felt a need to worship before some symbol that they believe identifies God or their religion. Since Constantine's time, the steeple and cross are symbols of Christ and Christianity.

The cherubic figure had been mistakenly identified as God or God's representative during the period prior to the flood. The cherubs were the beings that humans encountered guarding the entrance to the Garden of Eden. It is no wonder that the awesome power and presence of these cherubs were thought to be some type of god watching over the Garden of Eden and preventing man's return.

Since these cherubic figures were well known by the pre-flood men, we must assume that this knowledge carried through the flood with Noah and his family.

Legends began to flourish concerning these cherubs, and as legends will do, the line between fact and fiction became blurred. Except for those with whom God was dealing directly, the concept developed that the best representation of God was the figure of a cherub.

The cherub, described in Ezekiel and Revelation, is a most unusual creature. However, the most notable feature of the cherub's body is that it has the form of an ox, the wings of an eagle, the face of a man and a lion. Therefore, the concept of a golden calf or cow could easily be substituted for the oxen appearance of the cherub.

Over the process of time, the golden cow or calf became the ultimate symbol representing the highest god being in the minds of men. Throughout all human history, most religious beliefs include multiple gods and goddesses which were generated in the minds of men, but did not represent the actual fact.

In ancient Egypt, the chief god who had the appearance of a golden calf represented the Egyptian god, Apis. Today, we still see a large number of people who continue to revere cows and cattle as deities; this is the basis for the Hindu religion, as practiced by those in modern-day India.

The Israelites came to believe that Moses would not return from Mount Sinai. (Exodus 32:1–4) No doubt, Aaron created what he thought was symbolic of god as represented by the cherubim or golden calf. Interestingly enough, when Moses returned from the mountain and found what Aaron and the Israelites had done, it greatly angered him because he realized they were reverting to the type of worship they had learned in Egypt, which degenerated into a sexual orgy.

> And it came to pass, as soon as he came nigh unto the camp, that he saw the calf, and the dancing: and Moses' anger waxed hot, and he cast the tables out of his hands, and brake them beneath the mount. (Verse 25) And when Moses saw that the people were naked;

(for Aaron had made them naked unto their shame
among their enemies:) (Exodus 32:19, 25)

At this point, Aaron and the Israelites decided how *they* wanted
to worship God, rather than waiting for the specific instructions on
how God wanted to be worshipped.

People still believe they may worship God in any way they
choose and that it will satisfy God. This is not the case, just as it
was not the case with the Israelites at the foot of Mount Sinai. God
does not give us the right to determine when, where and how we
will worship him. God specifies how and when we are to worship
Him. However, God does give us the option as to whether we will
worship him or not. The Israelites fell victim to their own carnal
nature of desiring to worship something or someone, rather than
being patient and waiting for the return of Moses to receive God's
instructions on worship and all other aspects of human life.

ISRAEL REBELS

After two years in the shadow of Mount Sinai, the Israelites began
their long trek across the desert toward the land of Canaan. As
they approached the land, God instructed Moses to send twelve
spies, one from each of the twelve tribes of Israel, into the Promised
Land to scope it out in preparation for the conquest of Canaan by
the Israelites. These Israelite spies searched the land for a period of
forty days. Ten of the twelve scouts came back with a bad report;
the giants and walled cities disheartened them. (Numbers 13:25–
29) Only Joshua and Caleb gave a good report, encouraging the
people to go in and take the land. But, the people believed the ten
spies with the discouraging report and were convinced God had led
them out to this forsaken area to be slaughtered by their enemies.
They feared this in spite of the fact that the spies brought back rich
fruit from the Promised Land. The people again murmured against
Moses, Aaron and God.

Moses pleaded with the people to take the land and not be discouraged by the fearful scouts. Joshua and Caleb begged the people

not to rebel against God, nor to fear the people of Canaan. "Only rebel not ye against the LORD, neither fear ye the people of the land; for they are bread for us: their defence is departed from them, and the LORD is with us: fear them not." (Numbers 14:9)

The entire congregation wanted to stone Moses, Aaron, Joshua and Caleb. Then, God descended into the tabernacle before the congregation of Israel. God spoke to Moses and asked him, "How long will these people continue to rebel and provoke Me?" God told Moses that He was ready to destroy all of them, disinherit them and make a new nation out of Moses' descendants. At this point, Moses began to reason with God in an effort to change His Mind. God threatened to destroy all of the Israelites because of their rebellion. (Number 14:11–18)

Moses convinced God to change His mind and God agreed not to destroy all of the Israelites on the spot. However, He did decree that they would be punished because of their rebellion. As a result, God declared He would lead them back into the desert where they would live as vagabonds for the next forty years, one year for one day that the scouts spied out the land of Canaan, and until all of that generation died. (Numbers 14:34) However, the punishment for the ten spies who gave a bad report was *death by plague.* (Verses 36–37) God said that out of that generation only Joshua and Caleb would be allowed to go into the Promised Land. (Verse 30)

The travels and hardships of the Israelites because of their rebellion against and distrust of God are well documented throughout the books of Numbers and Deuteronomy. At the end of the forty years of travel through the desert, God brought the next generation of Israelites with Moses, Joshua and Caleb to the edge of the Promised Land. God told Moses he would not enter the Promised Land. However, God did take Moses up on a hill and allowed him to see across the Jordan River into the promised land that God was about to give this new generation of Israelites.

> And the LORD said unto him, This is the land which I
> sware unto Abraham, unto Isaac, and unto Jacob, say-
> ing, I will give it unto thy seed: I have caused thee

to see it with thine eyes, but thou shalt not go over thither. (Deuteronomy 34:4)

Moses, a devoted servant to God, died there in the land of Moab according to the word of the Eternal. God buried him in the valley of Moab over against Bethpeor, but to this day no man knows of a sepulcher or where his bones may be found. At the time of his death, Moses was 120 years old; the Bible says his eyes were still quite sharp and his natural abilities were unabated.

The children of Israel mourned for Moses thirty days after his death.

GOD KEEPS HIS PROMISES

I t had been almost five hundred years since God made the promise to Abraham that his descendants would inherit a land of their own. The scriptures show how God repeatedly urged the Israelites to keep their end of the bargain. Israel was warned, in Leviticus 26, concerning what God would do if the Israelites failed to keep their end of the bargain.

> Ye shall make you no idols nor graven image, neither rear you up a standing image, neither shall ye set up any image of stone in your land, to bow down unto it: for I am the Lord your God. Ye shall keep my sabbaths, and reverence my sanctuary: I am the Lord. If ye walk in my statues, and keep my commandments, and do them ..." (Leviticus 26:1–3)

God stated in Leviticus 26 that He would bless the Israelites and give them prosperity, and the land would forever belong to them. He warned them in Leviticus 26:14–18 what would happen if they rejected God and His Law.

> But if ye will not hearken unto me, and will not do all these commandments; And if ye shall despise my statutes, or if your soul abhor my judgments, so that ye

will not do all my commandments, but that ye break my covenant: I also will do this unto you; I will even appoint over you terror, consumption, and the burning ague, that shall consume the eyes, and cause sorrow of heart: and ye shall sow your seed in vain, for your enemies shall eat it. And I will set my face against you, and ye shall be slain before your enemies: they that hate you shall reign over you; and ye shall flee when none pursueth you. And if ye will not yet for all this hearken unto me, then I will punish you seven times more for your sins. (Leviticus 26:14–18)

The term "seven times" used in verse 18 refers to seven prophetic years of prophetic days. In a seven-year prophetic time frame, there are 2,520 days. Throughout the scriptures, we find the term "day" as another way of saying "a year." Therefore, God told the Israelites that, if they turned away from Him, He would punish them for a period of 2,520 days which equaled 2,520 actual years of punishment, at which time the fulfillment of God's Promise to Abraham would be suspended. Just because God made His promise unconditional to Abraham, as indicated in Genesis 22:17–18, God did not say that He would not punish the descendants of Abraham when they were disobedient.

We mentioned this time period of 2,520 years because it is very important for you to understand this point as we prove the modern-day identity of those people who were Abraham's descendants, especially those whom God calls Israel today!

FINAL PREPARATIONS

Just prior to Israel moving into the Promised Land, God used Moses to give final instructions to the Israelites before crossing the Jordan River. During that time, while the Israelites camped in the plains east of the Jordan River, the people didn't remain idle. Besides their regular duties, they had to oversee thousands of Midianite captives now in their midst, as well as take care of their added livestock.

They had to repair their worn or broken weapons in preparation for the war that would surely ensue once the Israelites crossed the Jordan River.

God left specific instructions through Moses that, when the Israelites crossed the Jordan River into the land of Canaan, one of their primary duties was to execute the inhabitants of the land and destroy all of their idols and pagan alters which God detested. In fact, God pointed out that these people actually burned some of their own children as offerings unto heathen gods.

> Speak unto the children of Israel, and say unto them, When ye are passed over Jordan into the land of Canaan; Then ye shall drive out all the inhabitants of the land from before you, and destroy all their pictures, and destroy all their molten images, and quite pluck down all their high places: And ye shall dispossess the inhabitants of the land, and dwell therein: for I have given you the land to possess it. (Numbers 33:51–53)

God told them that, if they spared any Canaanites, those Canaanites would give them trouble as long as any of them lived. Furthermore, God stated that He would punish the Israelites as He had planned to punish the Canaanites if Israel worshipped Canaan's gods.

> When the LORD thy God shall cut off the nations from before thee, whither thou goest to possess them, and thou succeedest them, and dwellest in their land; Take heed to thyself that thou be not snared by following them, after that they be destroyed from before thee; and that thou inquire not after their gods, saying, How did these nations serve their gods? even so will I do likewise. Thou shalt not do so unto the LORD thy God: for every abomination to the LORD, which he hateth, have they done unto their gods; for even their sons and their daughters they have burnt in the fire to their gods. What thing soever I command you,

observe to do it: thou shalt not add thereto, nor dimin-
ish from it. (Deuteronomy 12:29–32)

God wanted to make sure that the Israelites did not incorpo-
rate idolatrous methods of worship practiced by all of the heathen
nations. He intended to destroy the heathen nations using the
Israelite armies.

GOD DEFINES THE BOUNDARIES
AND THE CITIES OF REFUGE

God established a system of justice that was swift and effective.
The justice system was executed under the precept of "an eye for
an eye and a tooth for a tooth." When God gave the civil laws to
the Israelites, He specified punishments commensurate with the
infractions of both the civil law and God's Law. Some of these civil
laws can be found in Deuteronomy 22. An example of one of the
civil laws which God gave Israel to help control the society for the
safety and benefit of all is found in Deuteronomy 22:8, "When thou
buildest a new house, then thou shalt make a battlement for thy
roof, that thou bring not blood upon thine house, if any man fall
from thence." This law simply stated that, if you build any structure
high above the ground on which people will be standing, place a
fence around the edge to keep people from falling off and injuring
themselves.

Another example of laws for the good of the people can be
found in Verse 9. "Thou shalt not sow thy vineyard with divers
seeds: lest the fruit of thy seed which thou hast sown, and the fruit
of thy vineyard, be defiled." Verse 10 also is a law for the benefit of
farmers. "Thou shalt not plow with an ox and an ass together." If
you disobey this law, your fields will not be in straight rows. There
is nothing spiritual about this law; it is merely a good farming
practice.

Another law that God implemented for the Israelites to ensure
the health and welfare of the society is found in Deuteronomy
23:17–18.

There shall be no whore of the daughters of Israel, nor a sodomite of the sons of Israel. Thou shalt not bring the hire of a whore, or the price of a dog, into the house of the LORD thy God for any vow: for even both these are abominations unto the LORD thy God. (Deuteronomy 23:17–18)

As you can see, God wanted the people to avoid the moral degradation that comes about as a result of allowing prostitution and open homosexuality in the land.

Sometimes there arises a situation where an accidental death occurs. Under the laws given to Israel—"eye for an eye, tooth for a tooth"—the relatives of the slain victim could take revenge on the perpetrator. Even though it was an accident, God allowed for a swift retribution by the offended upon the offender. However, God also made a way of escape; He indicated that six towns of safety would be set up and administered by the Levites as places of safety for citizens who had accidentally killed or maimed someone. These were called "cities of refuge." This did not include habitation for a murderer.

God established these six *cities of refuge* for the protection of anyone who accidentally killed a person. This, of course, was necessary because angered relatives of the dead person might try to kill the one who caused the death. An example of an accidental death would be if two men were building a shed and one man accidentally dropped a beam which killed the other man. The man who dropped the beam would have to flee at once to the closest "city of refuge" where he would be protected from avengers who might seek his life. God condemned violence and expected the leaders of Israel to deal swiftly and effectively with anyone causing violence to any other person. Whatever the case, the man would be tried by the authorities. If he were found guilty, he would be either slain or allowed to fall into the hands of those who were set up to avenge the dead person. If he were found innocent, he would stay in the town for his own protection until the death of the high priest. Meanwhile, if he ventured out of his protective town and was found by an avenger, he would no long have protection. There were to be no jails or prisons in the land of Israel.

Before his death, Moses assigned three towns for refuge purposes east of the Jordan River. They included Bezel in the plain country of the Reubenites, Ramoth for the Gadites, and Golan for the Manassehites. The other three cities of refuge were to be set up later by Joshua. (Numbers 35:6–34; Deuteronomy 4:41–43: Deuteronomy 19:1–13; Joshua 20)

God reminded Israel to remember the Sabbath because it was the outward identifying sign between God and His people.

> And the LORD spake unto Moses, saying, Speak thou also unto the children of Israel, saying, Verily my sabbaths ye shall keep: for it is a sign between me and you throughout your generations; that ye may know that I am the LORD that doth sanctify you. Ye shall keep the sabbath therefore; for it is holy unto you: every one that defileth it shall surely be put to death: for whosoever doeth any work therein, that soul shall be cut off from among his people. Six days may work be done; but in the seventh is the sabbath of rest, holy to the LORD: whosoever doeth any work in the sabbath day, he shall surely be put to death. Wherefore the children of Israel shall keep the sabbath, to observe the sabbath throughout their generations, for a perpetual covenant. It is a sign between me and the children of Israel for ever: for in six days the LORD made heaven and earth, and on the seventh day he rested, and was refreshed. (Exodus 31:12–17)

After the death of Moses and the end of the mourning period by the Israelites, Joshua took command of this mighty nation as Israel prepared to take the Promised Land.

RAHAB AND THE SPIES

In the tradition of any good military commander, Joshua needed to know the strength and the ability of the opposing side; therefore, he dispatched scouts into the city of Jericho to spy out the city before the coming attack. Jericho's officers of the king learned of these Israelite spies and came to arrest them at the house of Rahab the harlot. Rahab knew that these two men were spies from Israel on a mission.

> Then Joshua sent two spies from the Israeli camp at Acacia to cross the river and check out the situation on the other side, especially at Jericho. They arrived at an inn operated by a woman named Rahab, who was a prostitute. They were planning to spend the night there, but someone informed the king of Jericho that two Israelis who were suspected of being spies had arrived in the city that evening. He dispatched a police squadron to Rahab's home, demanding that she surrender them. They are spies, he explained. They have been sent by the Israeli leaders to discover the best way to attack us. But she had hidden them, so she told the officer in charge, The men were here earlier, but I didn't know they were spies. They left the city at dusk as the city gates were about to close, and I don't know where they went. If you hurry, you can probably catch up with them! But actually she had taken them up to the roof and hidden them beneath piles of flax that were drying there. (The Layman's Bible) (Joshua 2:1–4)

Even though Rahab had a dubious reputation, she knew and understood who God was and what He was about to do to her fellow countrymen. As a result of this, Rahab the harlot repented and her life was spared with her family when Israel conquered her city.

Now before they lay down, she came up to them on the roof, and said to the men: I know that the LORD has given you the land, that the terror of you has fallen on us, and that all the inhabitants of the land are fainthearted because of you. For we have heard how the LORD dried up the water of the Red Sea for you when you came out of Egypt, and what you did to the two kings of the Amorites who were on the other side of the Jordan, Sihon and Og, whom you utterly destroyed. And as soon as we heard these things, our hearts melted; neither did there remain any more courage in anyone because of you, for the LORD your God, He is God in heaven above and on earth beneath. Now therefore, I beg you, swear to me by the LORD, since I have shown you kindness, that you also will show kindness to my father's house, and give me a true token, and spare my father, my mother, my brothers, my sisters, and all that they have, and deliver our lives from death. So the men answered her, Our lives for yours, if none of you tell this business of ours. And it shall be, when the LORD has given us the land, that we will deal kindly and truly with you. Then she let them down by a rope through the window, for her house was on the city wall; she dwelt on the wall. And she said to them, Get to the mountain, lest the pursuers meet you. Hide there three days, until the pursuers have returned. Afterward you may go your way. So the men said to her: We will be blameless of this oath of yours which you have made us swear, unless, when we come into the land, you bind this line of scarlet cord in the window through which you let us down, and unless you bring your father, your mother, your brothers, and all your father's household to your own home. (Joshua 2:8-18)

After the two scouts escaped from Jericho, they returned to

Joshua and reported that the Canaanites' morale was shattered and that they were living in total fear of what the Israelites were about to do.

Joshua ordered the people to break camp and prepare to move. The tabernacle tent and all the ornaments of the tabernacle were packed and the Israelites set out in a march toward the Jordan River. They stopped on the eastern side of the Jordan River.

Even though the Jordan River wasn't a large river such as the Nile, it was the largest river this new generation of Israelites had ever seen. Spring rains and snow melt-off from the mountains caused the river to swell and flow swiftly. It was evident to the Israelites that only strong swimmers would be able to make it across; building rafts to cross the river would take much time which would allow the armies of Canaan to concentrate upon the Israelite's crossing spot. This caused a great deal of concern among the people because here they saw an insurmountable barrier in this fast-flowing Jordan River.

ISRAEL BAPTIZED AGAIN

God revealed to Joshua exactly how He intended to take the Israelites across the Jordan River. God intended to work the same miracle with this second generation of Israelites as He had done with their fathers to deliver them from the land of Egypt through the Red Sea forty years before.

Joshua told the priests that they should personally take up the Ark of the Covenant and bear it to the river just ahead of the Israelite congregation. (Joshua 3:1–7) As God had commanded Joshua, he then told the priests that they should wade into the edge of the overflow water only a foot or so with Ark of the Covenant and then stand still while God intervened to stop the flow of the river.

Meanwhile, the evening before, Joshua had gathered the people around him to tell them they must have clean garments for what they would see the next day. He told them there was a swift and swollen river that they would cross. He pointed out that he had already heard that some of them were saying they did not think it would be possible to cross the swollen river. Joshua chided them because some had lost faith in "your God" who had brought them through many situations far worse than this. Joshua assured them that God would again prove His great power by taking them safely over the river. He told them the Ark of the Covenant would be carried to the river by the priests almost a mile in front. He said that, when the priests walk into the Jordan River carrying the Ark of the Covenant, the stream would cease to flow past the Ark! He indicated that part of the river south of the ark would drain away leaving a waterless river bed which would be dry for the people to walk across to the west bank!

Joshua instructed each of the twelve tribal leaders to select a husky man from his tribe to send him to Joshua for a special task. Each selected man, when he passed over the river bed, was to pick up a good-sized stone from the river bottom and carry it to the west bank for the building of a monument. (Joshua 3:8–13)

Sure enough, as the priests started out with the Ark early the next day, none of the Israelites followed until the priests were almost a mile away, which put them at the edge of the river. As the priests waded into the water up to their knees, the water suddenly and abruptly changed. As it stopped flowing from their right hand side, it flowed away to the left. In fact, its direction of movement was actually reversed as the priests continued to march into the midst of the Jordan. The Jordan River gradually grew higher and spread farther out on its flooded banks to the north. Thus, with water receding in both directions, a growing expanse of an empty river bed was exposed in view of the marveling priests and those of the waiting Israelites who could see the miracle from a distance.

The bearers of the Ark went into the middle of the river bed and then obediently stood where they had been instructed. They were awed to be able to participate in such a great miracle. When Joshua had made certain that all was ready, he signaled the Israelites to move into the river. This latest miracle proved to the people that God had now chosen Joshua to be their new commanding general.

WALLS OF JERICHO

It was the tenth day of the first month (Abib) when Israel crossed the Jordan River and made camp in Canaan at a spot called Gilgal. The western edge of the camp wasn't much more than a mile from the city of Jericho, a thick walled city swarming with enemy soldiers. (Joshua 4:19–24) The first month of God's New Year always begins in the spring about the latter part of March or early April, according to our calendar. This month of Abib is the time God set aside for His Passover on the evening of the first month on the fifteenth day. Israel was now celebrating its first Passover in the land of Canaan. It had now been forty years since Israel fled Egypt. Now, this next generation celebrating this first Passover in the Promised Land was about to take possession of the land God had promised Abraham.

The Israelites camped just east of the city of Jericho for several days to keep the Passover and the Days of Unleavened Bread. After a few days, while Israel was camped at Gilgal, Joshua went alone toward the city of Jericho to take a closer look at the city they were about to conquer. Suddenly, he found himself face to face with a high-ranking military man holding a gleaming sword and gazing intently at him. Joshua was, no doubt, surprised by this figure suddenly appearing in front of him and he approached the military man very cautiously; he asked him if he was "a friend of Israel or an enemy?" (Joshua 5:13) In a very firm voice, the figure answered, "I am here as the commander of the army of God!!" The man to whom Joshua was speaking was the God of the Old Testament. He was, in fact, the one who became Jesus Christ of Nazareth of the New Testament. This was Joshua's closest contact with God. When he realized to whom he was speaking, he fell fearfully forward and placed his forehead on the ground and asked, "What would you ask of me, my Lord?" It is clear that this was God because He allowed Joshua to worship Him and angels would never allow one of God's servants to worship them.

This great Leader of God's Army also told him to remove his

shoes and He said, "I will now instruct you on how to take Jericho!!" Upon receiving his instructions, Joshua rushed back to the camp, confident that Israel would win. (Joshua 6:2–7)

THE SIEGE OF JERICHO

The battle of Jericho began in a very unusual way. The Canaanites were surprised when they saw the growing columns of Israelites marching toward the city and, yet, not seeming to prepare for an attack. Perhaps the Canaanites thought that the Israelites intended to bypass their city and continue in a westerly direction.

As the Israelites began marching past the city, the Canaanites were encouraged until suddenly the Israelites began to turn and march around the city walls. It became clear that the city was being surrounded by thousands upon thousands of Israelites.

Undoubtedly, the Canaanites were baffled because the Israelites remained at a good distance from the city as they marched. Day after day the Israelites marched around the city with seven long-robed men blowing ram's horns which emitted shrill blasts that echoed from the hills to the west. Behind these horn-blowers marched four more robed men carrying what appeared to be a very large box. Of course, the Canaanites had no way of knowing that this object was the Ark of the Covenant and that the robed men were priests who had been instructed to blow special horns. The trumpet blasts were the only sound that came from the Israelites as they marched around the city. The usual habit of soldiers was to shout or sing as they marched to battle. In this case, the Israelites had been told not to utter a word during the march around Jericho.

The inhabitants watched uneasily as the Israelite enemy paraded around their city and returned to the Israelite camp. Jericho's ruler remained on the wall, puzzling over such weird demonstrations. (Joshua 8:8–11)

For six days, the Israelites marched around the city, to the bewilderment of the Canaanites, each day encircling Jericho just a little after sunrise. The Canaanite sentries were surprised when they saw the marching column approaching at early dawn on the seventh day. This slight change in tactics alerted the Canaanite officers who feared that this might indicate some drastic change in Israel's plan and the king was immediately notified of what was happening outside the wall. The Israelites went around the city the same as usual, but the more interesting fact was that, instead of returning to the camp they began to encircle the city once again. In fact, they spent almost the whole day marching around Jericho. By mid-afternoon they had made six rounds and were starting on the seventh. (Joshua 6:15) Next, thousands of soldiers marched out from Israel's camp to join the marchers. The plains around Jericho gradually grew darker with the growing number of the Israelite forces approaching.

At this point, the challenging shouts which had been heard coming from the Canaanites began to die away as the Israelite military strength was displayed. Many people fell into a state of panic when they realized how many fighting men were confronting them.

Late in the afternoon, when the Israelites had finished marching around the city for the seventh time, the Ark and the trumpet blowers stayed in position before Jericho; they stopped and all the marchers came to a halt. At that moment, seven horn-blowers, who had not sounded for several minutes, blew an unusually long, shrill blast. This was followed by a chilling surge of shouts from the Israelites surrounding Jericho, as well as those left in Israel's camp, as Joshua had commanded them to do. (Joshua 6:16–19) The noise that resulted from the millions of shouts was like the thunder of a tidal wave crashing against a rocky cliff.

GOD INTERVENES

Within a few seconds of all the noise emanating from the Israelites, their voices were drowned out by another great sound of a deep rumbling like the approaching reverberation of hooves of millions of horses! Following this commotion, the walls began to sway and those inside the city were terrified to see widening cracks appear in the cobbled and bricked streets. Screaming people began to pour out of the buildings and those on the walls began to race down to a firmer footing. Unfortunately for the Canaanites, it was far too late and the walls and the streets of the city began to heave and then tumbled down.

In the midst of all the ear-splitting noise, the king and his officers were among the first to realize in their last moments of life that the mighty God of Israel did not recognize their puny, powerless gods and the idols of this world. Archaeologists have found the ruins of Jericho just where God said the city was. After careful excavations of the city for several years, archaeologists have found the earth has preserved an amazing record of God's miraculous destruction of Jericho.

The walls of that city, which fell in Joshua's day, fell outward and flat as stated in Joshua 6:20. This record of the walls falling outward has been described in many books dealing with the fall of Jericho. There was only one place in the wall which was left partially standing. That place must have been where Rahab's house was located in the wall because the Israelite spies had promised protection for Rahab and her family because of her faith. (Hebrews 11:30–31)

THE ISRAELITES ATTACK

The army of Israel, under the leadership of this great General Joshua, raced into the city where the walls had been knocked down and killed all of the inhabitants, every man, woman and child with the exception of Rahab and her family. Rahab's house was identified by a *scarlet piece of cloth* that she hung outside her dwelling as she was instructed to identify her location to the soldiers of Israel. Only Rahab and her family survived the utter destruction of the city of Jericho.

The news of the fall of Jericho swiftly spread over the land. Joshua became famous in that part of the world because of his leadership in the Jericho Conquest. As a result, fear of Israel mounted in the surrounding nations. (Joshua 6:27)

God had His own public relations. He used the Battle of Jericho to notify the land of Canaan that Israel and *The God of Israel* had arrived in the land and they were victorious fighters. Other city-states, each with its own king, wondered if they too were in the path of the Israelites.

The next city Joshua intended to conquer was Ai. It was about twelve miles from Jericho in a westerly direction and, though it was considerably smaller, Joshua had no intention of bypassing any fortress that might eventually prove troublesome. All good military leaders know they cannot pass by any army without conquering it; otherwise, as they move toward the next battle, they would have an enemy in front of and behind them.

Joshua used scouts to reconnoiter the city of Ai as he had done with Jericho. When they returned from Ai, the scouts reported that this Amorite fortress was not very large or strong and it would be easy for Israel to attack and destroy it. The scouts reported that the walls were not very high and that the city was too small to contain very many fighting men. They believed that 2000 or 3000 Israelite soldiers would be able to conquer the city of Ai. (Joshua 7:2–3)

Joshua decided it would not be necessary to deploy the full army against Ai as he had done against Jericho. Remember, Joshua was trained in military strategy by Moses, who had been trained in the most sophisticated country at that time, Egypt. God had known, in those years when Moses was living in the house of Pharaoh, that one day Moses would mold the shepherds and cattle herders of Israel into one of the fiercest fighting machines the world had ever seen. While Moses had directed all the battles in the forty years the children of Israel roamed the desert, his lieutenant was Joshua. So, in turn, Joshua had been in training for forty years to learn military strategy and logistics. Looking at the size of the city, Joshua concluded that it would only be necessary to send 3000 men to conquer Ai. As the Israelite soldiers neared Ai, located on a ridge overlooking the Jordan Valley, it was evident that the army could be seen by the Amorites in Ai and that a surprise attack would be impossible. But, the soldiers were confident now because of what God had done for them in Jericho and they marched boldly up to Ai. Joshua was certain that the Amorites would surrender when they were told to give up without a fight or be set upon by the whole Israelite army. Suddenly, the gate of Ai swung open and thousands of Amorite soldiers rushed out. The Israelites thought that all of the inhabitants of Ai would be quaking with fear; this abrupt turn of events surprised them and they momentarily froze in their tracks. By the time they got into action, spears and arrows from on-rushing Amorites were raining on the ranks of the Israelites and some of the weapons were finding fatal marks. On top of that, rock catapults propelled huge stones down upon the Israelites.

Of course, the Israelites wondered where God was in their time of need. It became shamefully obvious to them that God's protection, since the crossing of the Jordan River, was not there! Unfortunately, faith in God swiftly fled and so did the Israelites. Instead of fighting back, they turned and raced away through a hail of stone, arrows and spears. This cowardly move spurred the screaming Amorites with greater boldness and they pursued their enemies all the way back to the road over which the Israelites had come.

When, at last, the routed and panic-stricken Israelites were clear of their pursuers, they found that the Amorites had slain thirty-six of their number and had wounded many more. No doubt, this was a dejected and disgraced army that returned to camp. When the people heard what had happened, their confidence in God dropped to a new low. They could not understand why God would promise them swift victory with all their enemies, and then allow about 3000 of their solders to be totally demoralized and chased by the idol-worshipping Amorites. (Joshua 7:4–5)

After the defeat, Joshua went to God in sincere and fervent prayer asking, What went wrong? He knew that God had not been on their side and he also knew there was a reason why God was not there when the Israelites needed Him. True enough, God had withheld His protection from Israel because sin had found its way into the camp. God reminded Joshua that He had ordered that no spoils should be taken from Jericho by any of the soldiers for personal gain. In fact, this is what had happened and God instructed Joshua how to identify the guilty person and bring him to justice. Indeed, the guilty man was found and his name was Achan; he had chosen to keep for himself some of the spoil taken in the battle of Jericho. The man was stoned to death by his fellow citizen Israelites because of his sin. God used this example to once again show the people that He would not help them if they disobeyed and failed to completely follow His instructions.

God told Joshua not to be discouraged. Now that the guilty man had been dealt with, Ai would now fall under the hands of the Israelites. God promised Joshua that He would help him in the second attempt to conquer this Canaanite city. Joshua was instructed to choose 30,000 soldiers for the strategy God had in mind. This time, God intended to use a surprise attack and a diversion to destroy the Canaanite city of Ai.

The Israelites, under the command of Joshua and God as their Supreme Commander, marched across the land conquering city after city as they drove the Canaanites out of the land God had promised for Israel.

THE LAND IS DIVIDED

The land of Canaan was divided into sections according to the size of each one of the tribes. There were twelve tribes to receive territory, but the Levites were only to receive the forty-eight cities that would be dispersed throughout the entire land.

When Israel was settled, Manasseh was split into two parts. The first part was east of the Jordan River; the second part of Manasseh was west of the Jordan. The tribe of Ephraim was located due south of Manasseh and west of the Jordan River. The city of Jerusalem was located in the tribal area of Benjamin. This is an important fact, as you will later see when the Kingdom is divided. Judah was located directly south of Benjamin.

Under the great General Joshua, Israel established its new nation in the Promised Land, according to the promise God had made to Abraham almost 500 years earlier.

As Israel settled into the new land and Joshua's life ended, Israel began to experience a long period of conquering the land and establishing itself as a nation under a government of God and controlled by a series of judges.

DOING RIGHT IN
THEIR OWN EYES

J oshua led the Israelites into the Promised Land circa 1407 BC. The only two surviving members of the Israelite men of war, who came out of the land of Egypt and were allowed by God to go into the Promised Land, were Joshua and Caleb. (Joshua 5:6) Moses died before going into the Promised Land at the age of 120 years.

As you may recall, God instructed the Israelites to totally rid the land of the inhabitants as Israel occupied their new territory. Unfortunately for Israel, they did not follow God's specific instructions under Joshua. In 1385 BC, the last of the tribes received their inheritance in the Promised Land. It had now been 400 years since the first Israelites originally left the land of Canaan going into Egypt.

At the age of 110, Joshua died. The Israelites had relied upon his leadership to guide and direct their nation as they engaged in battles to subdue the land. You can imagine the confusion and despair when their leader died. Even the name "Joshua" means in a broad sense–"the deliverer," just as the name of Jesus can also be pronounced in Hebrew as "Joshua." Joshua delivered the people into the Promised Land just as Jesus Christ will deliver the True

Christians into the Promised Land of eternal life and the Kingdom of God. Joshua was a type of Jesus Christ, therefore, God rightly chose his name to be Joshua.

As we continue the saga of ancient Israel, the very first thing we see in Judges 1:1 reflects the apprehension of the Israelites concerning their leadership. They asked, "Who shall go up for us against the Canaanites, first to fight against them?" (Judges 1:1) God continued to have great influence over the Israelites and the people were informed, through His priests, that the tribe of Judah would lead the next battle against the Canaanites. (Judges 1:2–3) The remaining verses of Judges 1 describe briefly the battles fought by the Israelites as they conquered the land of Canaan.

THORNS IN YOUR SIDES

In spite of the fact that God clearly instructed the Israelites to destroy all of the inhabitants of the land of Canaan, the Israelite soldiers failed to obey God's command resulting in problems throughout all generations for the Israelites. (Judges 1:19–36) God chronicles this fact, starting with the tribe of Ephraim. Because the Israelites failed to drive out the inhabitants of the land, these surviving Canaanites would plague Israel for centuries; they would be as "thorns in their sides." (Judges 2:3) In fact, God stated that these people would become a snare to the Israelites.

The generation that knew Joshua and remembered the miracles God performed to bring the children of Israel through the desert and into the Promised Land, soon died. This next generation grew up not knowing the God of Israel and the miracles He had performed to save the nation. As this next generation came to power, they turned away from God. The young Israelite men and women began to marry the sons and daughters of Canaan, whom the Israelites allowed to survive. (Judges 2:10) Unfortunately, we will see this pattern repeated over and over again throughout the early history of the nation of Israel until finally they were taken into captivity.

God chose the Israelites to be a people unto Himself. He chose Abraham because of his obedience; therefore, God chose Abraham, Isaac and his son Jacob who became Israel, and Israel's sons. God did not choose the other sons of Abraham or Isaac, but only Israel. God wanted a people for Himself—a people who would honor and obey Him as Abraham had done, a people who would be the example to the whole world, showing all mankind the correct way to live and worship God.

As we look from this vantage point into the past, it seems hard to understand how these people, who were selected by God and given the Promised Land, would ever turn away from the God of their fathers and lose their national identity.

IDOLATRY IS INSIDIOUS

People who first know God and then go into idolatry don't wake up one morning and decide to change their belief system from God to Paganism. It is a gradual process which generally takes about a generation to develop. However, in some cases, the conversion from the true worship of God to idolatry can occur in a much shorter period of time.

The change always begins when leaders, either in government or the church, introduce so-called "new ideas" into their worship. In most cases, these new ideas come straight from Paganism and are idolatrous. In just a few years, these new idolatrous ways are accepted as the proper way to worship God. The ancient Israelites, as well as the modern-day Christian church experienced exactly the same deception. History records that Emperor Constantine, in 325 AD, in order to make the Christian church "more palatable" to his sun-god worshipping subjects, decreed that the new Christian church accept the pagan holidays of Christmas and Easter and redefine their meaning into "Christianity." It was then that the "true" Christian church gave up keeping the weekly Sabbath Day and replaced it with the sun-god worship day of Sunday and substituted the pagan holidays of Christmas and Easter for God's Annual Holy Days, as listed in Leviticus 23.

Over time, the Israelites began to adopt the worship styles of the Canaanites in the land. True enough, there would have been Israelites who objected to this change, but they became the minority and the new religion was accepted by the majority. God labeled this change as "Baal and Ashtoreth worship." In fact, God had warned the Israelites against just such actions.

> When the LORD thy God shall cut off the nations from before thee, whither thou goest to possess them, and thou succeedest them, and dwellest in their land; Take heed to thyself that thou be not snared by following them, after that they be destroyed from before thee; and that thou inquire not after their gods, saying, How did these nations serve their gods? even so will I do likewise. Thou shalt not do so unto the LORD thy God: for every abomination to the LORD, which he hateth, have they done unto their gods; for even their sons and their daughters they have burnt in the fire to their gods. What thing soever I command you, observe to do it: thou shalt not add thereto, nor diminish from it. (Deuteronomy 12:29–32)

As a result of this idolatry, God allowed the inhabitants of the land, whom the Israelites did not drive out, to rise up and fight. In many cases, their enemies overcame them and made tributaries out of them. Wherever they went, the hand of the Lord was against them because they turned their backs on Him and chose the path of *idolatry*. Israel was following the religion of those people they should have displaced. In spite of this, God still loved Israel and, when they cried out to Him, because of the pain of servitude, God would show them great mercy by sending a strong leader to once again deliver those distressed tribes of Israel out of bondage from their enemies. The book of Judges derives its name from those men and women God chose from time to time to deliver all or part of the tribes of Israel from their distress and imminent demise.

NOTABLE JUDGES

The Israelites were faced with a growing number of enemies within their borders, namely the Philistines and all of the Canaanites, Hittites, Amorites, Perizzites, Jebusites, Sidonians and Hivites. (Judges 3:3–5) The fact that the Israelites lived among these heathen people and intermarried with them caused Israel continually to fall back into idolatrous worship. This always resulted in military defeat and, in some cases, captivity.

Such an occurrence manifested itself when God sent the first leader whom He called a judge to rescue the Israelites. The man's name was Othniel, a son of Caleb's younger brother.

> And the children of Israel did evil in the sight of the LORD, and forgat the LORD their God, and served Baalim and the groves. Therefore the anger of the LORD was hot against Israel, and he sold them into the hand of Chushan-rishatha'im king of Mesopotamia: and the children of Israel served Chushan-rishatha'im eight years. And when the children of Israel cried unto the LORD, the LORD raised up a deliverer to the children of Israel, who delivered them, even Othniel the son of Kenaz, Caleb's younger brother. And the Spirit of the LORD came upon him, and he judged Israel, and went out to war: and the LORD delivered Chushan-rishatha'im king of Mesopotamia into his hand; and his hand prevailed against Chushan-rishatha'im. (Judges 3:7–10)

Under Othniel, peace and prosperity returned to the land and the people began to root out the idolatrous worship and again serve God. This lasted for forty years until Othniel's death, when the Israelites returned to the same idolatrous practices as they had done before. As a result, Eglon, the king of Moab overcame them; Israel served Eglon for eighteen years in a form of slavery. After eighteen years of servile punishment, the people cried out to God and, once again, He sent them a new leader, Ehud, who killed Eglon, king of Moab, and delivered Israel from the Moabites. (Judges 3:30)

After the death of Ehud, Israel reverted to her old ways that had gotten the nation into trouble before. As a result, God allowed Jabin, king of Canaan, to subdue the Israelites and oppress them for twenty years. God then chose Deborah, a prophetess, to lead Israel out of its hardship. (Judges 4:4) Deborah and her military leader, Barak, subdued the Canaanites and once again freed Israel.

Time and again, Israel repeated the same mistake which always ended up with the same result. Israel fell back into its old, familiar idolatrous ways of making *groves* dedicated to Baal and Ashtoreth. At one such time, the Midianites fought Israel and caused them to retreat into the mountains for protection. It was at this time God chose a young man by the name of Gideon to deliver the people from their captors.

The story of Gideon and his 300 chosen warriors is well known and is found in Judges 7.

As you read through the book of Judges, God continues to deliver the various tribes of Israel after they had fallen into idolatry and then captivity.

Another famous deliverer was a man from the tribe of Dan called Samson. Samson was chosen by God, before his birth, for the specific purpose of delivering his people from their Philistine over-lords. (Judges 13:3–5) God gave Samson unusual physical powers which enabled him to punish the Philistines for their terrorist acts against his tribe, the Danites, and others. The events of Samson's life have been well documented in Hollywood movies, as well as covered in detail in Judges, chapters 14–16. Soon after Samson's death, the Israelites were lured back into idolatry.

After several other judges, God picked the final judge for Israel; his name was Samuel.

Even before Samuel was born, his mother, Hannah, promised God that, if she was allowed to have a child, she would give her child to God's service totally after the child was weaned. God heard Hannah's prayer and soon she bore Samuel. True to her word, Hannah committed her son to God's service and delivered him to the tabernacle at Shiloh to be trained and guided by the High Priest, Eli. Once a year, his mother came to visit Samuel, bringing him a little coat which she had made when she and her husband came to offer their required seasonal sacrifices. (I Samuel 2:19) However, God knew of the empty feeling that Hannah experienced each year as she left her little boy behind. God had mercy upon Hannah and she had three sons and two daughters because of her commitment and generosity to God in turning her firstborn over to Him for His Service. (I Samuel 2:20–21)

Samuel became a prophet and Israel's last judge.

FIRST DEMOCRACY

God granted Israel its freedom for approximately 300 years from the time Israel entered the Promised Land. The Bible says that "every man did what seemed right in his own eyes." (Judges 17:6)

During this time, God allowed Israel to make its mistakes and govern itself in the absence of a king. It was the Israelites who first developed the concept of a democracy, not the Greeks. (The Israelite kingdom predated the Greek empire by 400 years; the Israelite empire ended in 720 BC and the Greek empire came into power circa 320 BC.) Even so, the Israelites could not leave "well enough" alone and they wanted a government like the heathen nations that surrounded them. The heathen nations around them had kings. They had grown weary of God ruling over them through the judges with the help of the Levites. The Israelites thought a king would make things better for them and unite their nation to fight off their enemies.

God began to work with Samuel when he was a child, as evidenced in the scriptures where God contacted Samuel on three different occasions in a "very small voice." Finally, Eli instructed

Samuel to answer God. "And the LORD came, and stood, and called as at other times, Samuel, Samuel. Then Samuel answered, Speak; for thy servant heareth." (I Samuel 3:10)

God delivered an astounding statement in the ears of Samuel.

> And the LORD said to Samuel, Behold, I will do a thing in Israel, at which both the ears of every one that heareth it shall tingle. In that day I will perform against Eli all things which I have spoken concerning his house: when I begin, I will also make an end. For I have told him that I will judge his house for ever for the iniquity which he knoweth; because his sons made themselves vile, and he restrained them not. And therefore I have sworn unto the house of Eli, that the iniquity of Eli's house shall not be purged with sacrifice nor offering for ever. (Samuel 3:11–14)

The next morning, Eli asked Samuel what God had said. Obviously, Samuel was troubled over the message God had given him, but at Eli's urging, Samuel revealed the message. From that point forward, God revealed His plans to Samuel concerning Israel.

ELI'S SONS

Even though Eli was a man of God, he had a major shortcoming that God had warned him about through the dreams of Samuel. Eli had two wicked sons, Hophni and Phinehas.

When Eli was ninety-eight years old, Israel was fighting a battle against the Philistines, Israel's worst enemy at that time. Because the Philistines were winning the battle, the Israelite soldiers sent to Shiloh to fetch the Ark of the Covenant and brought it to the battlefield on the night before the battle, thinking that would cause God to turn the battle in their favor. When the Ark of the Covenant was brought into the camp, the soldiers shouted with joy. When the Philistines realized that the Ark of the Covenant was in the midst of the army of Israel, they remembered how God had dealt with the Egyptians on Israel's behalf hundreds of years before. The Bible says "fear struck the Philistines," but soon they overcame their fear and the next day they defeated the armies of Israel. They killed 30,000 soldiers and chased the remainder back into their own tents. They also captured the Ark of the Covenant for a prize. Eli's two sons were killed. When the messenger brought the news to Eli that the Ark of the Covenant had been taken by the Philistines and that his sons had been killed, Eli fell backwards off his chair, breaking his neck and killing him instantly. (I Samuel 4:18)

Eli judged Israel 40 years. With the death of Eli and his sons, this brought to an end the high priestly line of Aaron.

THE ARK AND THE PHILISTINES

The Philistines took the Ark of God and brought it from the battle site at Ebenezer to the temple of Dagon in Ashdod. The next morning, the people of Ashdod found the fish god, Dagon, had been knocked over on its face before the Ark of the Covenant. The people set Dagon back on his place again, but the next day, the people again found that Dagon had fallen over before the Ark of the Lord. This time, the head and both the palms of his hands were cut off and only the stump of Dagon was left. The Philistines recognized that the God of Israel was unhappy with this situation and they feared retaliation from God. Sure enough, God began to strike the people with various ailments until they realized the Ark of God had to be removed from their land; otherwise God might destroy them totally as well as their god, Dagon.

The men of Ashdod sent the Ark of the Covenant to a neighboring town called Ekron. When the Ark of the Covenant came into Ekron, the Ekronites became alarmed because they had heard of the problems associated with Ashdod when the Ark was there. The Philistines moved the Ark from town to town in their land for seven months, while asking their priests and soothsayers what they should do. They advised the Philistines to send the Ark back to Israel, but "do not send it away empty; make sure it returns with a trespass offering." They felt it should be taken out of the land to stop the plagues and other problems they had endured. Their soothsayers and priests instructed them to take the Ark and put it upon a new cart pulled by two milk cows. The calves of these milk cows were taken away from the cows and shut up at home. They also instructed the people to take the jewels of gold and other offerings to satisfy the God of the Israelites for a trespass offering and send it on its way.

They devised this plan to see if the evil had come upon them by the God of Israel or if it was all just a huge coincidence. The Philistines released the Ark to see which direction it might go. They were really hedging their bets by tying up the calves at home; ordinarily, a cow with calves will find her way to her calves for feeding. The Philistines said that if the cows pulling the cart came back home, then it was all a happenstance. However, they said, if the cows pulling the cart went toward Israel's territory, Bethshemesh, they would admit that God had done this great thing to them in punishment for stealing the Ark of God.

When the Philistines released the cart pulled by the milk cows, the cows went straight toward Bethshemesh lowing as they went. With this turn of events, the Philistines knew without a shadow of a doubt that it was the God of the Israelites who was punishing them.

As the cart containing the Ark approached the border of Bethshemesh, it stopped and remained there until the Levites came and took down the Ark and the coffer with the gold and jewels in it. The men of Israel greatly rejoiced that the Ark of God had been returned to Israel.

SAMUEL, THE LAST JUDGE

Over many years, Samuel judged Israel according to God's Law. Samuel also had two sons. Apparently, Samuel did not remember, or he chose to ignore, the lesson that he had observed with the sons of Eli. Samuel's sons were just as evil as the sons of Eli and God could not allow Samuel's sons to replace him. Even the people could not accept the perversion of Samuel's sons. They believed their only way out was to change the form of government under which they had been living for these many years in the Promised Land. The elders of Israel came to Samuel and pointed out that his sons were evil and would not be righteous judges, therefore, they wanted a king just like the kings of all the nations surrounding Israel.

> And it came to pass, when Samuel was old, that he made his sons judges over Israel. Now the name of his firstborn was Joel; and the name of his second, Abiah: they were judges in Beersheba. And his sons walked not in his ways, but turned aside after lucre, and took bribes, and perverted judgment. Then all the elders of Israel gathered themselves together, and came to Samuel unto Ramah, And said unto him, Behold, thou art old, and thy sons walk not in thy ways: now make us a king to judge us like all the nations. (I Samuel 8:1–5)

Samuel took it personally that the people seemed to be rejecting him by desiring a king as their ruler. God knew the people felt the grass would be "greener on the other side" when they demanded that Samuel give them a king! God saw through this request and explained to Samuel that it was not Samuel they were rejecting, but it was, in fact, God Himself.

"And the LORD said unto Samuel, Hearken unto the voice of the people in all that they say unto thee: for they have not rejected thee, but they have rejected me, that I should not reign over them." (I Samuel 8:7)

God instructed Samuel to explain to the people what having a king would mean. Samuel told the people a king would take away their God-given freedoms and the right of self-determination. God instructed Samuel to warn the people, ahead of time, of these things that would happen if they chose to reject God as their king and have, in His place, an earthly king.

Samuel spoke the words of the Eternal unto the people who asked for a king. And this is what he said:

> A king shall reign over you and will take your sons and appoint for himself chariots and horsemen to drive his chariots. He will establish a hierarchy with captains over thousands, over hundreds and over fifties and will require you to grow crops for his people and to make instruments of war. He will take your daughters to be cooks. He will take your fields and your vineyards. He will take a tenth of all your seed and all your vineyards. He will take your menservants and your maidservants and he will take a tenth of all that you have. Ultimately, you will lose all of your freedoms. (I Samuel 8:11–18)

In spite of all this, the people refused to listen to Samuel and they chanted, "We want a king!" They wanted a king so that they would be "like everyone else."

God heard the words of the people and told Samuel to "hearken" to the people and give them a king.

GOD REVEALS THE KING

Throughout history, people are never happy with the status quo. People seem to think the "grass is always greener on the other side." As a result, change becomes inevitable—and this is exactly what the Israelites opted for after many years of God-given freedom under His government.

God set events in motion that would bring a Benjaminite by the name of Saul in contact with Samuel; this was the man whom God had chosen to be the King of Israel. As recorded in I Samuel 9, Saul was on a mission to recover some lost donkeys that belonged to his father. After traveling throughout the land, it occurred to Saul that he and his friends might approach the prophet of God and ask where they might locate the lost donkeys. God was working out a plan to introduce Saul to Samuel.

God revealed to Samuel that He would send a man to him from the tribe of Benjamin and that this man would become the first anointed king of Israel. When Samuel saw Saul coming, God informed him that this was the man he was to anoint king over all Israel. When Saul learned that Samuel intended to anoint him king over Israel, it shocked him. He informed Samuel that he was a Benjaminite, one of the smallest of the tribes of Israel and that his family was the least of all the families in the tribe of Benjamin. He wondered how he could have been chosen over all the other able-bodied men throughout Israel.

Samuel then took a vial of oil and poured it upon Saul's head, kissed him and said, "Is it not because the Lord hath anointed you to be captain over His inheritance?" And soon after that, God placed his spirit upon Saul as Samuel had promised when he anointed him.

THE KING IS PRESENTED

Samuel called all the people together at Mizpeh and announced to the tribes of Israel that God had chosen Saul, from the tribe of Benjamin, to be their king. Saul was presented to the people and all the people shouted, "God save the king!" (I Samuel 10:24)

After the ceremony, Samuel again told the people the manner of the kingdom and wrote in a book the confirmation of Saul being anointed king and the creation of the new Kingdom of Israel.

The people rallied around Saul because he was a very handsome man and stood a full head taller than all of the other Israelites. The Scripture said that he was a choice man who had good character. In fact, the Bible says there was " … none among the children of Israel a goodlier person than he," (I Samuel 9:2)

SAUL IS TESTED

New leadership is always tested by the enemy; it didn't take long until Saul's leadership was tested by the Amorites. The Amorites intended to enslave the men of Jabeshgilead and they appealed to the rest of Israel for help. When the news came to Saul, he was angry that these Amorites intended to take advantage of the men of Jabeshgilead. As a result, Saul recruited the first army under his command to fight against the Amorites. The battle was short, but Saul and his men prevailed, and the Amorites soon retreated in a scattered fashion.

After the battle, Samuel said to the people that they should all go to Gilgal and there Saul would begin his reign. All the people went to Gilgal and "made Saul king before the Lord." After this formal coronation, Saul and all the people of Israel rejoiced. Samuel said unto the people, "Behold I have hearkened unto your voice to give you a king and all you said unto me and now you have a king to rule over you."

Samuel also pointed out that, now that they had a king, the king would be their leader. Samuel acknowledged that he was old and gray. He felt somewhat down-hearted, feeling that his usefulness to Israel had probably come to an end. Yet, after giving a short speech, which sounded like a "farewell address," the people said to Samuel that they wanted him to remain an important part of their nation. In his address to the people, he reminded the Israelites of God saving them out of Egypt and the work of Moses and all of the leaders. He warned them of what had happened to the Israelites whenever they forgot God and went their own way.

Samuel reminded the people that, if they would continue to fear God and obey His voice and not rebel against His commandments, they would continue to prosper and the king would be their good leader. Samuel also reminded them of all of the curses that would come upon them if they did not obey God.

From that point on, Samuel's involvement with the people was primarily that of a spiritual advisor and the main contact between God and Israel.

SAUL REIGNS

Early in Saul's reign over Israel, the Israelites found themselves in numerous conflicts with their neighbors. In the first three years, Israel fought several major battles against the Philistines. On one such occasion, the Philistines seemed to be prevailing and the Israelites fled the battle scene into caves and rocks, rather than fight. Saul had contacted Samuel for advice and God's help in winning this battle against the Philistines. Samuel instructed Saul to remain at Gilgal for seven days, at which time Samuel would come to him and give him the latest words from God. Unfortunately for Saul, he made his first big mistake.

As Saul waited for Samuel at Gilgal, he became impatient because Samuel delayed his arrival. As a result, Saul was concerned that his army would disperse, allowing the Philistines to attack and defeat them. Therefore, Saul felt he should do something, so he decided to offer a burnt offering and a peace offering as a sacrifice to God. As soon as Saul finished the burnt offering, Samuel showed up and was astounded to find that Saul had been too impatient to wait for him. He asked Saul what on earth he had done. Saul answered that he did this because the people were scattering and he was becoming concerned about the Philistines, and besides that, he pointed out, Samuel was late in showing up.

Saul must have truly been stunned when Samuel spoke the following words:

> And Samuel said to Saul, Thou hast done foolishly: thou hast not kept the commandment of the LORD thy God, which he commanded thee: for now would the LORD have established thy kingdom upon Israel for ever. But now thy kingdom shall not continue: the LORD hath sought him a man after his own heart, and the LORD hath commanded him to be captain over his people, because thou hast not kept that which the LORD commanded thee. (I Samuel 13:13–14)

Can you imagine the utter amazement that Saul must have felt after being told that his kingdom would not stand and knowing that these were words coming directly from God through Samuel's mouth? This event occurred at a time when Saul had been ruling in Israel for only a little more than three years. As you will see, God allowed Saul to remain many more years as the anointed king of Israel.

SAUL ISSUES A FOOLISH ORDER

Again, Saul and his men faced the Philistines. In this case, some of the Israelites had joined forces with the Philistines to fight against Saul and his army. As a result, Saul was very concerned about victory and he issued an order forbidding any of his men to eat any food until the army could be avenged. Unknown to Saul, Jonathan, Saul's grown son who was in charge of a band of Israel's soldiers, had already routed the Philistines and had not heard Saul's order concerning the "fast" until the end of the day. As Jonathan was returning to Saul to report his victory, he found a honeycomb and tasted the honey to renew his strength.

When it was learned that Jonathan had eaten the honey in violation of the order, the people were fearful for Jonathan. Saul's foolish order to refrain from eating anything prior to the battle had caused the soldiers to be very physically weak and yet they were successful. Jonathan's men had already beaten the Philistines.

After the battle, Saul was disturbed that Jonathan had unknowingly disobeyed his order, which carried with it a "death penalty." However, the people rallied to Jonathan's side to convince Saul not to kill him because Jonathan had fought a great battle which caused Israel to carry the day. Saul revoked the penalty.

Soon after this, according to I Samuel 14:47, Saul became the undisputed king over the entire nation of Israel. The name of Saul and the power of Israel were exalted. He was greatly loved by the Israelites because of his stature (standing head and shoulders above the rest) and charisma. The people willingly followed Saul.

SAUL DISOBEYS

God instructed Samuel to issue Saul an order to fight against the Amalekites. God remembered the Amalekites from the time when they forbade Israel safe passage through their land after Israel left Egypt. This event occurred over 300 years before, but God still remembered and reserved His punishment of the Amalekites; now the time had arrived!

God wanted Saul and his army to attack the Amalekites and utterly destroy all of them; they were ordered to slay men, women, infants and all of their livestock. This order was issued to Saul and he readily pursued the Amalekites to carry out God's command.

But, Saul did not obey as he was instructed to do. Saul chose to save Agag, the king of the Amalekites and the best of the sheep, the oxen and the fatling of the lambs. All that was good was not destroyed. Saul proved to God that he could not be trusted to be a king over Israel. Saul would not follow God's commands; instead, he looked at this direct order from his own point of view.

As a result, God spoke to Samuel and expressed his anger against Saul for not performing all of the directives given to him. The next day, Samuel came to meet Saul, already knowing that he had disobeyed God. When Saul saw Samuel, he approached him, giving thanks to God for the great victory. He said to Samuel, "I have performed all the commandments of the Lord." At this point, Samuel again startled Saul with God's words. "And Samuel said, What meaneth then this bleating of the sheep in mine ears, and the lowing of the oxen which I hear?" (I Samuel 15:14)

Immediately, Saul knew that Samuel was displeased and, rather than taking the responsibility for his actions, he blamed the "people" for saving the sheep and oxen. (Verse 15) "And Saul said, They have brought them from the Amalekites: for the people spared the best of the sheep and of the oxen, to sacrifice unto the LORD thy God; and the rest we have utterly destroyed."

Samuel told Saul that God had a stern message for him!

> And Samuel said, When thou wast little in thine own sight, wast thou not made the head of the tribes of Israel, and the LORD anointed thee king over Israel? And the LORD sent thee on a journey, and said, Go and utterly destroy the sinners the Amalekites, and fight against them until they be consumed. Wherefore then didst thou not obey the voice of the LORD, but

didst fly upon the spoil, and didst evil in the sight of the LORD? (I Samuel 15:17–19)

Even after this, Saul protested by placing the blame directly upon the shoulders of the people.

> And Saul said unto Samuel, Yea, I have obeyed the voice of the LORD, and have gone the way which the LORD sent me, and have brought Agag the king of Amalek, and have utterly destroyed the Amalekites. But the people took of the spoil, sheep and oxen, the chief of the things which should have been utterly destroyed, to sacrifice unto the LORD thy God in Gilgal. (Verses 20–21)

God knew Saul's heart; He saw a spirit of rebellion in Saul against His direct orders. "For rebellion is as the sin of witchcraft, and stubbornness is as iniquity and idolatry. Because thou hast rejected the word of the LORD, he hath also rejected thee from being king." (Samuel 15:23)

Samuel had grown to love King Saul very much. He realized that God would not perpetuate the family of Saul as the rulers of Israel. He also knew this meant that Jonathan would never sit on the throne because of the disobedience of his father. Samuel grieved for many days over the fact that God was going to take the kingdom away from Saul and his family. God soon grew weary of Samuel's mourning for Saul.

> And Samuel came no more to see Saul until the day of his death: nevertheless Samuel mourned for Saul: and the LORD repented that he had made Saul king over Israel. And the LORD said unto Samuel, How long wilt thou mourn for Saul, seeing I have rejected him from reigning over Israel? fill thine horn with oil, and go, I will send thee to Jesse the Bethlehemite: for I have provided me a king among his sons. (I Samuel 15:35;16:1)

GOD CHOOSES ANOTHER

God told Samuel that He had chosen a man to be the new king over Israel and, of course, Samuel would anoint him. Even though Samuel would not live to see the end of Saul's reign and the new king take over, Samuel knew that the deed would be accomplished at some point and that a new line would reign in place of Saul and his descendants.

God directed Samuel to go to the family of Jesse, of the tribe of Judah, in Bethlehem. Samuel set apart Jesse and his sons and offered a sacrifice to God. Jesse presented seven of his sons to Samuel. God rejected each one. Finally Samuel asked if these were all of his sons.

> And Samuel said unto Jesse, Are here all thy children? And he said, There remaineth yet the youngest, and, behold, he keepeth the sheep. And Samuel said unto Jesse, Send and fetch him: for we will not sit down till he come hither. (I Samuel 16:11)

Soon, the last son of Jesse came to Samuel. He was of smaller stature than Saul; yet, he was a good-looking young man—ruddy with red or strawberry blond hair. As soon as he appeared before Samuel, God said, "This is the one!" David was a very young man, probably between sixteen and seventeen years old. The Bible says he was a boy of beautiful countenance. Samuel took the horn of oil and anointed him in the midst of his brothers and immediately the Spirit of God came upon David from that day forward. And, at the same time, God removed His Spirit from Saul. (I Samuel 16:13–14)

Samuel departed, having completed his mission and went home to Ramah to live out the remainder of his life.

GOD GROWS A KING

Saul's servants noticed a change in Saul's personality; an evil spirit often came upon him. One of his servants suggested that music might calm him and restore Saul's pleasant countenance. Saul agreed and instructed the servants to find a musician that could be brought into the court to play for him and "soothe the angry beast."

One of Saul's servants said he had seen a son of Jesse playing a stringed instrument (something like the guitar today) which might just fit the bill. Saul sent messengers to Jesse and requested David's presence at court.

David came and immediately Saul liked him. He even gave David the responsibility of being his armor-bearer. God had a hand in this arrangement because He wanted David to learn the ways of the kingdom by being in the king's court on a regular basis.

Sure enough the evil spirit left Saul while David was playing his instrument.

As time went by, David learned much about the inner workings of the palace and the duties and responsibilities of a king. David grew in Saul's favor, as well as those who had any contact with him.

DAVID AND GOLIATH

Israel's long-time enemy, the Philistines, were again challenging the army of Israel. This time the Philistines believed they had the ultimate weapon in the guise of a giant of a man; his name was Goliath of Gath. The Bible says he was six cubits and a span tall, which equates to about ten ft. He had a helmet of brass, a coat of metal which weighed approximately 100 lbs., brass shields on his legs and he carried an iron spear six inches in diameter and fifteen ft. long weighing at least twenty-five lbs.

This enormous individual taunted the armies of Israel to come out and fight him. In fact, he proposed a battle between the Philistines and Israel by only two men; Goliath proposed that he would represent the Philistine army and that one Israelite soldier would represent the Israelite army. It would be a battle to the death and the winner would be the victorious army.

While Saul and his armies were preparing to battle the Philistines, David went back home to his father to care for the sheep. However, Jesse's three eldest sons followed Saul into battle because they were over twenty years of age which qualified them to go to war. (Numbers 26:2)

This taunting by the Philistines lasted for about forty days. Jesse sent David with food to his three brothers encamped with Saul.

When David arrived at the camp and was talking to his brothers, Goliath came forward as he did every day to taunt the men of Israel. David was amazed to see the soldiers of Israel so afraid of this giant. However, the men of Israel said, "Have you seen this man that defies us and his great size?" David then heard that Saul had pledged to give any man who fought Goliath great riches, including his daughter in marriage and making his father's house free in Israel. All that was required was to kill Goliath. David went to Saul and volunteered for the task of fighting Goliath. Saul protested, saying that David was not capable of fighting this Philistine because he was not of age to be a soldier. David pointed out to Saul that he had developed a lot of strength over the years and, in fact, he had killed a lion and a bear that had taken lambs out of his flock. After convincing Saul, David then prepared to fight Goliath. Saul urged David to use the king's armor but it was too large. Instead, David took his staff in his hand along with his sling shot. He chose five smooth stones out of the brook and put them in his shepherd's bag.

When David reached Goliath, Goliath was insulted that the Israelites would send such a youth against him; the Philistines cursed David by their gods. Goliath said to David, "Come to me and I will give your flesh unto the fowls of the air and the beasts of the field." Then said David to Goliath, "Why don't you come to me with your sword, spear and shield and I will come to you in the name of the Lord of Hosts, the God of the Armies of Israel whom you have defiled." David boldly proclaimed that God would deliver Goliath into his hands on that day.

Incensed by this inexperienced soldier, Goliath charged toward David to slay him. At that moment, David fearlessly put his hand into his bag, took out a stone, placed it in his slingshot and hurled the stone directly at Goliath, hitting him in the forehead. Goliath fell to the ground in an unconscious heap. David then ran forward and grabbed Goliath's sword and cut off his head. As soon as the Philistines saw that Goliath was dead, they fled for fear of the Israelites.

When Saul saw David pursuing the Philistines with the rest of the army, he asked General Abner, "Who was the young man?" At this point, Abner did not know David. For some reason, Saul did not make the connection that this young man was the court musician who had played music for him in the past.

As David returned from the slaughter, Abner took him to Saul with the head of the Philistine, Goliath, in his hand.

From that point on, Saul took David into his house and would not let him go back to his father's home. Jonathan and David became the closest of friends. In fact, Jonathan stripped himself of his princely robe and gave it to David, along with his sword, his bow and his girdle (belt).

David was at Saul's side wherever he went. God placed David in this position to learn more about the kingship. Remember, God was growing a king!

Eventually (after David became of age to go to war), Saul set David over the men of war. (I Samuel 18:5)

SAUL IS JEALOUS OF DAVID

As Saul and his army returned from a great victory over the Philistines, some of the women of Israel came out singing and dancing to meet Saul with their musical instruments. These women were engaged to celebrate victories or to sing at funerals. They composed a song which included the words, "Saul hath slain his thousands, and David his ten-thousands."

When Saul heard the women praising David more than he was praised, he became jealous of David and, from that day forward, Saul became David's enemy.

The next day, when David was playing his instrument for Saul, Saul picked up a javelin and threw it at David, trying to kill him. Being very swift afoot, David jumped out of the way as the javelin struck the wall. David immediately left the palace, but Saul became even more jealous of David because Saul knew God was with David and no longer with him.

Saul, therefore, removed David from the position of Captain over thousands; thus began a long period of "bad blood" between David and Saul. To make matters worse for Saul, all of Israel and Judah loved David.

Saul dispatched David on dangerous missions which he thought would result in David's death. On one such mission, Saul demanded that David kill 100 Philistines, circumcise them and bring the foreskins to him. He thought David would be killed on this mission. However, if he returned, his reward would be the King's daughter, Michal, as his wife. David responded and fulfilled King Saul's request. Because Saul's devious plan did not work, he instructed his servant to kill David, but this information was given to Jonathan, who immediately went to David and advised him of Saul's plot.

Jonathan and David worked out a signal to warn David if his life was in danger from Saul. At the same time, Jonathan spoke to his father in an effort to change his mind and allow David to continue being part of Saul's army to fight the Philistines.

Soon, another war broke out between Israel and the Philistines; David once again was enlisted into the army of Saul to fight the Philistines. David was victorious and was allowed back into Saul's house.

Again, when the evil spirit came upon Saul, David played his instrument to soothe Saul. As Saul did previously, he picked up a javelin and threw it at David, still intent upon killing him. That night, David fled the palace to escape Saul's anger, with the help of Michal. Because Saul did not know David had escaped, he sent his servants with instructions to kill David.

DAVID GOES TO SAMUEL

Since Samuel was a prophet and had anointed him to be king, David felt he could seek his advice. He went to Ramah, Samuel's home and told Samuel all the attempts Saul had made on his life. David accompanied Samuel to the School of the Prophets at Naioth, where Samuel was the Headmaster.

When Saul heard that David was in Naioth, with Samuel, he sent his servants to capture David or kill him. When Saul's servants came to the School of the Prophets and observed the students speaking with inspiration concerning God, they also began to speak under inspiration, giving up on their mission to capture David. Saul sent additional messengers to capture David; they too joined the students speaking with inspiration. After this, Saul decided to take matters into his own hands. He went to Ramah to find Samuel and David. As he approached Ramah, suddenly, the Spirit of God came upon Saul and he too began to prophesy. He stripped off all of his armor and kingly robes, as a sign of humility, and started speaking under inspiration. The bottom line was—no one captured David!

David met Jonathan and asked, "What have I done? What is my iniquity? What is my sin before your father who seeks to kill me?" (I Samuel 20:1)

Jonathan told David that he would be his eyes and ears in Saul's palace, advising him of every move his father would take as it related to him. Jonathan professed his profound friendship and respect for David. "Then said Jonathan unto David, Whatsoever thy soul desireth, I will even do it for thee." (I Samuel 20:4)

THE SHEWBREAD

By now, David had a small following of loyal men who believed he would one day become king of all Israel. Some of these men, like David, were on the run for one reason or another. David and his soldiers came to a priest in Nob whose name was Ahimelech. The priest was fearful when he saw David approach because he knew of Saul's intentions to kill David.

David explained that he and his soldiers were hungry, asking the priest if he might provide the bread on the table for the men to eat. Shocked at this request, the priest pointed out to David that this was no ordinary bread, but bread set aside especially to be used as an offering to God. However, the priest understood the immediate need of David and his friends to have some food. The priest then asked several questions about whether the men had been with women over the past several days. When it was determined that they had not, the priest gave the "hallowed" bread to David and his men to eat.

This bread had been set aside for a specific use as a sacrifice.

> And the LORD spake unto Moses, saying, Command the children of Israel, that they bring unto thee pure oil olive beaten for the light, to cause the lamps to burn continually. Without the veil of the testimony, in the tabernacle of the congregation, shall Aaron

order it from the evening unto the morning before the LORD continually: it shall be a statute for ever in your generations. He shall order the lamps upon the pure candlestick before the LORD continually. And thou shalt take fine flour, and bake twelve cakes thereof: two tenth deals shall be in one cake. And thou shalt set them in two rows, six on a row, upon the pure table before the LORD. And thou shalt put pure frankincense upon each row, that it may be on the bread for a memorial, even an offering made by fire unto the LORD. (Leviticus 24:1–7)

Since David was not of the priestly line, it was unlawful for him or his soldiers to eat this bread. However, the priest agreed to give this shewbread to nourish David and his hungry men. Jesus Christ actually mentioned this event in Matthew 12 when He was responding to the Pharisees who accused Him of breaking the Sabbath after Jesus Christ and His Disciples had plucked ears of corn to eat on the Sabbath Day.

At that time Jesus went on the sabbath day through the corn; and his disciples were an hungred, and began to pluck the ears of corn, and to eat. But when the Pharisees saw it, they said unto him, Behold, thy disciples do that which is not lawful to do upon the sabbath day. But he said unto them, Have ye not read what David did, when he was an hungred, and they that were with him; How he entered into the house of God, and did eat the shewbread, which was not lawful for him to eat, neither for them which were with him, but only for the priests? Or have ye not read in the law, how that on the sabbath days the priests in the temple profane the sabbath, and are blameless? (Matthew 12:1–5)

Christ showed that David was blameless in this act even though he did profane the law and the rituals relating to the shewbread.

Ahimelech also gave David the sword of Goliath which David had captured years before. Then David and his followers departed, hoping to avoid Saul and his men.

Soon after David's departure, Saul and his band arrived to question the priests. Doeg, an Edomite servant, told Saul that Ahimelech allowed David and his men to eat the shewbread. Saul had Ahimelech and all of his family executed because he had befriended David, his most hated enemy. Saul used Doeg to execute the priests and their families. Doeg also killed the other priests in Nob, as well as men, women, children, sheep, oxen and donkeys. That day 85 priests died as a result of Saul's anger. However, one of the sons of Ahimelech, Abiathar, escaped and followed David to tell him what Saul had done to the priests of God. David told Abiathar that he knew the Edomite was responsible for this horrible massacre and David decided to deal with him later.

SAUL PURSUES DAVID

As each day passed, Saul realized that David was the one God was grooming to replace him as king. As Saul's hatred for David grew, his mind became more twisted with intense passion to kill him. Saul, in his tormented mind, thought he could derail God's plan by destroying David.

Saul pursued David throughout the land of Israel, with David staying just one jump ahead of him and his men. On one occasion, when Saul was hunting for David in the wilderness of Engedi, Saul went into a cave. This was the same cave in which David and his men were hiding. David and his men were astonished to see Saul alone. David's men urged him to kill Saul and put an end to this grave danger. "And the men of David said unto him, Behold the day of which the LORD said unto thee, Behold, I will deliver thine enemy into thine hand, that thou mayest do to him as it shall seem good unto thee...." (I Samuel 24:4)

However, David had no intention of killing the king. He slipped up behind Saul and cut a piece from Saul's garment. David would later use this piece of fabric to prove his loyalty toward Saul, to prove that he would not kill his king.

After Saul and his men left the cave, David emerged from the cave and began calling out to Saul. When Saul turned, David bowed to the ground in respect for his king in a gesture of sincerity toward Saul. David advised Saul that his men wanted David to kill him while he was in the cave. To prove that he was close enough to do it without Saul's knowledge, David held up the piece of the robe he had cut from Saul's garment. David informed Saul that the Lord had delivered him into his hands that day in the cave, but David reminded him that he would not put forth his hand against God's anointed king of Israel. (I Samuel 24:9–11)

When Saul realized the danger he had been in, it affected him emotionally and he began to weep and cry out that David was far more righteous than he.

> And it came to pass, when David had made an end of speaking these words unto Saul, that Saul said, Is this thy voice, my son David? And Saul lifted up his voice, and wept. And he said to David, Thou art more righteous than I: for thou hast rewarded me good, whereas I have rewarded thee evil. And thou hast shewed this day how that thou hast dealt well with me: forasmuch as when the Lord had delivered me into thine hand, thou killedst me not. For if a man find his enemy, will he let him go well away? herefore the Lord reward thee good for that thou hast done unto me this day. (I Samuel 24:16–19)

At this point, Saul had to admit God had chosen David to be king over Israel and his rule would eventually come to an end. "And now, behold, I know well that thou shalt surely be king, and that the kingdom of Israel shall be established in thine hand." (I Samuel 24:20)

After this, Saul asked David to swear to him that he would not destroy Jonathan or his family after he became king. It was always the custom, up until the last half of the Twentieth Century, that when kingships changed, the new king would attempt to kill the possible heirs to the throne. This could include cousins, brothers, even sons and other relatives. The thinking was that, if the heirs lived, they would raise an army, come in, and kill the present king, and take the crown for themselves. This scenario has happened many times in history. This was one reason for having an army—to protect the king and protect him from those trying to take the rulership away from him.

Saul knew that possibility arose because of how he had treated David for almost thirty-seven years. He also knew that David would keep his word; therefore, he asked him to swear to it. With this request, David readily agreed that he would protect Saul's family and descendants.

SAMUEL DIES

Samuel, the last judge of Israel and one of its greatest prophets, died in his old age. He saw Israel come together as a nation under its king and witnessed the nation reject God as its king in favor of an earthly king, giving up many of its God-given freedoms in favor of a human monarch. God sent Samuel at just the right time to judge Israel in preparation for the nation's transition from a God-centered government to a human-centered government. Samuel was well-known and respected throughout the land. Surely, Samuel watched the events unfolding between Saul and David with a great deal of sorrow and concern. Samuel loved Saul and one can only wonder if he ever got over the fact that Saul and his family would not continue to rule in Israel. All the Israelites gathered together and lamented the death of Samuel and they buried him in Ramah. Following this, David became concerned that Saul would once try to kill him.

DAVID REFUSES TO KILL THE KING

As David had suspected, Saul once again gathered his army together and began chasing him. Soon Saul heard that David was hiding himself in the hill of Hachilah, which is near Jeshimon. One night when Saul was camped out with his soldiers near the hill of Hachilah, David found himself in a position for a second time where he could take the life of Saul.

While Saul and his men were sleeping, David and one of his followers, Abishai, slipped into the camp and found Saul sleeping in a trench. David and Abishai approached Saul unnoticed. Abishai urged David to kill Saul and end this relentless pursuit. However, David again refused to lay a hand upon King Saul.

> Then said Abishai to David, God hath delivered thine enemy into thine hand this day: now therefore let me smite him, I pray thee, with the spear even to the earth at once, and I will not smite him the second time. And David said to Abishai, Destroy him not: for who can stretch forth his hand against the LORD's anointed, and be guiltless? David said furthermore, As the LORD liveth, the LORD shall smite him; or his day shall come to die; or he shall descend into battle, and perish. The LORD forbid that I should stretch forth mine hand against the LORD's anointed: but, I pray thee, take thou now the spear that is at his bolster, and the cruse of water, and let us go. (I Samuel 26:8–11)

Instead of killing Saul, David took Saul's spear and a small container of water from Saul's personal effects and crept away. After this, David began crying out to the people surrounding them so that they might hear him. When Saul and Abner, Saul's General, were awakened, David chided Abner for not protecting the king at all times.

And David cried to the people, and to Abner the son of

Ner, saying, Answerest thou not, Abner? Then Abner answered and said, Who art thou that criest to the king? And David said to Abner, Art not thou a valiant man? and who is like to thee in Israel? wherefore then hast thou not kept thy lord the king? for there came one of the people in to destroy the king thy lord. This thing is not good that thou hast done. As the LORD liveth, ye are worthy to die, because ye have not kept your master, the LORD's anointed. And now see where the king's spear is, and the cruse of water that was at his bolster. (I Samuel 26:14–16)

Immediately, Saul knew this was the voice of David and that, again, his life had been spared by his enemy, David. (I Samuel 26:17–18)

Following this encounter, Saul was remorseful. However, David knew in his heart that this was not the end of the pursuit by Saul and that Saul would not rest so long as David lived. As a result, David resolved to keep moving in order to avoid Saul.

Even though Saul was intent upon killing David, his attention was diverted because of continued attacks by the Philistines. On one occasion, when the Philistines had gathered to fight Israel at Shunem, Saul gathered his army together in the area of Gilboa. When Saul saw the size of the Philistine army, he became very afraid and remembered, in times past, that he would go to Samuel for guidance. Since Samuel was dead, Saul made a very foolish decision. He decided to consult a fortune teller much like many of the fortune tellers that are advertising on television today as psychics. Saul instructed his servants to seek out a psychic who had a spirit guide and inquire if he would win the battle against the Philistines. His servants found a psychic (witch) at Endor who had such a spirit. Saul approached the woman, but in disguise. He asked what he should do. The evil spirit knew who Saul was and revealed it to the woman. She recognized him as the king who had rid the land of other psychics; therefore, she was unwilling to provide her service to Saul. Saul assured her that he would not harm her if she would grant him this request to speak to Samuel, the deceased prophet. The woman then consulted her spirit world and the demons produced a figure that resembled Samuel. When she saw this figure, she was very much afraid and she said she saw demonic spirits ascending up from the earth. One of these spirits appeared and Saul thought it was Samuel. The spirit said to Saul, "Why are you bothering me?" Saul expressed his concerns about the outcome of the battle because he knew that God had departed from him. The evil spirit, posing as Samuel, confirmed that God had truly left Saul and He was now his enemy! The evil spirit reminded him that Samuel said God rent the kingdom from his hand and gave it to David. This spirit, which Saul thought to be Samuel, advised Saul that Israel would lose this battle to the Philistines.

After this, the psychic was very fearful for her life and she once again reminded Saul of his promise not to harm her because she was a witch.

SAUL DIES

Soon after seeking counsel with the "witch of Endor," Saul lost all touch with reality and the "die was cast" regarding his fate. The armies of Israel and the armies of the Philistines squared off. Since it became obvious the Israelites were losing, they began to flee in all directions. All of Saul's sons, including Jonathan, were slain by the Philistines and Saul himself was wounded by an arrow.

When Saul realized the battle was lost and he was about to be captured, he commanded his armor bearer to draw his sword and kill his king, lest Saul be captured by the Philistines. However, his armor bearer would not do it because, after all, this was the king of Israel. Then Saul took his own sword and fell upon it. When the armor bearer saw that Saul was dead, he too fell upon his own sword and died alongside his king. On that day, Saul died, as well as his three sons, his armor bearer and many of his men that surrounded him.

When the soldiers saw that Saul was dead, fear gripped them

and they fled in all directions from the Philistines. When the Philistines found Saul's body, they cut off his head, stripped him of his armor and sent it to the land of the Philistines to publish victory over Israel. In fact, they put his armor in the pagan temple of Ashtoreth, and fastened his body to the wall of Bethshan in a victorious salute over the Israelites.

At nightfall, some of Saul's soldiers went to the wall of Bethshan and took down his body and the bodies of his sons. They were buried under a tree in Jabesh and the soldiers fasted seven days in mourning for Saul and his sons; all the while they wondered what on earth would happen to Israel now that their king was dead.

DAVID MOURNS SAUL

While Saul had his hands full with the Philistines, David fought against the Amalekites and was victorious. A young man came to him who had torn clothes and dust upon his head, indicating a disaster had occurred. When David questioned him, he was shocked to hear that Israel lost the battle and that his beloved friend, Jonathan, was dead as well as the king and his other sons. David asked the young man how he knew of the deaths of the king and his sons. At this point, the soldier, who was an Amalekite, thought he might win great favor in David's sight by making up a story which he thought would please David.

The Amalekite said that Saul intended to kill himself, but that he could not do it, so supposedly he asked the Amalekite to slay him so he would not be captured. This soldier, thinking to win David's favor, told David that he took the sword and killed King Saul. He was certain David would be happy that he had killed Saul.

As soon as David heard the story, he rent his clothing and all the men with him did the same. They mourned, wept and fasted until evening for Saul and for Jonathan, his son. They also mourned for the House of Israel because it had been defeated by the Philistines.

David then turned to the Amalekite and asked, "Who are you?"

And the man answered, "I am an Amalekite." David said unto him, "Were you not afraid to kill God's anointed king over Israel?" At that point, David became so angry that he ordered the death penalty for the man. How dare he take it upon himself to kill the King of Israel!

Afterwards, David sorely lamented for his king and his dear friend, Jonathan. The following verses reflect David's true sorrow at the death of the king of Israel in such a horrible and untimely fashion.

The beauty of Israel is slain upon thy high places: how are the mighty fallen!

Tell it not in Gath, publish it not in the streets of Askelon; lest the daughters of the Philistines rejoice, lest the daughters of the uncircumcised triumph.

Ye mountains of Gilboa, let there be no dew, neither let there be rain, upon you, nor fields of offerings: for there the shield of the mighty is vilely cast away, the shield of Saul, as though he had not been anointed with oil.

From the blood of the slain, from the fat of the mighty, the bow of Jonathan turned not back, and the sword of Saul returned not empty.

Saul and Jonathan were lovely and pleasant in their lives, and in their death they were not divided: they were swifter than eagles, they were stronger than lions.

Ye daughters of Israel, weep over Saul, who clothed you in scarlet, with other delights, who put on ornaments of gold upon your apparel.

How are the mighty fallen in the midst of the battle! O Jonathan, thou wast slain in thine high places.

I am distressed for thee, my brother Jonathan: very pleasant hast thou been unto me: thy love to me was wonderful, passing the love of women.

How are the mighty fallen, and the weapons of
war perished! (II Samuel 1:19–27)

Saul was the first king of Israel. His reign was for forty years,
from circa 1000 BC until 960 BC. He was rejected by God after three
years into his kingship; therefore, God spent thirty-seven years
growing a new king, a man after God's own heart, a man chosen in
his youth to be Israel's greatest king—David!

DAVID–A KING AFTER GOD'S OWN HEART

G od gave Israel a king according to the wishes of the people. Israel's first king, Saul, ultimately rejected God and ruled according to the way of man, rather than according to the way of God! God brought to an end the rule of Saul's family and gave the kingdom to David and his heirs. Believe it or not, it is David's throne given to him by God that Jesus Christ will take over at His Return!

> For unto us a child is born, unto us a son is given: and the government shall be upon his shoulder: and his name shall be called Wonderful, Counsellor, The mighty God, The everlasting Father, The Prince of Peace. Of the increase of his government and peace there shall be no end, upon the throne of David, and upon his kingdom, to order it, and to establish it with judgment and with justice from henceforth even for ever. The zeal of the LORD of hosts will perform this. (Isaiah 9:6–7)

> He shall be great, and shall be called the Son of the Highest: and the Lord God shall give unto him the

throne of his father David: And he shall reign over the
house of Jacob for ever; and of his kingdom there shall
be no end. (Luke 1:32–33)

For Christ to return and sit upon the throne of David, as it says
in these two Biblical passages, it can only mean that throne must be
in existence at the return of Jesus Christ. God emphatically promised David that he and his heirs would always sit upon the throne
in Israel.

And when thy days be fulfilled, and thou shalt sleep
with thy fathers, I will set up thy seed after thee, which
shall proceed out of thy bowels, and I will establish his
kingdom. He shall build a house for my name, and
I will establish the throne of his kingdom for ever. I
will be his father, and he shall be my son. If he commit iniquity, I will chasten him with the rod of men,
and with the stripes of the children of men: But my
mercy shall not depart away from him, as I took it
from Saul, whom I put away before thee. And thine
house and thy kingdom shall be established for ever
before thee: thy throne shall be established for ever.
(II Samuel 7:12–16)

God's promises are sure and the fact that David's throne exists
today will be another clue to help you identify where the so-called
Lost Tribes of Israel presently reside. "The LORD hath sworn in
truth unto David; he will not turn from it; Of the fruit of thy body
will I set upon thy throne." (Psalms 132:11)

DAVID CROWNED KING OF JUDAH

The death of Saul did not end David's troubles. Before Saul's death,
David had formed an alliance with the Philistine king, Achish, and
as a result, he had almost become a traitor to his own country in his
effort to flee from Saul. David asked God what he should do and
where he should go. Even though David already knew that God

intended to make him king over all Israel, he chose not to ask God concerning his kingship. Instead, he asked for God's guidance and leadership. God instructed him to go to Hebron. When he arrived in Hebron, the men of Judah came and anointed him king over the house of Judah. David began to reign circa 960 BC.

But at the same time, Abner, who had been the captain of Saul's army, intended to maintain the house of Saul over the nation of Israel. As soon as it was practical, Abner took steps to make sure that Saul's son, Ishbosheth, took Saul's place. As a result, there was contention between the two kingdoms. Abner and the servants of Ishbosheth went to Gibeon where they met Joab, who was the captain of David's army. As they sat together at the pool, they suggested a competition should be held between the men of David and the followers of Ishbosheth. Unfortunately, this was a ruse and, after they formed a team of twelve men on each side, they engaged in a game that resulted in the servants of Ishbosheth killing the servants of David. Immediately, a fierce battle broke out and David's servants defeated Abner and his men.

Abner fled, pursued by one of David's servants—Asahel, Joab's brother. As Abner was fleeing on foot, Asahel pursued him with the intention of slaying him. Abner warned Asahel to stop chasing him; otherwise, he would be forced to kill him. When Asahel did not heed the warning, Abner killed the pursuing Asahel. (II Samuel 2:22–23)

Joab, David's captain, continued to pursue Abner because he had killed his brother. Soon, Joab had the full army in pursuit of Abner's men because of his treachery. When Abner saw that David's men were coming after him, he stopped and called out to Joab, asking for a truce. (II Samuel 2:25–26) In the course of the battle between Abner's followers and Joab's men, Joab's men killed 360 of Abner's men, but Joab only lost a total of 20 men, including Asahel. Unfortunately, this did not end hostilities and there was a long war between the House of Saul and the House of David. But, in the process of time, David became stronger and Saul's son became weaker and weaker.

As the weeks and months went by, Abner recognized his cause of supporting Saul's son, Ishbosheth, was hopeless. David and his men were winning everywhere and it now seemed that the people wanted David to be their king. In addition to Abner's other troubles, Ishbosheth accused Abner of sexual improprieties with Saul's concubine. As a result, Abner decided to switch sides and join David.

When David heard the news that Abner was coming over to his side, he knew this would mean an end to the war. Essentially, the kingdom of Judah, led by David, was fighting against the kingdom of Israel, led by Saul's son, Ishbosheth. Abner said that he would help bring all Israel under David's rule. David admired Abner as a good general and believed he would be loyal to him, as he was once to Saul. However, in order to test his loyalty, David made one condition for peace. Abner must bring Michal, David's first wife, to him. Abner agreed and made arrangements to send Michal to David.

Then, Abner got in touch with all the elders of Israel and told them of his plans to unite the kingdom under David. When the elders all agreed to the plan of uniting the kingdom, a state dinner was held. Abner and twenty men came to David in Hebron. It was a joyous occasion and David, with his forgiving nature, gladly overlooked all that Abner had done against him in the years gone by as a leader of Saul's army. Abner again promised to bring Israel under David's rule.

However, Joab was still angry with Abner because he had killed Joab's brother, Asahel. He was angry, beyond words, that David forgave Abner and planned to give him a very high position in his government. Joab deceitfully came to Abner under the pretext of speaking to him about official matters. Joab felt Abner was nothing more than a spy from Ishbosheth, and he hated him for killing his brother, Asahel. When Joab and Abner were alone, Joab killed Abner in exactly the same way Abner had killed Asahel. When David heard about the murder, he was saddened and he ordered Joab to put on sackcloth and mourn for the man he had killed.

When the funeral was held, King David himself followed the bier of the fallen general, Abner. David said of this great general, "Know you not that there is a prince and a great man fallen this day in Israel?" David was saddened and ashamed that one of his own men should have played such a deceitful trick upon a man David had forgiven.

Shortly after the news of Abner's death had spread across the country, two of Saul's captains, Bannah and Rechab, wanting to win David's favor, decided to get rid of David's rival, Ishbosheth. They killed Ishbosheth and took his head to David. David's outrage overtook him and he commanded that his young men slay Bannah and Rechab.

THE NATION UNITED

Many years now had passed since David had killed Goliath and he had spent most of his time on the battlefield. After Saul's death, David was anointed king over the people of Judah and ruled over Judah for seven and a half years until the death of Ishbosheth, Saul's son. With the help of Abner, before his untimely death, the elders of Israel realized that it would be better to once again unite the entire kingdom of Israel under a single leader. At that time, they publicly acknowledged and anointed David to be king over all Israel.

It turned out to be a great procession like the land had never seen before. (I Chronicles 12:23–39) Tens of thousands of people came to the ceremony. Every tribe sent its finest troops, all fully armed. As the procession moved to crown King David, 6800 soldiers of Judah led the procession of all the tribes coming to David to make him their king. After the ceremony, there was a great feast that lasted for three days. Israel was now at peace under its single king. David, the man whom God had chosen to lead Israel for the next thirty-three years, was now the King of Israel. (II Samuel 5:5)

After David was crowned king, he moved his headquarters to a city inhabited by the Jebusites. The name of the city later became Jerusalem, which was strategically located in Israel and could be fortified as a stronghold against outside attack. David attacked the city to drive out the Jebusites. They tried to defend the city against David's army; however, they did not count on the power and cunning of David as he led his troops against the city. When the city fell, David established his throne in Jerusalem. From then on, it was known as the City of David.

David built a beautiful city and fortified its walls against attackers. That same city exists today and is looked upon by the Jewish people as the beloved capital and the seat of their nation.

After David settled into the city, Hiram, king of Tyre, sent carpenters and masons to build David's palace. This was to be a magnificent structure and David realized God was exalting his kingdom as a reminder to the people that David was their king and Israel was to be a great nation under God.

DAVID MOVES THE ARK

Not long after David's coronation, he talked with the leaders of Israel concerning the Ark of the Covenant, which he had thought about for a very long time. Before Israel had a king, the Ark of the Covenant was transported ahead of the Israelite soldiers to strengthen them.

David thought the Ark should be brought to its rightful place, now the capital of Israel—Jerusalem. He soon brought the proposal to the leaders of Israel and they all agreed to the plan to return the Ark from Abinadab's house to a more suitable location.

The Ark would be placed on a new cart for the journey back to Jerusalem. Uzziah and Ahio, Abinadab's two sons, received the honor of being the drivers of the cart. As the cart began to move, there was a loud burst of music and David and all of Israel sang and danced before the Ark. As the cart crossed unstable terrain, Uzziah, concerned about the safety of the Ark, placed his hand against the Ark to stabilize it. Immediately, Uzziah was struck dead. (II Samuel 6:6–7) When God originally gave instructions to Moses regarding transporting the ark, He instructed that the Ark should be borne on rods or staves by the Levites on foot and that the Ark should never be touched. (Numbers 4:15)

As a result of God reacting so violently against Uzziah, David became afraid of God on that day and he determined not to move the Ark any farther into the city until he had a chance to consult God. The Ark was placed in the house of Obededom, the Gittite, for three months while David sought God's instructions. David realized that God was in favor of moving the Ark to Jerusalem, but under strict requirements about how and who would handle the Ark. Once again, as the ark was moved, David and the procession danced before the Ark as they brought it into Jerusalem. David, most of all, displayed his great happiness at the Ark coming to Jerusalem. Unfortunately, David was a little careless in covering his nakedness while dancing. As he was coming into the city, Michal, Saul's daughter and David's first wife, became highly agitated because of David's actions. She saw King David "leaping and dancing before the Lord; and she despised him in her heart." (II Samuel 6:16) When David returned to his household, Michal met him and accused him, "how glorious was the King of Israel today, who uncovered himself today in the eyes of the handmaids of his servants, as one of the vain fellows shamelessly uncovered himself!" (II Samuel 6:20) This outburst by Michal caused him to lose respect and love for her. She died in her old age without any children. (II Samuel 6:23)

GOD MAKES A PROMISE

After the Ark of the Covenant was moved to Jerusalem, the nation was at peace for a period of time. As David was living in his beautiful new palace, many times his thoughts were of God and the blessings he was enjoying. In fact, many of the Psalms written by David reflect his attitude toward God. An example can be found in Psalm 108 where David is praising and worshipping God in these poems put to melody called The Psalms.

O God, my heart is fixed; I will sing and give praise,

even with my glory. Awake, psaltery and harp: I myself will awake early.

I will praise thee, O LORD, among the people: and I will sing praises unto thee among the nations.

For thy mercy is great above the heavens: and thy truth reacheth unto the clouds. Be thou exalted, O God, above the heavens: and thy glory above all the earth;

That thy beloved may be delivered: save with thy right hand, and answer me.

God hath spoken in his holiness; I will rejoice, I will divide Shechem, and mete out the valley of Succoth.

Gilead is mine; Manasseh is mine; Ephraim also is the strength of mine head; Judah is my lawgiver;

Moab is my washpot; over Edom will I cast out my shoe; over Philistia will I triumph. Who will bring me into the strong city? who will lead me into Edom? Wilt not thou, O God, who hast cast us off? and wilt not thou, O God, go forth with our hosts? Give us help from trouble: for vain is the help of man. Through God we shall do valiantly: for he it is that shall tread down our enemies. (Psalm 108)

As you read the Psalm, you can discern David's attitude toward God—total commitment and a strong desire to be pleasing to Him. Recognizing this desire in David, God continued to prosper him.

As time went by, David wanted to build a sanctuary dedicated to God, one that would serve as a rallying point for Israel to come and worship before the Creator. David visualized a beautiful temple to honor God. David made this statement about his condition in II Samuel 7:1–2, "And it came to pass, when the king sat in his house, and the LORD had given him rest round about from all his enemies; That the king said unto Nathan the prophet, See now, I dwell in an house of cedar, but the ark of God dwelleth within curtains."

As David pondered about building a "house for God," he contacted the prophet Nathan who then received word from God concerning His House. God told Nathan what to say concerning David's progeny and the house for God in Jerusalem. God even gave Nathan a prophecy that has not yet been fulfilled, but will yet be fulfilled even in our future.

> Moreover I will appoint a place for my people Israel, and will plant them, that they may dwell in a place of their own, and move no more; neither shall the children of wickedness afflict them any more, as beforetime. (II Samuel 7:10)

The time spoken of in this particular verse is the time of the Millennium when David will once again rule in Israel under the King of Kings, Jesus Christ, on this earth.

David was astounded at the message from God delivered by Nathan. The message stated that God would set David's descendants upon a throne that He would establish and they would reign upon that throne *forever!*

> And when thy days be fulfilled, and thou shalt sleep with thy fathers, I will set up thy seed after thee, which shall proceed out of thy bowels, and I will establish his kingdom. He shall build an house for my name, and I will establish the throne of his kingdom for ever. (II Samuel 7:12–13)

He repeated this promise in verses 16–17: "And thine house and thy kingdom shall be established for ever before thee: thy throne shall be established for ever. According to all these words, and according to all this vision, so did Nathan speak unto David."

When he heard this proclamation from God through his servant Nathan, David was humbled.

> Then went king David in, and sat before the LORD, and he said, Who am I, O Lord GOD? and what is my house, that thou hast brought me hitherto? And this

was yet a small thing in thy sight, O Lord GOD; but thou hast spoken also of thy servant's house for a great while to come. And is this the manner of man, O Lord GOD? And what can David say more unto thee? for thou, Lord GOD, knowest thy servant. For thy word's sake, and according to thine own heart, hast thou done all these great things, to make thy servant know them. Wherefore thou art great, O LORD God: for there is none like thee, neither is there any God beside thee, according to all that we have heard with our ears.... And let thy name be magnified for ever, saying, The LORD of hosts is the God over Israel: and let the house of thy servant David be established before thee. (II Samuel 7:18–22, 26)

God made a *promise* to David and to all of his descendants that one of them would always have a position on the throne in Israel.

Even though God promised that David's descendants would rule forever on the throne of Israel, God did not want David to build a temple. In II Samuel 7:13, God informed David that it would be his son who would build a house which would stand in Jerusalem.

ISRAEL ENLARGED AND STRENGTHENED

David continued with a magnificent reign over the nation of Israel and was able to subdue all of the enemies surrounding it. David then placed garrisons in Syria of Damascus and the Syrians brought gifts to David; the Bible says David was preserved wherever he went. David dedicated to God much of the spoils of gold and silver that he had captured from the nations of Syria, Moab, Ammon, Philistia, Amalek and others. The Bible says David reigned over Israel and he executed justice and judgment for all the people.

DAVID THE KIND-HEARTED

One day David thought of his deceased friend, Jonathan, and wondered if there were any descendants who were alive from the House of Saul. David inquired about Saul's descendants and soon discovered that Jonathan had a son who was still alive. Jonathan's son had been injured when his nurse attempted to flee from David many years before, fearing for the life of the child. While fleeing, she dropped the child and he was lame in both feet as a result. The nurse had taken him to the house of Machir, the son of Ammiel in Lo-debar to hide from David. When David learned where the boy was living, he sent for him. The young man's name was Mephibosheth. When Mephibosheth came before David, he bowed with a subservient attitude. Because of David's great love for Mephibosheth's father, Jonathan, David told him not to fear, that he would show him great kindness for his father's sake. And so it was that Mephibosheth dwelt in Jerusalem and he ate at the king's table. (II Samuel 9:13)

David was well in control of his kingdom and he was loved by all of the Israelites who made up his realm. David ruled in a way that pleased God and the people. God blessed his family and the whole country because of King David's obedience and love for God. David had six sons born to him while he was in Hebron: Amnon, Chileab, Absalom, Adonijah, Shephatiah, Ithream. He had 11 sons and daughters born to him in Jerusalem: Shammuah, Shobab, Nathan, Solomon, Ibhar, Elishua, Nepheg, Japhia, Elishame, Eliada, Eliphalet. Tamar, David's daughter, had the same mother as Absalom, but it is not recorded where she was born.

Israel prospered, becoming ever stronger and was recognized by all of the surrounding countries as a formidable power. David became legendary as a great king, dispensing justice and mercy according to God's Way.

According to Acts 13:21–22, God found in David, the son of Jesse, a man after his own heart! A greater compliment could never be said of any man.

THE PENALTIES OF SIN

After David became king over all Israel, his main focus was to consolidate its power and to defeat its enemies. Much of his time was spent chasing non-Israelites from the land God had promised the children of Israel so many years earlier when they crossed the Jordan River and began to conquer the land of Canaan. As David and his armies extended the boundaries of the nation of Israel from the Euphrates to Egypt, the prestige and power of Israel was well-known throughout the region and King David was seen as a mighty warrior who followed the ways of God in ruling over the nation of Israel.

The Israelites loved King David because he dealt with them justly and according to God's Law. They knew David followed God in all of his ways. A study about the different kings of Israel and Judah shows that God deals with the nation based on the king's relationship to God. The history of Israel and Judah continually points out that, when the king followed God, the people would follow the king and God would greatly prosper the nation under the rule of a good king. Whenever a new king came to power and rejected God, the nation experienced God's curses. God looks to the national leadership first and foremost when He begins to deal with a people. A leader who truly follows God will bring blessings and prosperity to a nation. A leader who rejects God and follows his own carnal, human lusts will cause his nation to suffer many consequences at the hands of its enemies and, yes, God also.

The Bible reveals that David was a man "after God's own heart," which meant that he tried to order his life as much as possible in the way God would have him live. As a result, the nation of Israel and its army became such a powerful force that those nations surrounding Israel sued for peace. However, there were occasions when foolish leaders over these Gentile nations allowed themselves to be drawn into conflicts against the mighty army of Israel.

As Israel grew stronger and became more consolidated, David had to spend more time administering the kingdom and dealing with the government. David, a man of action, came to realize it was not necessary for him to lead every battle, but he could rely on his leading general, Joab, to execute a battle. This inaction on David's part may have led to the boredom which ultimately turned out to be David's darkest hour. There is an old saying that an "idle mind is the devil's workshop," and no truer words have been spoken than these as they apply to King David during a battle when he chose not to go, but to stay behind in his capital city.

Even though David did many wonderful things, he was not without blemish and his record became tarnished as he succumbed to the carnal drives of lust and greed. King David made a serious mistake and his nation paid for his sin!

The problem began, at a point in time, when the king of Ammon died. The Ammonites had been on less than friendly terms with David. He saw this as an opportunity to win the friendship of the king's son and reduce the hostilities between the two nations. Therefore, David intended to show his respect for the dead king of Ammon by sending an envoy of Israelites to wish his son well and to show kindness to the Ammonites. (II Samuel 10:1–2) Unfortunately, the Ammonites' paranoia overcame the new king Hanun and he suspected that David was sending his men into the land of Ammon to spy it out for a future conquest.

REBUFFED AND SHAMED

As David's men came into Ammon, the princes of the Ammonites convinced Hanun that David had sent his servants to search out the city and spy on the people, preliminary to an attack. Hanun believed his servants and, as a result, he took David's men and shaved off half of their beards and cut their garments off on the back side, exposing even down to their buttocks.

When the men returned to Israel and David learned what Hunan had done, he was angry because Hanun had attacked the dignity of David's soldiers. David sent a message to his servants and told them to remain in Jericho until their beards had grown back and then they should return.

The Bible said that, after a year had expired, David intended to punish Ammon for its treachery against his servants and against the nation of Israel. However, at this time, David chose not to follow his armies into battle, but sent Joab to besiege Rabbah, while he remained in Jerusalem (II Samuel 10:7–19), conducting the business of the kingdom.

DAVID WEAKENS

One evening, when David had completed his administrative duties, he strolled out on his terrace which overlooked the houses immediately surrounding his palace. No doubt, he was curious about the people living in the houses. He noticed a beautiful young woman bathing herself in his plain view. At this point, David should have acted as the King of Israel and returned into his house and ignored her; but, in this case, David allowed his carnal, human nature to win out. As we have said before, carnal human nature is made up of vanity, jealousy, lust and greed. David allowed his lustful nature to gain control of him, as he fantasized about this woman. Christ makes it very clear in Matthew 5:28 that lust begins with the eyes, "...whosoever looketh on a woman to lust after her hath committed adultery with her already in his heart."

After David watched this beautiful woman bathing, he wanted to meet her. He inquired who the woman was from one of his servants. He was told that her name was Bathsheba, the wife of Uriah, one of his generals.

Many have speculated that Bathsheba may have been a Hittite, since she was married to Uriah, the Hittite. However, Biblical evidence supports just the opposite. In fact, her father and grandfather had served David as some of his closest advisors. Notice II Samuel 11:3, "And David sent and inquired after the woman. And one said, Is not this Bathsheba, the daughter of Eliam, the wife of Uriah the Hittite?"

Also notice II Samuel 23:34, "... Eliam the son of Ahithophel the Gilonite," Eliam is one of the 30 advisors to David. Ahithophel, Bathsheba's grandfather, was from Giloh, in the mountainous region of Judah. Ahithophel was a statesman of great brilliance in David's government. Therefore, Bathsheba was from the tribe of Judah, the same tribe from which David came.

In spite of the fact that David knew Bathsheba was married, he still sent for the woman because his lust overcame his ability to flee this evil act. Sure enough, Bathsheba came to the king as he had wished. As a result of adultery, as is so often the case, serious consequences follow. In this case, Bathsheba conceived a child.

When Bathsheba discovered she was pregnant, she sent a message to David telling him that she was carrying his child. To protect oneself from being found out, the act of adultery requires another sin—lying. At this point, the same carnal, human nature that grips so many modern-day public officials also gripped King David and he attempted a *cover-up* of his sin.

The problem he faced was that Uriah, Bathsheba's husband, was away from Jerusalem, fighting for his king against Ammon while Israel's armies besieged the city of Rabbah.

THE COVER-UP

David realized his evil deed of adultery would soon be known by everyone when Bathsheba appeared in public showing her pregnancy. Those in the palace who had summoned Bathsheba to David's residence would quickly put two and two together and realize that the child Bathsheba was carrying was none other than David's! It was then that David concocted a plan to cover up his evil deed. "And David sent to Joab, saying, Send me Uriah the Hittite. And Joab sent Uriah to David." (II Samuel 11:6)

Soon, Uriah reported to his king and commander-in-chief. David sought to cover up his evil deed by having Uriah return from the field of battle and visit his wife. Then, David surmised, the child conceived in adultery would appear to be Uriah's child. Unfortunately, David's plan failed.

> And David said to Uriah, Go down to thy house, and wash thy feet. And Uriah departed out of the king's house, and there followed him a mess of meat from the king. But Uriah slept at the door of the king's house with all the servants of his lord, and went not down to his house. And when they had told David, saying, Uriah went not down unto his house, David said unto Uriah, Camest thou not from thy journey? why then didst thou not go down unto thine house? And Uriah said unto David, The ark, and Israel, and Judah, abide in tents; and my lord Joab, and the servants of my lord, are encamped in the open fields; shall I then go into mine house, to eat and to drink, and to lie with my wife? as thou livest, and as thy soul liveth, I will not do this thing. And David said to Uriah, Tarry here to day also, and to morrow I will let thee depart. So Uriah abode in Jerusalem that day, and the morrow. And when David had called him, he did eat and drink before him; and he made him drunk: and at even he went out to lie on his bed with the servants of his lord, but went not down to his house. (II Samuel 11:8–13)

As you can see from these scriptures, Uriah, in loyalty to David and the army of Israel, refused to go in to his wife while his comrades were fighting for their king and Israel. This, unfortunately, sealed his "death warrant."

THE COVER-UP LEADS TO MURDER

When David realized that his plan did not work, it became necessary for him to take drastic measures to hide his sin of adultery. But, as in many cases, the innocent party of an adulterous relationship is hurt even more than the adulterers.

Because Uriah did not visit Bathsheba, David formulated a new plan which would result in the murder of his loyal soldier. Not only did it involve David, but now it would also involve David's top general, Joab.

David wrote Joab a letter that he asked Uriah to deliver. In this letter, David laid out the plan whereby Uriah would be killed. (II Samuel 11:14–17)

Sure enough, the messenger came to David with a report from Joab that Uriah was dead. David then sent a message back to Joab, encouraging him not to be displeased over the death of Uriah. (II Samuel 11:25)

It appeared that David's plan had worked. After Bathsheba's period of mourning, David sent for her and made her his wife. At this point, David believed that no one would ever know what really happened. However, God, who has his eyes on His servants, was fully aware of David's sin. It would not go unpunished!

GOD REACTS

The time passed and Bathsheba gave birth to David's son. At this point, David thought he was home free. Many people believe that, just because God doesn't react instantly to our sins, He either doesn't notice or doesn't care about the situation. In some cases, as with God's vengeance upon the Amalekites for the evil they had done to Israel when they came out of Egypt, it was several hundred years before God finally acted. In David's case, God decided not to act until after the child was born. Soon after the birth of the child, David sent Nathan the Prophet on a mission that, no doubt, Nathan anguished over as he came before King David.

Nathan came to David with a scenario against which David reacted strongly. Notice II Samuel 12:1–6. After Nathan related his story to David and got his reaction, David must have been stunned when Nathan indicated that he, David, was the character in the story.

> And I gave thee thy master's house, and thy master's wives into thy bosom, and gave thee the house of Israel and of Judah; and if that had been too little, I would moreover have given unto thee such and such things. Wherefore hast thou despised the commandment of the LORD, to do evil in his sight? thou hast killed Uriah the Hittite with the sword, and hast taken his wife to be thy wife, and hast slain him with the sword of the children of Ammon. Now therefore the sword shall never depart from thine house; because thou hast despised me, and hast taken the wife of Uriah the Hittite to be thy wife. Thus saith the LORD, Behold, I will raise up evil against thee out of thine own house, and I will take thy wives before thine eyes, and give them unto thy neighbour, and he shall lie with thy wives in the sight of this sun. For thou didst it secretly: but I will do this thing before all Israel, and before the sun. (II Samuel 12:1–6)

DAVID REPENTS

As soon as David heard God's punishment, David accepted all of the responsibility—he did not try to blame it upon "that woman!" David knew that the sin was his and his alone. Because he immediately accepted responsibility and repented, he displayed the char-

acter that made God love him so very much. He reacted exactly
the opposite way Saul had reacted when Samuel confronted him.
Notice David's answer. "And David said unto Nathan, I have sinned
against the LORD. And Nathan said unto David, The LORD also
hath put away thy sin; thou shalt not die." (II Samuel 12:13)

David's repentance is expressed in Psalms 51:

Have mercy upon me, O God, according to thy lov-
ingkindness: according unto the multitude of thy tender mercies blot out my transgressions.

Wash me thoroughly from mine iniquity, and
cleanse me from my sin. For I acknowledge my transgressions: and my sin is ever before me.

Against thee, thee only, have I sinned, and done
this evil in thy sight:

that thou mightest be justified when thou speak-
est, and be clear when thou judgest.

Behold, I was shapen in iniquity; and in sin did
my mother conceive me.

Behold, thou desirest truth in the inward parts:
and in the hidden part thou shalt make me to
know wisdom.

Purge me with hyssop, and I shall be clean: wash
me, and I shall be whiter than snow.

Make me to hear joy and gladness; that the bones
which thou hast broken may rejoice.

Hide thy face from my sins, and blot out all mine
iniquities.

Create in me a clean heart, O God; and renew a
right spirit within me.

Cast me not away from thy presence; and take not
thy holy spirit from me.

Restore unto me the joy of thy salvation; and
uphold me with thy free spirit.

Then will I teach transgressors thy ways; and sin-

ners shall be converted unto thee. Deliver me from
bloodguiltiness,
 O God, thou God of my salvation: and my tongue
shall sing aloud of thy righteousness.
 O Lord, open thou my lips; and my mouth shall
shew forth thy praise.
 For thou desirest not sacrifice; else would I
give it: thou delightest not in burnt offering.
The sacrifices of God are a broken spirit: a
broken and a contrite heart, O God, thou wilt
not despise.
 Do good in thy good pleasure unto Zion:
build thou the walls of Jerusalem.
 Then shalt thou be pleased with the sacrifices of
righteousness,
 with burnt offering and whole burnt offering:
then shall they offer bullocks upon thine altar.

THERE ARE CONSEQUENCES TO PAY

Even though David repented, God still exacted a *penalty* for this sin
David had committed. Notice II Samuel 12:14, "Howbeit, because
by this deed thou hast given great occasion to the enemies of the
LORD to blaspheme, the child also that is born unto thee shall
surely die." Immediately after Nathan departed David's palace, God
struck the child with a terminal illness.

 In spite of David begging to spare the child, it was not to be
so. After seven days, the child died and David realized it was God's
hand that had executed it. Unfortunately, this was not to be the end
of David's misery. In spite of the fact that God forgave David of the
spiritual side of this sin, He did continue to punish David the rest
of his days. In fact, David's worst problems came from within his
own family.

 David's sin brought upon his family vexation and problems that began when a problem arose between his daughter Tamar and his son Amnon.

Tamar was the sister of Absalom and the half-sister of Amnon. Amnon developed strong feelings toward Tamar, to the point that he became obsessed with her. He told his cousin, Jonadaab, about this lustful obsession. Jonadaab suggested a plan which might allow Amnon to have an intimate relationship with Tamar. Following Jonadaab's suggestion, Amnon pretended to be sick and asked for Tamar to come and take care of him. While Tamar was attending to Amnon, he raped her in spite of her pleas to the contrary. (II Samuel 13:14) Immediately after the sexual affair, he hated her. She begged him not to cast her away, causing her more dishonor. Amnon cast her out. Tamar tore her garments and placed ashes on her head as a sign of mourning.

When Absalom, her brother, asked her what had happened, she told him about the rape. When King David heard the news, he was upset, to say the least. However, Absalom, who kept his "cool" outwardly, developed a strong hatred for Amnon because of this action.

Two years later, Absalom, still bearing this grudge against Amnon, devised a plan which would result in Absalom having his servants kill Amnon. He had a dinner, inviting all of the traitors.

> Now Absalom had commanded his servants, saying, Mark ye now when Amnon's heart is merry with wine, and when I say unto you, Smite Amnon; then kill him, fear not: have not I commanded you? be courageous, and be valiant. And the servants of Absalom did unto Amnon as Absalom had commanded. Then all the king's sons arose, and every man gat him up upon his mule, and fled. (II Samuel 13:28–29)

So it was that David lost another son, which was only the beginning of the punishments he and his family would have to suffer throughout the rest of his reign.

ABSALOM, THE BEAUTIFUL

Absalom, among David's sons, was the one who stood out above all the others. He was very good-looking and had a great personality to go along with his good looks. He is described by the Bible in II Samuel 14:25, "But in all Israel there was none to be so much praised as Absalom for his beauty: from the sole of his foot even to the crown of his head there was no blemish in him."

Absalom had a full head of hair. In fact, each year, he would have his hair cut and weighed according to the king's weight. Absalom had a great deal of pride in being able to grow so much hair—more than most of those around him. However, his vanity about his hair was his undoing.

When Absalom had Amnon killed, he knew it would make David angry and he fled Jerusalem, fearing his father. Absalom stayed away from David for three long years. Finally, David's number one general and Absalom's friend, Joab, came to David and pleaded with him to allow Absalom to return to Jerusalem. David allowed Absalom to return to Jerusalem, but he refused to see Absalom. Apparently, during this period of exile, Absalom began to harbor in his mind the prospect of becoming king and replacing his own father. Absalom was a young man full of vanity, lacking in wisdom, but he had charisma which appealed to the Israelites. Absalom allowed his carnal, human nature to overcome his better judgment. He began a conspiracy against his own father.

ABSALOM'S CONSPIRACY

I Samuel 15:1, "And it came to pass after this, that Absalom prepared him chariots and horses, and fifty men to run before him." In an effort to create the illusion that he was somebody important, Absalom used this method to announce his arrival into the city each day. His intent was to under-cut David and ultimately to foster an insurrection against his own father. Each day, Absalom would go to the gates of the city to meet those who had a controversy and were coming before David for judgment. Absalom would call to them, pretending to be their servant, saying what he would do if he were king.

> And Absalom rose up early, and stood beside the way of the gate: and it was so, that when any man that had a controversy came to the king for judgment, then Absalom called unto him, and said, Of what city art thou? And he said, Thy servant is of one of the tribes of Israel. And Absalom said unto him, See, thy matters are good and right; but there is no man deputed of the king to hear thee. Absalom said moreover, Oh that I were made judge in the land, that every man which hath any suit or cause might come unto me, and I would do him justice! And it was so, that when any man came nigh to him to do him obeisance, he put forth his hand, and took him, and kissed him. And on this manner did Absalom to all Israel that came to the king for judgment: so Absalom stole the hearts of the men of Israel. (II Samuel 15:2–6)

Absalom began to execute his plan designed to overthrow his father. He sent spies throughout all the tribes of Israel to inform his friends and, hopefully, his followers, that, at a given signal of "blowing the trumpets" to proclaim that Absalom was now king in Hebron, they should all rise up against David. (II Samuel 15:10) Many of David's followers, unaware of what Absalom was really up to, came to Absalom and began to follow this son of David. Eventually, David learned what Absalom was doing and how the people were beginning to follow him. At this point, David and his servants decided to flee Jerusalem rather than fight with his favorite son. Among those who conspired with Absalom was Bathsheba's grandfather, Ahithophel.

It was not to be that Absalom would replace his father as king. Absalom's conspiracy was not as complete among the people as he thought and many professed their allegiance and loyalty to ensure that David's reign would continue. David, in his usual manner, did not take things in his own hands. He went to God and asked Him for guidance as to what he should do. The whole country wept with a loud voice when they heard that David had fled the city and had passed over the brook Kidron into the wilderness.

Zadok, the high priest, and the other priests went with David and his band of men, transporting with them the Ark of the Covenant. David said to Zadok that the Ark should be carried back to the city of Jerusalem rather stay in the wilderness. David did not want the Ark of the Covenant exposed in a military confrontation where it could suffer damage. Therefore, Zadok and his sons carried the Ark of the Covenant to Jerusalem and waited to see the outcome of the battle. David then went to the Mount of Olives where he wept and cried out to God, asking what he should do.

ABSALOM OCCUPIES JERUSALEM

With David and his men fleeing Jerusalem, the city opened up and Absalom arrived to take over the kingdom. After Absalom moved into Jerusalem, he consolidated his power. Absalom disgraced his father as was prophesied by Nathan the prophet.

> Thus saith the LORD, Behold, I will raise up evil against thee out of thine own house, and I will take thy wives before thine eyes, and give them unto thy neighbour, and he shall lie with thy wives in the sight of this sun. (II Samuel 12:11)

Absalom had become twisted and demented in his thoughts and actions. He was advised by Ahithophel, Bathsheba's grandfather and former advisor to David, that Absalom should go to visit his father's concubines who remained in the king's house and all Israel then would know that Absalom now ruled with a strong hand. Absalom spread a tent on top of the palace and went in to his father's concubines so that all Israel could pass by and see. The prophecy given to David by Nathan had come true.

Absalom had become very evil and God had used this once fine son of David to bring about more punishment upon David for his adultery with Bathsheba and his murder of Uriah. This same Ahithophel then counseled Absalom to take 12,000 men and pursue David with the intent of killing him.

THE BATTLE BETWEEN FATHER AND SON

Ahithophel became Absalom's chief advisor in his drive to establish himself as the new king of Israel. He urged an immediate attack before David could gather his loyal armies around him. Absalom had 12,000 men under his command. A second advisor, Hushai, suggested that Absalom would be ensured success if he mobilized all Israel and led them against David. Hushai had remained in Jerusalem when David fled. He had now sworn an allegiance to Absalom, but he actually remained secretly loyal to King David. At this point, Hushai was stalling for time, hoping he could give David enough time to build up his forces.

Hushai pointed out to Absalom that David and his men were mighty men and experts at warfare. This may have caused Absalom to think back to the time when his father was in his prime and the greatest general in Israel. Hushai was trying to make Absalom unsure of his own victory, thereby giving David enough time to rally his forces.

When the battle began, Absalom and his men were no match for Joab and the other generals who had remained loyal to David and who were "battle-tested" veterans. Absalom, who had unseasoned troops and rebels, was utterly defeated and thousands died in the battle, though David had instructed that the life of his son, Absalom, be spared.

When Absalom was advised that the battle was going against him and that David's armies were, as Hushai had advised, seasoned soldiers who were defeating Absalom's men, he decided to make a deal with David's servants. As he was riding his donkey through the forest, his long, flowing hair became caught in the boughs of an oak tree and he was unable to free himself. General Joab came to him and found him dangling in the tree. Joab took three darts or spears and thrust them through the heart of Absalom, while he was hanging alive from the oak tree.

There were also ten aids to Joab who also joined in and took part in executing Absalom for treason. They took him down from the tree and cast him into a pit in the woods and buried him.

"Now Absalom in his lifetime had taken and reared up for himself a pillar, which is in the king's dale: for he said, I have no son to keep my name in remembrance: and he called the pillar after his own name: and it is called unto this day, Absalom's place." (II Samuel 18:18)

Ahithophel, hearing of Absalom's punishment for his treachery, knew that he too would be punished because he had chosen to follow Absalom rather than remain loyal to King David. He went back to the land of his lineage, Gihon in Judah, and hanged himself.

When the news came to David that his favorite son was dead, he wept greatly for him. David would have been willing to forgive Absalom, but his treachery had now cost him his life. David stayed in an area known as Mahanaim until the trouble over Absalom had finally died down in Jerusalem.

David's army at last reached Jerusalem and one can only imagine how happy David was to once again be back in the capital city of Israel. In fact, he composed a Psalm about the very event. (Psalms 18)

FINAL YEARS

The remainder of David's reign was touched with famine and threats of violence from the Philistines and others who surrounded Israel. David lived out his life in Jerusalem and, when he was near death, he disclosed that his son Solomon, whose mother was Bathsheba, would rule in his stead.

David ruled in Israel for forty-seven years, including the time that he was king in Hebron. He truly was a man after God's own heart, even though he made many human mistakes. It is David who will be resurrected at the end of this age when God will once again restore the Kingdom, with David ruling directly under Jesus Christ. David had ruled over the entire nation of Israel in a magnificent way. However, because of David's sin, his family was plagued with trouble.

The throne of David has been preserved and its lineage can be traced, which adds even greater fascination to this incredible true history, as we uncover our Lost National Identity.

SOLOMON

During David's reign, he consolidated the power of Israel and its territory stretched to rule over kingdoms from the Euphrates to the land of the Philistines, and to the borders of Egypt. The nations that surrounded Israel now had been subdued and they paid tribute to David and the Israelites.

One of the last acts David performed before he died was to reconfirm the fact that Bathsheba's son, Solomon, would, in fact, rule Israel upon his death.

> Then king David answered and said, Call me Bathsheba. And she came into the king's presence, and stood before the king. And the king sware and said, As the LORD liveth, that hath redeemed my soul out of all distress, Even as I sware unto thee by the LORD God of Israel, saying, Assuredly Solomon thy son shall reign after me, and he shall sit upon my throne in my stead; even so will I certainly do this day. (I Kings 1:28–30)

Soon after this, David's long reign and life came to an end. David had left Israel secure from military threat without.

> Judah and Israel were many, as the sand which is by the sea in multitude, eating and drinking, and making

merry. And Solomon reigned over all kingdoms from
the river unto the land of the Philistines, and unto
the border of Egypt: they brought presents, and served
Solomon all the days of his life. (I Kings 4:20–21)

Notice, even at this juncture, the Bible refers to Judah and
Israel as two separate entities. However, Judah and Israel considered Solomon as their united king. The Bible points out that King
Solomon had dominion over the region from the river Tiphsah,
even Azzah, and over all the kings on this side of the river, and he
had peace on all sides round about him.

Judah and Israel dwelt in safety; every man lived his life as he
chose all the days that Solomon reigned. Solomon had been trained
by David, his father, and Bathsheba, his mother, in God's way and
how to be a good ruler. When you study the books of Psalms and
Proverbs, you will notice that many verses were written for his
instruction.

The fact that Solomon had been trained according to God's
Way probably accounts for the fact that he chose the gift of wisdom, when God offered to bless him as he might desire. Solomon
was granted the gift of wisdom beyond any man that had lived.
According to the scripture in I Kings 3:3, Solomon truly started out
trying to follow God. "And Solomon loved the LORD, walking in
the statutes of David his father: only he sacrificed and burnt incense
in high places."

We also find that God appeared to Solomon in a dream offering to bless him;

In Gibeon the LORD appeared to Solomon in a dream
by night: and God said, Ask what I shall give thee.
And Solomon said, Thou hast shewed unto thy servant David my father great mercy, according as he
walked before thee in truth, and in righteousness,
and in uprightness of heart with thee; and thou hast
kept for him this great kindness, that thou hast given
him a son to sit on his throne, as it is this day. And

now, O LORD my God, thou hast made thy servant king instead of David my father: and I am but a little child: I know not how to go out or come in. And thy servant is in the midst of thy people which thou hast chosen, a great people, that cannot be numbered nor counted for multitude. Give therefore thy servant an understanding heart to judge thy people, that I may discern between good and bad: for who is able to judge this thy so great a people? And the speech pleased the Lord, that Solomon had asked this thing. And God said unto him, Because thou hast asked this thing, and hast not asked for thyself long life; neither hast asked riches for thyself, nor hast asked the life of thine enemies; but hast asked for thyself understanding to discern judgment...And I have also given thee that which thou has not asked, both riches, and honour; so that there shall not be any among the kings like unto thee all thy days. (I Kings 3:5–13)

SOLOMON ANSWERS A FOOL ACCORDING TO HER FOLLY

Solomon's wisdom and understanding were known throughout the world and his wisdom was soon tested. Two women claimed the same child.

Then came there two women, that were harlots, unto the king, and stood before him. And the one woman said, O my lord, I and this woman dwell in one house; and I was delivered of a child with her in the house. And it came to pass the third day after that I was delivered, that this woman was delivered also: and we were together; there was no stranger with us in the house, save we two in the house. And this woman's child died in the night; because she overlaid it. And she arose at midnight, and took my son from beside me, while thine handmaid slept, and laid it in her bosom, and laid her dead child in my bosom. And when I rose in the morning to give my child suck, behold, it was dead: but when I had considered it in the morning, behold, it was not my son, which I did bear. And the other woman said, Nay; but the living is my son, and the dead is thy son. And this said, No; but the dead is thy son, and the living is my son. Thus they spake before the king. Then said the king, The one saith, This is my son that liveth, and thy son is the dead: and the other saith, Nay; but thy son is the dead, and my son is the living. And the king said, Bring me a sword. And they brought a sword before the king. And the king said, Divide the living child in two, and give half to the one, and half to the other. Then spake the woman whose the living child was unto the king, for her bowels yearned upon her son, and she said, O my lord, give her the living child, and in no wise slay it. But the other said, Let it be neither mine nor thine, but divide it. Then the king answered and said, Give her the living child, and in no wise slay it: she is the mother thereof. And all Israel heard of the judgment which the king had judged; and they feared the king: for they saw that the wisdom of God was in him, to do judgment. (I Kings 3:16–28)

SOLOMON BUILDS THE TEMPLE

The land of Israel prospered and the people loved Solomon. Solomon loved God and it became his desire to build a temple suitable for the God of Israel. David, Solomon's father, wanted to build the temple, but God instructed David that he was to design the building, but Solomon would actually build the facility.

Solomon set about gathering the materials and workmen to

construct the first permanent House dedicated to God. Solomon went to Hiram, king of Tyre, who had long been a friend of David, to assist in building the temple. Solomon entered into an agreement where the king of Tyre and his servants would assist in the building of the temple of God in Jerusalem. (I Kings 5:6–10)

The temple was to be the finest structure the world had ever seen and, in order to accomplish this, Solomon raised taxes and recruited 30,000 men to build this Great House for God. A joint project between Solomon's builders and Hiram's builders started the construction of the first temple in Jerusalem. The temple was started 418 years after Israel came out of Egypt and in the fourth year of Solomon's reign, in the month of Zif.

David had provided the blueprints for the structure, which he had received directly from God. I Kings 6 describes much of what the new temple was to look like. Notice that the temple was to contain two very large cherubim made of olive tree wood, each standing ten cubits high. This would equate to approximately 17 and 1/2 feet high. These two wooden cherubim were to be overlaid with gold and they were to be replicas of the arch-cherubs standing at the very throne of God in Heaven. These large statues depicting these two angelic beings were to be situated inside the temple with the ark. The walls and doors were also carved with cherubim, palm trees and open flowers within and without the temple. (I Kings 6:23) "And within the oracle he made two cherubim of olive tree, each ten cubits high."

> And the priests brought in the ark of the covenant of the LORD unto his place, into the oracle of the house, to the most holy place, even under the wings of the cherubim. For the cherubim spread forth their two wings over the place of the ark, and the cherubim covered the ark and the staves thereof above. (I Kings 8:6–7)

The floor of the temple was overlaid with gold within and without. The magnificence of this house is astounding as you read the description of it in I Kings 6 and 7. When the temple was completed, Solomon assembled all the elders of Israel and all of the heads of the tribes and all the leaders to come to Jerusalem in preparation for the ceremony to dedicate the temple. The priests brought the Ark of the Covenant, the tabernacle of the congregation, and the holy vessels that were in the tabernacle to become part of the temple. The Ark was to be placed in the most holy place—even under the wings of the cherubim.

When the arrangements for the temple dedication were set, Solomon stood before the altar of God in the presence of the congregation, spread forth his hands toward the heavens and uttered a beautiful prayer of invocation, found in I Kings 8:22–61. This dedication occurred during the Seventh month, at the Feast of Tabernacles and on the eighth day of the Feast of Tabernacles the people blessed the king. They returned to their homes very joyful that now they had a permanent location for the Ark of the Covenant and a building dedicated solely to the God of Israel.

After the dedication of the temple, God appeared to Solomon a second time in a dream and indicated that He had heard his prayer and invocation he had made for himself and the nation. God reconfirmed to Solomon that he could be as great as his father and, if he walked in the statutes and commandments of God, He would establish the throne of Solomon upon Israel forever as He had promised David, his father.

SOLOMON'S NAVY

As King Solomon grew in power and the nation prospered, he sought to increase Israel's influence and develop its commerce by constructing large sea-going ships. Solomon teamed up with King Hiram's navy. It was King Hiram's men who came to be known as the Phoenicians. They sailed with the Israelites and taught them their maritime navigational skills, allowing for deep water navigation. The Bible records that the Phoenicians and the Israelites jointly crewed the Israelite ships. In fact, many times, Phoenician sailors would command Israelite ships and vice versa. Solomon's ships traversed the oceans of the world. The Bible indicates in I Kings 10 that he also teamed up with the ships of Tarshish to bring gold, silver, ivory, apes and peacocks back to the kingdom. The scripture says that King Solomon's riches exceeded all the kings of the earth and his wisdom was unmatched, "Now the weight of gold that came to Solomon in one year was six hundred threescore and six talents of gold." (I Kings 10:14)

> For the king's ships went to Tarshish with the servants of Huram: every three years once came the ships of Tarshish bringing gold, and silver, ivory, and apes, and peacocks. And King Solomon passed all the kings of the earth in riches and wisdom. (II Chronicles 9:21–22)

The Israelites from the tribe of Dan were the ones who were the seafaring men of Israel. The tribe of Dan was prophesied to be a "serpent by the way." A wake of a ship appears to be a serpent's trail. Dan always left his trail wherever he went, particularly in Europe and the British Isles. We will cover this later in another chapter, but suffice it to say here that Dan was the tribe which traveled with the Phoenicians. One group of Danites lived in the north of Israel near the area where King Hiram did; the other group of Danites lived on the Mediterranean itself.

At this point, the Bible adds very little to the exploits of Solomon's ships. However, archaeological history is able to add some insight as to what the ships of Solomon may have been doing.

Solomon was not content to be a land power alone, but he wanted to make Israel a major maritime force known throughout the entire world. Notice that his fleet was based on the Red Sea near Ezion-Geber, as stated in I Kings 9:26. "And King Solomon made a navy of ships in Eziongeber, which is beside Eloth, on the shore of the Red Sea, in the land of Edom."

It is interesting to note that this location on the Red Sea was in an area where there was great industrial activity. Since Solomon's fleet was located in the Red Sea, it could, of course, trade with Africa and Asia through the Indian Ocean. As the Israelites and Phoenicians continued to join forces on both land and sea, they became, for all intents and purposes, a single entity under Solomon's leadership.

As Solomon's fame grew and Israel was developing into what one might consider a super-power today, its Egyptian neighbors chose to join forces with the Israelite-Phoenician alliance to be part of this great naval trading fleet. As a result of this, Egypt, King Hiram's Phoenicia and Israel became a tri-lateral naval force.

By understanding the fact that the Egyptians, Israelites and Phoenicians now had a joint naval force on whose ships the sailors could be from one or all of these nations, we now can understand some of the great archaeological finds in this last half of the 20^{the} Century, which have proved to be truly amazing.

AMERICA BC

I have chosen this heading because it is the name of a book written by a noted archaeologist, Dr. Barry Fell. His book, *America* BC is a truly amazing story based on extensive archaeological research concerning the early settlers of the American continent as far back as 1000 BC. Dr. Fell attributes many of the archaeological finds to the Phoenicians, to the Egyptians and to the Celtics (Israelites).

Substantial colonies of Israelites and Phoenicians were planted in America by the seafaring navies of Israel and King Hiram's Phoenicians, as remains of their presence have been found in New England and in other parts of America. A large temple observatory site has been located in what has been known as "Mystery Hill" in North Salem, New Hampshire. This site covered approximately twenty acres and included shrines dedicated to the Phoenician/Israelite god, Baal. A temple site of twenty acres gives us a clear indication that the Phoenicians had a major presence in the new world. Dr. Fell dated the inscriptions to this temple of Baal to be approximately 800 to 600 BC.

The site of this ancient temple has endured much physical damage because it was not recognized as an ancient temple site. It has priceless archaeological worth proving the existence of an old world civilization in the new world. The ancient site was composed of "stone slab chambers and associated hinge stones" for determining the times of the spring and winter solstices. Unfortunately, these stone structures were substantially dismantled during the 1800s and the stones were reused to build walls, dams and bridges in New England. Indeed, during the years of 1823 through 1843 alone, about forty percent of the stone structures were destroyed by building contractors. Dr. Fell observed, concerning walls built with stones from this ancient site, their original use as an ancient temple site was "abundantly attested to by the number of temple dedications we have found in these stone walls." This ancient old world civilization built a large temple observatory complex in ancient America indicating that they were colonizing, not merely exploring. The dates of this civilization are consistent with the Bible accounts of the Israelite/Phoenician commercial shipping and worldwide trade.

The ships of Tarshish referred to in Ezekiel 27:25 and Jonah 1:3 were also regular callers to the new world and inscriptions and tablets of their involvement in colonizing were preserved in Rhode Island, Ohio and West Virginia. This identification is dependent upon "Tarshish" being the same as ancient "Tartissus" on the Iberian peninsula of ancient Europe. Dr. Fell noticed Tartessin inscriptions in ancient America are a "dialectal variant" of the Phoenician language. This confirms these early American visitors were also from the region of the nation of Israel in the Mediterranean.

One might justifiably wonder, given the existence of old world civilizations in ancient America, why American history books haven't been inundated with this new information. Unfortunately, history revisionists choose not to go past the history of the American Indians. The American Indians are NOT the descendants of these people. Archaeologists know the North and South American Indians came from Asia and are of the Oriental (Japheth) race.

Dr. Fell has noted that some archaeologists have tried to dismiss the clearly readable ancient American inscription as "accidental markings made by plowshare and roots of trees." Unfortunately, the concept that Columbus discovered America in 1492 has become such a cherished doctrine that it appears to demand an almost superstitious devotion by modern academics. Even that is known to be untrue, in that Leif Erickson sailed to North America in 1000 AD, long before Christopher Columbus was born.

Ancient Egyptians, who were allied with King Solomon, also left their mark. The Egyptian sailors were also skilled in deep water oceanic navigation and they too plied the oceans of the world. The ancient Egyptian/Libyan fleets also sailed across the Indian Ocean and sent explorers on mining expeditions into the Pacific Ocean. The Egyptians bought gold in the area now known as Sumatra, and records of their Pacific explorations are found as far as the Hawaiian Islands. It is also noted that the Egyptians roamed the Indian and Pacific oceans in search of gold in 1000 BC.

The time period of 1000 BC is extremely important because it is the same time frame of the United Kingdom of Israel under David and Solomon when that nation moved into world prominence.

America BC includes much evidence of the exploration of American soil by ancient people with the many language groups common to the Middle East in 1000 BC. Apparently, the ancient explorations and settlements from Israel and the Middle East were concentrated on the major eastern inland waterways of America as much of the evidence of their presence has been found in such locations. A major archaeological find was a stele (a slab or pillar of stone used to bear an inscription) inscribed with ancient old world languages, found in 1874, near Davenport, Iowa, by M. Gass. Unfortunately, this new world equivalent of the Rosetta Stone has largely been ignored because no one could read it. Also, the false dogma that "no old world explorer, prior to Columbus, had been on our continent" affected the perception of most people. If this stele had been discovered in Europe, it surely would have been recognized for what it was, a trilingual archeological stele of ancient cultures. Since it was found in Iowa, it had to wait approximately a century to be understood. One of the reasons the stele, or slab of stone, was originally rejected was that it contained some signs resembling Hebrew and others resembling Phoenician.

This ancient artifact contains joint inscriptions in three ancient languages: Iberian Punic (a language related to the descendants of Phoenician and Hebrew), Egyptian and ancient Libyan. These are the language groups of the three-nation alliance between King Solomon's Israel, King Hiram's Tyre and Egypt. These ancient artifacts show that these groups were traveling and working together as far from the Middle East as the interior of North America.

In his book, Dr. Fell describes this stele as "one of the most important ever discovered." Why, then is this priceless evidence of ancient exploration in North America not in textbooks anywhere? The answer is that the truth as it relates to the true identity of the modern-day Americans has been suppressed and continues to be hidden from the public eye. Modern scholastic elites have a most superstitious attachment to the false dogma that nobody could have discovered America before Columbus. This dogma has been believed so long that all evidence of old world exploration and colonization prior to Columbus is conveniently lost upon the educated elitists.

Further evidence of international commercial contacts is found in the discovery of copper ingots in ancient burial mounds in Ohio, West Virginia, Indiana and Kentucky. The same type of copper ingots, shaped like four-legged animal hides, were also found in old world archaeological sites, indicating they served as an acceptable form of ancient currency on both sides of the Atlantic Ocean. There is also very clear evidence that Baal worship appeared among the ancient Hebrew/Phoenicians who were in ancient America. One might ask, why are there not relics to the worshippers of the True God as there are inscriptions to Baal? The answer is found in Exodus 20:24–25,

> An altar of earth thou shalt make unto me, and shalt sacrifice thereon thy burnt offerings, and thy peace

offerings, thy sheep, and thine oxen: in all places where I record my name I will come unto thee, and I will bless thee. And if thou wilt make me an altar of stone, thou shalt not build it of hewn stone: for if thou lift up thy tool upon it, thou hast polluted it.

The Israelites were specifically forbidden by God to make carvings upon stones as a form of worship. Therefore, the Baal worshipping sailors who traveled with the Israelites left the insignia of their god rather than the God of Israel upon the stone artifacts.

There is evidence that worshippers of the God of Israel were present in ancient America. Near Albuquerque, New Mexico, there are ancient Hebrew inscriptions (called the Los Lunas inscriptions) recorded on stone. The inscription is the Exodus 20 version of the Ten Commandments. Another example is the famous *Moabite Stone* found in the Middle East referring to a war between Israel and Moab in the Ninth Century BC, during the time of the separate kingdoms of Israel and Judah. Dr. Fell noted that the Los Lunas inscription of the Ten Commandments was written in ancient Hebrew letters in the same style as the Moabite Stone (from about 1000 BC) which was not translated until 1949. The dating of 1000 BC would place the inscription during the reigns of Kings David and Solomon of the United Kingdom of Israel when Israel was indeed serving the God of the Bible.

It is obvious that the Los Lunas Hebrew inscriptions could have occurred only with the backing and support of a wealthy Hebrew-speaking nation such as ancient Israel dating the inscription between 1000 and 720 BC. Since the Los Lunas inscription indicates the makers were devoted to the God of the Ten Commandments, we are limited to the kings of Israel who could have funded international exploration during a period when the nation was loyal to God. This requirement then limits the respective dating of the Los Lunas inscriptions to the reigns of King David and/or King Solomon. The kings of Israel who followed King Solomon were almost universally dedicated to serving Baal and other false gods.

KING SOLOMON'S MINES

No doubt, this evidence coupled with the truth of the Bible clearly proves that God prospered ancient Israel under the leadership of King David and King Solomon far beyond what is recognized in the world today. King Solomon collected gold from all parts of the world, possibly including gold mined in the Appalachian Mountains of North America. There are ancient Cherokee stories which indicate the Cherokee Indians located in the areas today of North Georgia and western North Carolina mined gold and moved it to the sea via the Savannah River for transport on ships from a great eastern kingdom. Indian legends are still told today among the Cherokees concerning trade between a great eastern king and the Cherokee nation thousands of years ago. It is true that there is gold in North Georgia; in fact, the dome of the state capitol of Georgia, was overlaid in gold from Dahlonega, the old gold mining town in North Georgia. People still pan for and find gold in that region. Before gold was discovered in California in 1849, most of the gold in North America came from North Georgia.

Other archaeologists have discovered ancient inscriptions found on the North American continent. A noted epigrapher, Gloria Farley, has made notable finds of ancient inscriptions left by Libyans, Celts and Phoenicians who navigated the Mississippi, Arkansas and Cameroon Rivers. The evidence presented shows conclusively that Mediterranean civilizations, beginning in the time of King David and afterwards not only were present in North America, but also in the lands of the Indian and Pacific Oceans.

The onset of significant old world exploration of the new world from 1000 to 800 BC parallels the period when the Bible states there was a great deal of international travel and commerce with many monarchs coming from around the world to visit Solomon in Jerusalem. This time frame exactly parallels the beginning of the Golden Age of Israel and includes much of the time when the Kingdom of Israel was a major power. The conclusion is inescapable and ancient history verifies the Biblical accounts that Israel was a great and powerful nation in its day.

PHOENICIANS WERE NEIGHBORS OF ISRAEL

Dr. Fell confirms the beginning of the first millennium BC as a Golden Age for Phoenicia. He indicated "Phoenician trade was on an international scale in textiles, metal, pottery, glass, timber, wheat and wine...."

Historical evidence that Phoenician greatness began around 1000 BC is critically important since it coincides precisely with the period during which King Hiram of Tyre allied his people with Israel under the great power of King David. In fact, it was Israel's Golden Age "rubbing off" on the Phoenician city-states that produced Phoenicia's prosperity. Israel was the dominant partner in the alliance and the Phoenicians served as junior partners of Israel!

The term "Phoenicia," when applied to the ancient world in the time frame of 1000–700 BC designates the combined alliance of the Israelites and the city-states led by Tyre and Sidon. It must also be realized that the people known as the *Phoenicians* did not give themselves that name. The name "Phoenician" is derived from a Greek word, which the Greek historians used to describe many people living on the eastern shores of the Mediterranean Sea. This is according to George Rawlingson who wrote, "At first the term 'Phoenician' was used by the Greeks with a good deal of vagueness, of the Syrian coast generally between Asia Minor and Egypt." The *Encyclopedia Judicia* states, "The Greek name 'Phoinike' was first mentioned by Homer and though the exact extent of the region called Phoenicia cannot be determined, the name is clearly the equivalent of Canaan."

It is also interesting to note that, at the same time King Solomon's reign began, the technical skills of the Phoenicians took a great leap forward. Who was it that caused this sudden advance in technical skills? The Bible tells us that God gave Solomon the gift of unprecedented wisdom and understanding. (I Kings 3:12)

The Bible adds, "... all the earth sought to Solomon, to hear his wisdom, which God had put in his heart." (I Kings 10:24)

It was obvious that Solomon's wisdom was not limited to ethical and sociological applications. The Israelites invented the Bessemer process. A large blast furnace complex was built during Israel's Golden Age. Solomon was a genius in all fields and his inventions not only allowed him to be held in awe by other nations, but also revolutionized the culture and commerce of that day! The fact that the above technologies "suddenly developed" within Israel and Phoenicia around 1000 BC, indicate the presence of a genius who "accelerated their culture." The Bible openly tells us of this genius which belonged to King Solomon.

> I the Preacher was king over Israel in Jerusalem. And I gave my heart to seek and search out by wisdom concerning all things that are done under heaven: this sore travail hath God given to the sons of man to be exercised therewith. I have seen all the works that are done under the sun; and, behold, all is vanity and vexation of spirit. That which is crooked cannot be made straight: and that which is wanting cannot be numbered. I communed with mine own heart, saying, Lo, I am come to great estate, and have gotten more wisdom than all they that have been before me in Jerusalem: yea, my heart had great experience of wisdom and knowledge. (Ecclesiastes 1:12–16)

Solomon was acknowledging the great gift he had received from God. This great gift of knowledge and understanding can now be seen in archaeological history. The Bible is not overplaying the unparalleled knowledge and genius of King Solomon.

In the late 1970s and early 1980s, a few more Tartessian inscriptions were discovered in North America associated with large burial tumuli, or burial mounds, resembling those of the Iberian Bronze Age. Large burial grounds point to the fact that important American colonies of these Phoenician navigators and merchant princes were there long enough to have buried masses of their dead. The first Tartessian inscription discovered in America is engraved on a rock on the seashore of Mount Hope Bay, Bristol, Rhode Island. In 1780, it was described by Ezra Stiles who later became president of Yale College. According to Dr. Fell, the inscription could not be accurately dated, but it was most likely done between 700 and 600 BC. The voyagers were probably not explorers, but merchants trading with the New England Celts who, by that date, were already established fur trappers and miners of precious metals on those sites where ancient workings were discovered. Ample evidence also proves a large Celtic migration from the old world took place around 1000 BC. The Celts came from several of the ten northern tribes after the nation was divided and taken captive in 721 BC, as will be shown in later chapters.

The periodic arrival of Phoenician ships on the New England coast was attested to by the Ogam inscription on Monhegan Island, off the coast of Maine. According to Dr. Fell, the inscriptions suggested that organized international maritime commerce was well established in the late Bronze Age and that North American ports were listed on the sailing timetables of the overseas vessels of the principle Phoenician shipping companies. This same information was circulated to customers in America. As Monhegan Island was some ten miles offshore, it seems likely that the whole island was a trading station used by the Phoenician/Israelite captains with some organized ferry system for the transfer of goods to and from the mainland.

What, then, became of the many ships of Tarshish that frequented these same coasts 2000 to 3000 years ago? Certainly some, probably many, must lie on the bottom of the ocean, for sea travel was more dangerous in ancient times and the storm waves could overpower the timbered hulls of Phoenician galleys more easily than the steel plates of modern ships.

In the Sixth Century BC, shipping was more highly organized than we have heretofore believed. Letters were discovered written on metal sheets concerning trade. The style is concise and polished,

sometimes legalistic, as if drawn up by lawyers. Indeed, this is probably for the signatures of the writers or consenting parties to a trade
contract, because the matters referred to are readily understandable
and the decipherment of the text is made much easier than in the
case of religious writings.

In 1973, Dr. Fell was able to decipher a letter written on sheets
of gold leaf by Hiram, king of Tyre. The language is Etruscan, as he
is writing to a king of Levinia, near Rome. The letter was excavated
in Pergi, Italy in 1964. The text shows that the Etruscan language is
a member of the Anatolian group of tongues, related thus to Hittite
and Urartian.

WHAT HAPPENED TO THOSE COLONIES?

The archaeological information provided by Dr. Fell and others lead
us to the question, were the native American Indians the descendants of these ancient Middle Eastern peoples of Israel, Tyre and
Egypt? And, if the Indians are not the descendants of those early
arrivals, then where were those from the Middle East when the
New World began to be colonized in the 1600s?

The races of people that made up the so-called Native
Americans (American Indians) are believed to have come from
Asia, due to their oriental appearance. Their facial features and
body characteristics are much closer to the descendants of Japheth
and Ham than those of Shem. The Israelites were generally fair-
skinned people with hair colors including blonde, red and brown.
Unlike the American Indians who all have black hair similar to
those of Asians, the Israelites and the descendants of Shem were
fairer skinned peoples.

No one can rightly say what happened to these early colonists
(800–100 BC), but they were extinct by the time the American colonies began to flourish in the 1600s. The question as to what happened to these people is unanswerable at this time. However, it is
quite obvious that the American Indians were not descendants of
these people. It is entirely possible that the American Indians were

responsible for total annihilation of these people and the ending of their civilization. Just as no one knows what happened to the original colonists who came to Roanoke Island, North Carolina, in 1585–87, the same can be said for the colonists that came in 1000 BC.

From a Biblical perspective, the land of the Americas was not yet to be given to the descendants of ancient Israel. There still lay in front of Israel a 2520 year punishment for their sins as will be explained in chapter 23. This, most likely, is the real explanation why that civilization did not continue to flourish in the Middle East, nor did it flourish in the Americas at that time.

All of these newly discovered archaeological finds further support the greatness King David and King Solomon enjoyed as rulers over a United Israel.

GOD BLESSED SOLOMON

The fact that Solomon chose *wisdom*, when God offered him any gift he might have desired, turned out to be the greatest gift of all. Not only did God bless Solomon with wisdom beyond all measure and in all facets of life, but He also blessed Solomon and the Kingdom almost beyond belief. Israel reached far beyond its borders to influence world happenings. Since God intended to bless Abraham's descendants through Israel because of Abraham's obedience, he continued to bless Israel as long as Solomon was obedient to God.

However, as Solomon and the nation were blessed, they soon forgot from whom all of their blessings flowed. Just as America has prospered, we have systematically rejected God from whom all of our blessings flow.

Today, our political leaders, who often feel they are above the law, allow themselves to be entrapped by sexual misconduct and other evil deeds. The result was disastrous to ancient Israel and will also spell disaster for modern-day America in the Twenty-first Century. The parallels between ancient Israel and modern-day

America are inescapable. Our histories seem to be following the same paths.

God warned Israel that, if she followed the paths of unrighteousness, He would punish her seven times for her sins. God called for Israel to repent for hundreds of years, but the people were stiff-necked and would not listen.

SOLOMON'S IDOLATRY

In the last chapter, concerning the archaeological discoveries of the settlements in America of about 1000 BC, the archaeological evidence confirms that people from the Middle East came to our shores about the same time period Israel, under King David and King Solomon, reached its zenith.

This leads to the question: What happened to these ancient peoples?

PAGAN GODS AND DIPLOMACY

The fame and wealth of King Solomon and Israel were known throughout the world. Solomon was sought out by world leaders. Many nations wanted to have diplomatic alliances with King Solomon and the United Kingdom of Israel.

Those who aligned themselves with Israel benefited militarily and commercially. The settlements in North America attest to that fact. Unfortunately for Israel, the decision to establish diplomatic relations with these Gentile nations played a crucial role in the destruction of the kingdom of Israel and its North American settlements.

King Solomon interacted with his neighbors on joint commercial and diplomatic fronts. It was through these joint ventures that these nations introduced the Israelites and King Solomon to their pagan gods, goddesses and religious customs.

It is clear that Israel's relationship with other nations did not cause those nations to turn to the true God of Israel, but just the reverse occurred. There is no evidence that Israel's interaction with these people caused them to reject their pagan gods and follow the God of Israel. In fact, the scriptures clearly show that toward the end of Solomon's reign, he allowed the many women in his life to influence him to follow their pagan gods. Notice that many of these women were given to Solomon to enhance the diplomatic relationships between the United Kingdom of Israel and the Gentile nations. Consider God's reaction to this development in the latter years of Solomon's life.

But king Solomon loved many strange women, together with the daughter of Pharaoh, women of the Moabites, Ammonites, Edomites, Zidonians, and Hittites; Of the nations concerning which the LORD said unto the children of Israel, Ye shall not go in to them, neither shall they come in unto you: for surely they will turn away your heart after their gods: Solomon clave unto these in love. And he had seven hundred wives, princesses, and three hundred concubines: and his wives turned away his heart. For it came to pass, when Solomon was old, that his wives turned away his heart after other gods: and his heart was not perfect with the LORD his God, as was the heart of David his father. For Solomon went after Ashtoreth the goddess of the Zidonians, and after Milcom the abomination of the Ammonites. And Solomon did evil in the sight of the LORD, and went not fully after the LORD, as did David his father. Then did Solomon build an high place for Chemosh, the abomination of Moab, in the hill that is before Jerusalem, and for Molech, the abomination of the children of Ammon. And likewise did he for all his strange wives, which burnt incense and sacrificed unto their gods. And the LORD was angry with Solomon, because his heart was turned from the LORD God of Israel, which had appeared unto him twice. (I Kings 11:1–9)

The previous chapters of I Kings revealed the great wealth King Solomon accumulated during his forty years reigning over Israel. God was blessing Solomon and the United Israel in an unprecedented way. It was during this Golden Age that God allowed Israel to expand its influence to include settlements in North America. However, God constantly warned Israel that, if they rejected Him and began following pagan gods, He would bring punishments upon the nation.

Notice Leviticus 26:1, "Ye shall make you no idols nor graven image, neither rear you up a standing image, neither shall ye set up any image of stone in your land, to bow down unto it: for I am the LORD your God."

This was exactly what Israel was doing by following other gods. God warned Israel in Leviticus 26:14–19 what would happen as a result of embracing pagan gods.

But if ye will not hearken unto me, and will not do all these commandments; And if ye shall despise my statutes, or if your soul abhor my judgments, so that ye will not do all my commandments, but that ye break my covenant: I also will do this unto you; I will even appoint over you terror, consumption, and the burning ague, that shall consume the eyes, and cause sorrow of heart: and ye shall sow your seed in vain, for your enemies shall eat it. And I will set my face against you, and ye shall be slain before your enemies: they that hate you shall reign over you; and ye shall flee when none pursueth you. And if ye will not yet for all this hearken unto me, then I will punish you seven times more for your sins. And I will break the pride of your power; and I will make your heaven as iron, and your earth as brass ... (Leviticus 16:14–19)

Notice, God indicated that He would punish Israel because of these sins and He would, in fact, break the pride of their power they had built during the time of King David and King Solomon.

WIVES INFLUENCE SOLOMON

Solomon's character and personality deteriorated as he grew older. As he embraced more and more Gentile women, he also embraced their false gods and erected temples where his Gentile wives could worship these pagan gods.

It is unthinkable that Solomon, who had spoken directly with God and had been blessed so much by Him, would turn from the True God and begin worshipping the pagan gods associated with human sacrifices and sexual indulgences. As Solomon's harem of women grew and his exposure to false gods grew, he became more perverted in his outlook and his approach to God.

Notice Solomon's own words in Ecclesiastes 1:1–11,

The words of the Preacher, the son of David, king in Jerusalem.

Vanity of vanities, saith the Preacher, vanity of vanities; all is vanity.

What profit hath a man of all his labour which he taketh under the sun?

One generation passeth away, and another generation cometh: but the earth abideth for ever.

The sun also ariseth, and the sun goeth down, and hasteth to his place where he arose.

The wind goeth toward the south, and turneth about unto the north; it whirleth about continually, and the wind returneth again according to his circuits.

All the rivers run into the sea; yet the sea is not

full; unto the place from whence the rivers come, thither they return again.

All things are full of labour; man cannot utter it: the eye is not satisfied with seeing, nor the ear filled with hearing.

The thing that hath been, it is that which shall be; and that which is done is that which shall be done: and there is no new thing under the sun.

Is there any thing whereof it may be said, See, this is new? it hath been already of old time, which was before us.

There is no remembrance of former things; neither shall there be any remembrance of things that are to come with those that shall come after.

Solomon grew despondent about his life even though he was living in the lap of luxury and had experienced every blessing God could lavish upon a human being. Here was a man who could experience a different woman every night for a thousand nights and still he would not have slept with all of the women available to him. As his sexual appetite grew, so did his perversion and life-style. Solomon describes his situation in Ecclesiastes 2:1–11,

I said in mine heart, Go to now, I will prove thee with mirth, therefore enjoy pleasure: and, behold, this also is vanity.

I said of laughter, It is mad: and of mirth, What doeth it?

I sought in mine heart to give myself unto wine, yet acquainting mine heart with wisdom; and to lay hold on folly, till I might see what was that good for the sons of men, which they should do under the heaven all the days of their life.

I made me great works; I builded me houses; I planted me vineyards:

I made me gardens and orchards, and I planted trees in them of all kind of fruits:

I made me pools of water, to water therewith the wood that bringeth forth trees:

I got me servants and maidens, and had servants born in my house; also I had great possessions of great and small cattle above all that were in Jerusalem before me:

I gathered me also silver and gold, and the peculiar treasure of kings and of the provinces: I gat me men singers and women singers, and the delights of the sons of men, as musical instruments, and that of all sorts.

So I was great, and increased more than all that were before me in Jerusalem: also my wisdom remained with me.

And whatsoever mine eyes desired I kept not from them, I withheld not my heart from any joy; for my heart rejoiced in all my labour: and this was my portion of all my labour.

Then I looked on all the works that my hands had wrought, and on the labour that I had laboured to do: and, behold, all was vanity and vexation of spirit, and there was no profit under the sun.

King Solomon considered all material things as worthless and unable to fulfill his insatiable lust and desire for more and more hedonistic satisfaction. He had turned so far away from God that he considered suicide in his old age. King Solomon proved that all the material wealth in the world could not satisfy or soothe the spirit within man. The eye of man can never be satisfied, apart from first satisfying the spiritual needs of man. The life of Solomon provides us with ample evidence that material wealth cannot satisfy the true human desire to have peace and tranquility. Many believe that, if they suddenly had a million dollars at their disposal, they would live as it says in the fairy tales—"happily ever after." Unfortunately, material wealth will never bring total physical and spiritual satisfaction. Apart from God's Spirit, as part of the individual's life, real wealth can bring unbelievable unhappiness.

GOD'S WRATH AGAINST SOLOMON AND ISRAEL

As we have seen in these modern times, people tend to reflect the immorality of their government leaders or entertainment celebrities. During the last half of the Twentieth Century, America was plagued with presidents who lied and cheated their way into power. Some of them committed adultery or other immoral acts as sitting presidents. For years, newspapers chose to ignore their actions rather than to expose all the ugliness and indecency. No wonder the moral fabric of America has declined so dramatically since 1950.

The same can be said of ancient Israel as we now look back on the history of King Solomon. During the latter part of his reign, King Solomon rejected God and became a very immoral person, his character traits spreading to his subjects in the United Kingdom of Israel. Such activity was summarily condemned by God. God warned Solomon that turning away from Him and worshipping the false gods brought by his many wives and concubines would precipitate God's wrath. As a result of Solomon's evil actions, God passed this sentence upon him. Notice I Kings 11:11–13,

> Wherefore the LORD said unto Solomon, Forasmuch as this is done of thee, and thou hast not kept my covenant and my statutes, which I have commanded thee, I will surely rend the kingdom from thee, and will give it to thy servant. Notwithstanding in thy days I will not do it for David thy father's sake: but I will rend it out of the hand of thy son. Howbeit I will not rend away all the kingdom; but will give one tribe to thy son for David my servant's sake, and for Jerusalem's sake which I have chosen.

God was about to break the pride and the power of this great empire by splitting up the nation into two parts. At the same time, God prepared another man who would replace Solomon and his descendants. Notice, however, that God did indicate that Solomon's son, David's progeny, would have at least one tribe to rule over. This, of course, was a far cry from the great United Kingdom of Israel that reached its zenith during the time of David and Solomon.

God was behind the division of the Kingdom of Israel, creating two kingdoms, Israel and Judah. He chose the successor to the king of Israel to be Jeroboam. Jeroboam, an Ephramite (Ephrathite), was the ruler over the tribes of Joseph (Ephraim and Manasseh) in the United Kingdom under King Solomon.

God sent the Prophet Ahijah to Jeroboam to tell him of God's intention. "And Ahijah caught the new garment that was on him, and rent it in twelve pieces:" (I Kings 11:30) After Ahijah tore the new garment into twelve pieces, he told Jeroboam to pick up ten pieces, signifying that God intended to give Jeroboam ten tribes and leave the remainder for Solomon's descendants.

God made the same covenant with Jeroboam that he had made with David. Notice in I Kings 11:35, God reassures Jeroboam that He will give him ten tribes of the kingdom, but that He was reserving the remainder for the descendants of David.

> And it shall be, if thou wilt hearken unto all that I command thee, and wilt walk in my ways, and do that is right in my sight, to keep my statutes and my commandments, as David my servant did; that I will be with thee, and build thee a sure house, as I built for David, and will give Israel unto thee. (I Kings 11:38)

God promised Jeroboam that He would build an everlasting kingdom and his descendants would rule over Israel if he followed God as David had done. God also told Jeroboam that He intended to punish Solomon, but not forever. Verse 39, "And I will for this afflict the seed of David, but not for ever."

God restates why He was destroying the United Kingdom of Israel and why He intended to bring that empire down.

> Because that they have forsaken me, and have worshipped Ashtoreth the goddess of the Zidonians, Chemosh the god of the Moabites, and Milcom the god of the children of Ammon, and have not walked in my ways, to do that which is right in mine eyes, and to keep my statutes and my judgments, as did David his father. (I Kings 11:33)

The news came to Solomon that God intended to split up the kingdom and make Jeroboam king over ten tribes. Solomon intended to do something about it; he and his armies pursued Jeroboam in an attempt to kill him, thinking this would prevent the split. Jeroboam heard of the plot and fled to Egypt. It wasn't long after this that King Solomon died, ending his forty-year reign over Israel.

KINGDOM IN TURMOIL

Soon after the death of King Solomon, his son Rehoboam was anointed king over all of Israel. The kingdom was still intact, but God's plan was going forth nevertheless. The leaders of Israel approached Rehoboam to air their grievances and to see what sort of leader he would be. As of yet, the majority of the Israelites did not realize what God was about to do.

The people spoke to Rehoboam indicating their need for "tax relief" and an easing of the hardships imposed by Solomon. During the last 40 years, the nation had struggled and worked hard under Solomon to build a great empire which extended all the way to the Americas. The people were now weary of these taxes and the harsh treatment many received under Solomon's leadership. Toward the end of Solomon's life, he had become a harsh ruler over the people.

The Israelites approached Rehoboam and asked to have their

burden made lighter. Notice I Kings 12:4, "Thy father made our yoke grievous: now therefore make thou the grievous service of thy father, and his heavy yoke which he put upon us, lighter, and we will serve thee."

Rehoboam listened to the people and promised them that he would give them an answer in three days regarding which way his government would rule. Unfortunately, Rehoboam made a fatal mistake which ensured the breakup of the United Kingdom of Israel. I Kings 12 points out that King Rehoboam consulted with the old men who had been with Solomon when he was alive. These older men gave him sage advice, which, if he had followed, may have saved the kingdom. However, being headstrong and immature in governing, he forsook the counsel of the old men and consulted with the young men with whom he had grown up. They counseled Rehoboam to be even harsher with the people than Solomon had been. They advised him to let the people know who was boss and thereby keep them under control!

> And he said unto them, What counsel give ye that we may answer this people, who have spoken to me, saying, Make the yoke which thy father did put upon us lighter? And the young men that were grown up with him spake unto him, saying, Thus shalt thou speak unto this people that spake unto thee, saying, Thy father made our yoke heavy, but make thou it lighter unto us; thus shalt thou say unto them, My little finger shall be thicker than my father's loins. And now whereas my father did lade you with a heavy yoke, I will add to your yoke: my father hath chastised you with whips, but I will chastise you with scorpions. (I King 12:9–11)

When the people heard the harsh words from Rehoboam, they decided it was time to end the United Kingdom. From that point forward, Israel rebelled against Rehoboam and the house of David. The people of Israel chose Jeroboam to be their king, but in fact

God had chosen Jeroboam. This rebellion occurred circa 933 BC and just as God had prophesied through the Prophet Ahijah, ten tribes joined King Jeroboam to form the northern kingdom of Israel and the remainder stayed with King Rehoboam to form the kingdom of Judah. The tribes which remained with Rehoboam were the tribes of Judah and Benjamin. Later, the Levites, who were scattered throughout all the tribes, migrated south to join Judah.

Immediately, Rehoboam intended to stop the rebellion and to crush Jeroboam and his followers. However, the word of God came to Rehoboam and told him that He, God, had caused the separation to be complete and that Rehoboam could not stop it.

> Thus saith the LORD, Ye shall not go up, nor fight against your brethren the children of Israel: return every man to his house; for this thing is from me. They hearkened therefore to the word of the LORD, and returned to depart, according to the word of the LORD. (I Kings 12:24)

WHAT ABOUT THE AMERICAN SETTLERS?

With the dividing of the United Kingdom of Israel, Rehoboam did not possess the clout nor the material wealth to support the worldwide ventures of his father, Solomon. The early settlers who had been in America just for a few years found themselves cut off from their mother country. God intended to punish Israel and Solomon's descendants, including its colonial satellites in America. This was part of God breaking the pride of Israel's power.

When the kingdom of Israel was divided in 933 BC, the supplying and maintenance of these colonial outposts became impossible. As a result, the other American settlers who had come from Asia, whom we know as the American Indians, began to overrun these white Middle Eastern settlements to drive them from the land. In a short time, these white settlers were completely lost.

A KINGDOM DIVIDED

From this point forward, there were two nations of Israelites. There was the *northern kingdom* of Israel with its headquarters located in Samaria; and the *southern kingdom* of Judah with its headquarters remaining in Jerusalem.

Most people totally overlook the fact that Israel was made up of thirteen tribes and only one of the tribes was the tribe of Judah or Jews. The northern kingdom of Israel, now split, was an independent nation, no longer united with Judah. Judah and Israel were now two separate nations, with two separate kings. The history of Judah is well documented in the pages of the Bible, but only a little more than 200 years of the history of Israel have been documented through the books of I and II Kings and I and II Chronicles. Israel and Judah were now about to embark on separate courses as a "divided house."

From the very beginning, God warned Israel of impending destruction if they turned away from Him and began to follow pagan gods. God fulfilled His Promise in Leviticus 26: 19 when He broke the pride of the great nation of Israel because of the disobedience and the idolatry of King Solomon.

God loved Israel above all people on the earth. They were His chosen people through whom He intended to bless all mankind. This was made evident during the reign of King Solomon, when God allowed the nation of Israel to extend its influence beyond its own borders, even to the New World. It is precisely because of this great love God had for Israel and His willingness to give them multiple chances that he did not destroy the nation at King Solomon's death.

This initial punishment of breaking up the United Kingdom into two separate entities was designed to give Israel and Judah another chance. Just as God is willing to forgive individuals many times over for their sins, if they repent!

JEROBOAM

God intended to establish the northern kingdom of Israel separate from the southern tribes to be a beacon unto the Gentiles. With the split-up of the United Kingdom, God intended to give Rehoboam and the Kingdom of Judah an opportunity to once again become the nation of God. By the same token, He was extending the same opportunity to the Ten Northern Tribes of the kingdom of Israel under Jeroboam to become as great a nation as they had been under King Solomon. All that was required was for the leaders and the people to stay focused on God, to remain steadfast in their obedience to Him, and reject the gods of the gentile nations who had made diplomatic alliances with King Solomon and the United Kingdom of Israel. God was giving the nations a second chance, even though it was now a nation divided. God promised Jeroboam all the greatness and the longevity of his family dynasty just as He had promised David if he would walk in the ways of God and do that which was right in His sight.

God emphasizes His covenant again in Jeremiah 33:17, "For thus saith the LORD; David shall never want a man to sit upon the throne of the house of Israel." God did not forget His covenant and, because this covenant is everlasting, it will help us to identify the children of Israel and where they migrated after they were taken captive circa 721 BC.

The new nation of Israel under Jeroboam began its existence circa 933–932 BC.

At the time God determined to break up the kingdom of Israel because of Solomon's sins, He selected Jeroboam to lead the Northern Tribes. In the beginning, there were eleven tribes that made up the Northern Kingdom. Many Levites lived in the northern kingdom which included the tribes of Dan, Reuben, Gad, Issachar, Simeon, Zebulon, Asher, Naphtali, Ephraim, and Manasseh.

In the beginning, God had chosen the men of Levi to be the priests and teachers of Israel. In order for them to do this, they were scattered throughout the country to provide spiritual training and physical leadership for all the tribes of the Israelites.

Jeroboam did not take into account the importance of the Levites. Soon after the separation of the two kingdoms, Jeroboam made a decision which would come back to haunt him and Israel until their final demise circa 721 BC. God had promised Jeroboam that He would make his lineage as everlasting as that of King David if Jeroboam would follow God's laws and commandments. Jeroboam, either through total ignorance or rebellion against God, made a fatal mistake in an effort to protect his kingdom, rather than rely on God to fulfill His promise.

Some months after the split-up occurred, it came time for the Fall Holy Days known as the Feast of Tabernacles. Since the temple was constructed in Jerusalem, all the people across Israel would travel to Jerusalem to observe the Feast of Tabernacles, which occurred each year in the seventh month beginning on the fifteenth day. As this time approached, Jeroboam reasoned that the people traveling to Jerusalem to keep the Feast of Tabernacles could present imminent danger to him and his kingdom.

> And Jeroboam said in his heart, Now shall the kingdom return to the house of David: If this people go up to do sacrifice in the house of the LORD at Jerusalem, then shall the heart of this people turn again unto their lord, even unto Rehoboam king of Judah, and

they shall kill me, and go again to Rehoboam king of Judah. (I Kings 12:26–27)

Jeroboam, in an effort to make sure the people of Judah and the northern kingdom of Israel did not get back together, decided to modify the true religion of God. The first thing that he did wrong was to make replicas of the golden cherubs in the temple in Jerusalem. After constructing these two large golden images he placed one in Bethel and the other in Dan.

Just as modern Christendom places a *cross* or a *steeple* on a building to signify that it is a church, so did Jeroboam make copies of the golden cherubs located in the temple at Jerusalem so the people would understand there were "church sites" located in Bethel and Dan, "Whereupon the king took counsel, and made two calves of gold, and said unto them, It is too much for you to go up to Jerusalem: behold thy gods, O Israel, which brought thee up out of the land of Egypt. And he set the one in Bethel, and the other put he in Dan."(I Kings 12:28–29)

When Jeroboam took on this unauthorized project, the building of these two golden images, he immediately drew the anger of the God of Israel, who referred to them as *golden calves.*

The Levites living in Jeroboam's kingdom immediately knew that Jeroboam had committed an idolatrous deed. They came to him demanding that this idolatry should stop. Jeroboam realized that the Levitical priests would never go along with the establishment of his "brand" of God's Church, therefore, he chose those who would have no scruples about following Jeroboam's way, even though it was idolatrous. "And this thing became a sin:... And he made an house of high places, and made priests of the lowest of the people, which were not of the sons of Levi." (I Kings 12:30–31)

Not only did Jeroboam establish new meeting places for the Israelites to keep the Feast of Tabernacles, but he also changed it from the fifteenth day of the seventh month to the fifteenth day of eighth month.

And Jeroboam ordained a feast in the eighth month,

on the fifteenth day of the month, like unto the feast
that is in Judah, and he offered upon the altar. So did
he in Bethel, sacrificing unto the calves that he had
made: and he placed in Bethel the priests of the high
places which he had made. So he offered upon the
altar which he had made in Bethel the fifteenth day
of the eighth month, even in the month which he had
devised of his own heart; and ordained a feast unto the
children of Israel: and he offered upon the altar, and
burnt incense. (I Kings 12:32–33)

GOD RESPONDS

Immediately, God dispatched a prophet from Judah to go to
Jeroboam and demand that he cease this idolatrous practice and
destroy the two golden images and the new altar he had built for
sacrificing.

And, behold, there came a man of God out of Judah
by the word of the LORD unto Bethel: and Jeroboam
stood by the altar to burn incense. And he cried
against the altar in the word of the LORD, and said, O
altar, altar, thus saith the LORD; Behold, a child shall
be born unto the house of David, Josiah by name; and
upon thee shall he offer the priests of the high places
that burn incense upon thee, and men's bones shall be
burnt upon thee. And he gave a sign the same day,
saying, This is the sign which the LORD hath spoken;
Behold, the altar shall be rent, and the ashes that are
upon it shall be poured out. (I Kings 13:1–3)

As soon as Jeroboam heard the denouncement of his altar in
Bethel, he stretched out his hand commanding that his guard capture the prophet of God. As soon as he did this, his hand became
leprous, indicating God's strong disapproval of Jeroboam's actions.

Jeroboam realized immediately that he had made a mistake and he asked that the prophet of God appeal to God to restore his hand. The prophet did so and God answered the prayer and his hand was restored. Unfortunately, Jeroboam misunderstood the healing and apparently assumed that God approved of what he was doing.

You will see in subsequent chapters how the sin of Jeroboam never departed from the land of Israel until it was taken captive circa 721 BC. Since the Levites saw that they had no part in the religious community of Israel (the northern tribes), they began to migrate back down to the kingdom of Judah. In so doing, Rehoboam was now king over three tribes, which included Levi, Judah and Benjamin. Jeroboam remained king over the remaining ten tribes, just as the Prophet Ahijah had proclaimed. Note: Joseph had two tribes, making a total of 13 tribes.

Jeroboam hardened his heart and soon proved to God that he was not worthy to have his house established as David's house had been.

> After this thing Jeroboam returned not from his evil way, but made again of the lowest of the people priests of the high places: whosoever would, he consecrated him, and he became one of the priests of the high places. And this thing became sin unto the house of Jeroboam, even to cut it off, and to destroy it from off the face of the earth. (I Kings 13:33–34)

PUNISHMENT COMES TO JEROBOAM

Soon after the events with the prophet at Bethel, Jeroboam's son became gravely ill. It appeared that there was no cure for his son, so he instructed his wife to travel to Shiloh and meet with the prophet Ahijah and ask for God's intervention for his son. Jeroboam instructed his wife to go to Ahijah in a disguise and inquire about his son and the possibility that he might recover.

Jeroboam's wife did as she was instructed and, even before she came to Ahijah's house, God revealed to Ahijah that the woman approaching him was, in fact, Jeroboam's wife in disguise. As she entered the room, Ahijah welcomed her and immediately informed her that he knew who she was. Ahijah then revealed the bad news and punishment from God because of Jeroboam's disobedience.

> Go, tell Jeroboam, Thus saith the LORD God of Israel, Forasmuch as I exalted thee from among the people, and made thee prince over my people Israel, And rent the kingdom away from the house of David, and gave it thee: and yet thou hast not been as my servant David, who kept my commandments, and who followed me with all his heart, to do that only which was right in mine eyes; But hast done evil above all that were before thee: for thou hast gone and made thee other gods, and molten images, to provoke me to anger, and hast cast me behind thy back: herefore, behold, I will bring evil upon the house of Jeroboam, and will cut off from Jeroboam him that pisseth against the wall, and him that is shut up and left in Israel, and will take away the remnant of the house of Jeroboam, as a man taketh away dung, till it be all gone. Him that dieth of Jeroboam in the city shall the dogs eat; and him that dieth in the field shall the fowls of the air eat: for the LORD hath spoken it. Arise thou therefore, get thee to thine own house: and when thy feet enter into the city, the child shall die. (I Kings 14:7–12)

Most would believe the actions of Jeroboam did not warrant God's anger, since he was actually making changes in the True Religion of God that would, by some standards, make obedience to God more convenient for the people. Some might say, "What difference would it make that Jeroboam simply changed the Feast Month from the seventh to the eighth month of the year and made it more convenient for the Israelites to keep the Feast of Tabernacles in their own land rather than travel so far back to the temple in Jerusalem?" This is exactly the same argument used in religion today; people claim that it makes no difference how you worship God, so long as you worship Him on any day you choose. But, we see that it does make a difference to God in the way that we worship Him. God has never given us the right to determine how we will worship him and in what form or manner. God has prescribed the way He is to be worshipped and there is to be no deviation from His words. When we deviate from the way God tells us to worship Him, we commit idolatry. Those who claim that you can worship God on any day that you choose are in violation of God's direct command in the Fourth Commandment to "Remember the Sabbath Day." There are those who claim men changed the Sabbath to Sunday-keeping and, since they were supposedly men of God, it must be all right. Here again, man does not have any authority to change the Word of God, especially when it is a direct command. As we go through the History of Israel, we realize those people never came to understand that God, and God only, can prescribe the method and time that we are to worship Him.

By changing the location and time of the celebration of God's annual Festival of Tabernacles, Jeroboam created a sin from which Israel never departed. In fact, the Bible makes this statement about each king after Jeroboam, which shows us conclusively that none of these Israelite kings ever repented from the original sin of Jeroboam. Not only did they *not* depart from the original sin of Jeroboam, each successive king added even more abominations which increased the anger of God against Israel. Jeroboam became so great "in his own eyes" that his vanity caused ultimately the downfall of Israel.

JEROBOAM'S FATE IS SEALED

From this point on, Jeroboam was a man living on borrowed time. God abandoned Jeroboam and he became reprobate in his mind. Just as had been predicted, the child died and all Israel mourned for him.

God promised Jeroboam and Israel that he would smite the nation as a reed that is shaken in the water and, ultimately he would root Israel up out of the land he had given them and scatter them beyond the waters because they had provoked Him to jealousy by building their houses of worship with their raised obelisks and secretly worshipping the goddess Astarte and the heavenly bodies of the sun and crescent moon, symbolic of Nimrod and Semiramis.

The Israelites sank into immoral lifestyles and built more places of worship with images and steeples on every high hill and under every green tree throughout the land. They practiced all the abominations so hated by the God of Israel. (I Kings 14:23–24)

THERE WAS NO PEACE

During all the days of Jeroboam, the king of Israel, and Rehoboam, the king of Judah, there were skirmishes and battles between the Northern Kingdom (*Israel*) and the Southern Kingdom (*Judah*). This internal fighting among the tribes of Israel greatly weakened the Israelite Empire that had been so highly developed under the kings David and Solomon.

After Rehoboam's death, he was succeeded to the throne by Abijah, his son and the hatred between Israel and Judah continued as indicated in II Chronicles 12:16,

> And Rehoboam slept with his fathers, and was buried in the city of David: and Abijah his son reigned in his stead. II Chronicles 13:1–2, Now in the eighteenth year of king Jeroboam began Abijah to reign over Judah. He reigned three years in Jerusalem. His mother's name also was Michaiah the daughter of Uriel of Gibeah. And there was war between Abijah and Jeroboam.

Israel and the Southern Kingdom of Judah—the Jews—now fought a major war against each other that engaged hundreds of thousands of soldiers.

Although Jeroboam's Israelites outnumbered the Jews by approximately two to one, God gave the victory to the kingdom of

Judah in which roughly one-half million Israelites were killed. The hatred that had developed between Israel and Judah had become so great that these warring factions were intent upon savagely destroying each other. These wars occurred circa 910–920 BC.

As a result of these devastating wars, Israel's military might and its political power were diminished. The surrounding nations realized that Israel was no longer the great power it had been. It was during this time that its many colonies, especially those in the Western Hemisphere, could no longer depend on the mother country to support them and provide them with help in the New World. Without this help, no new settlers came to those ancient colonies; therefore, those who were stranded there were killed or died out and Israel's influence and control came to an end.

In the Middle East, at that time, Assyria began to build its military strength virtually unhindered by Israel or any other nation. The vacuum that had been left as a result of the civil war that split Israel and Judah allowed Assyria to move in line to fill that vacuum. The same would have occurred had the United States of America, 1,900 years later, been split into two countries by the American Civil War. France, England and Spain looked lustfully to the American shores, expecting to have the pickings if the United States was split up into two small countries. However, God intervened because of plans He had for this country.

WAR CLOUDS

The stage was now being set, even though it would be almost 200 years in the future, for the ultimate demise of the Empire of Israel.

Her power became diminished because of the many skirmishes and battles, while her neighbors mounted threats against her sovereignty. For 200 years, Israel had to fight for survival against its neighbors who saw an opportunity to take a spoil from a weakened great empire.

Jeroboam outlived his rival, Rehoboam, but in a few years he too died and his son, Nebab, became the second king of Israel. Jeroboam reigned as king of Israel for 22 years.

ALL ISRAELITES ARE NOT JEWS

The world has failed to recognize, and even modern-day Jews today do not acknowledge, the fact that not all Israelites are Jews, but that only racial Jews are Israelites. The Jews were the most populous tribe that remained in the Southern Kingdom; therefore, it was called the Kingdom of Judah. Only the direct descendants of their father, Judah, made up the tribe of the Jews. The Levites were not Jews, but were the descendants of Levi, just as the Benjaminites were not Jews, but descendants of their father Benjamin. The Bible later describes a battle between Israel and the Jews which correctly differentiates between the southern kingdom of Judah and the northern kingdom of Israel.

Notice, God mentioned the house of Israel and the house of Judah. The two nations are mentioned in Jeremiah 33:7, "And I will cause the captivity of Judah and the captivity of Israel to return, and will build them, as at the first."

In Jeremiah 33:14, we find, "Behold, the days come, saith the LORD, that I will perform that good thing which I have promised unto the house of Israel and to the house of Judah."

The two houses are mentioned again in Jeremiah 30:3–4, "And these are the words that the LORD spake concerning Israel and concerning Judah." See also Jeremiah 32:30, "For the children of Israel and the children of Judah have only done evil before me from their youth…"

The term "Jew" comes from a perversion of the name given to the descendants of Judah. Judah was one of the sons of Jacob; Jacob's name was changed to Israel. The term "Israel" could apply to all of the tribes of Israel; however, after the split, it applied to the house of Israel which made up the Ten Northern Tribes and did not include the Jews.

Notice that, in some cases, the scripture will refer to Jerusalem as representing the Jews. You will also notice that God refers to *Samaria*, which was the capital city of Israel, when speaking of the northern kingdom of Israel. On other occasions, He speaks of *Ephraim* when He is referring to the Ten Northern Tribes. Hosea 7:1, "When I would have healed Israel, then the iniquity of Ephraim was discovered, and the wickedness of Samaria: for they commit falsehood; and the thief cometh in, and the troop of robbers spoileth without."

It is important to understand the concept that the Ten Northern Tribes may be referred to as the *house of Israel*, *Samaria*, and *Ephraim;* the southern tribes can be referred to as the *kingdom of Judah*, *Jews*, and even *Jerusalem*.

You must understand these distinctions before you can ever understand prophecy. By understanding that the name *Ephraim* can refer to the Kingdom of Israel and that *Judah* is the Kingdom of Judah, we can then understand prophetic scriptures such as Hosea 6:4, "O Ephraim, what shall I do unto thee? O Judah, what shall I do unto thee? for your goodness is as a morning cloud, and as the early dew it goeth away."

Again, notice these two different names are used in Hosea 5:12–15.

> Therefore will I be unto Ephraim as a moth, and to the house of Judah as rottenness. When Ephraim saw his sickness, and Judah saw his wound, then went Ephraim to the Assyrian, and sent to king Jareb: yet could he not heal you, nor cure you of your wound. For I will be unto Ephraim as a lion, and as a young lion to the house of Judah: I, even I, will tear and go away; I will take away, and none shall rescue him.

BIRTHRIGHT AND SCEPTER

With the break-up of the two kingdoms, the *scepter*, which is an indication that the line of kings was to remain with Judah, while the *birthright* which included all the many great blessings given to the two sons of Joseph, Ephraim and Manasseh, would go with the Ten Northern Tribes making up the House of Israel. These promises are given in Genesis 48:13–19,

> And Joseph took them both, Ephraim in his right hand toward Israel's left hand, and Manasseh in his left hand toward Israel's right hand, and brought them near unto him. And Israel stretched out his right hand, and laid it upon Ephraim's head, who was the younger, and his left hand upon Manasseh's head, guiding his hands wittingly; for Manasseh was the firstborn. And he blessed Joseph, and said, God, before whom my fathers Abraham and Isaac did walk, the God which fed me all my life long unto this day, The Angel which redeemed me from all evil, bless the lads; and let my name be named on them, and the name of my fathers Abraham and Isaac; and let them grow into a multitude in the midst of the earth. And when Joseph saw that his father laid his right hand upon the head of Ephraim, it displeased him: and he held up his father's hand, to remove it from Ephraim's head unto Manasseh's head. And Joseph said unto his father, Not so, my father: for this is the firstborn; put thy right hand upon his head. And his father refused, and said, I know it, my son, I know it: he also shall become a people, and he [Manasseh] also shall be great: but truly his younger brother [Ephraim] shall be greater than he, and his seed shall become a multitude of nations.

This was the *birthright* given to Ephraim and Manasseh, two of the tribes of the kingdom of Israel. The *scepter,* which is a promise of kingship, would remain with Judah—this was promised to him by Israel in Genesis 49:8–10,

> Judah, thou art he whom thy brethren shall praise: thy hand shall be in the neck of thine enemies; thy father's

children shall bow down before thee. Judah is a lion's whelp: from the prey, my son, thou art gone up: he stooped down, he couched as a lion, and as an old lion; who shall rouse him up? The sceptre shall not depart from Judah, nor a lawgiver from between his feet, until Shiloh come; and unto him shall the gathering of the people be.

Understanding the concept of which direction the birthright went and which direction the scepter went will absolutely nail down the location of the Lost Ten Tribes of Israel. That scepter is in existence today, as was promised to David by God in Jeremiah 33:17, "For thus saith the LORD; David shall never want a man to sit upon the throne of the house of Israel;"

ISRAEL LOST ITS
NATIONAL IDENTITY

Od did not immediately reject Israel during the more than 200 years she existed as a separate nation from the kingdom of Judah. In fact, God sent many prophets, whose messages are recorded in the pages of the Old Testament, in an effort to awaken the Israelites before it was too late. One of these great prophets received a commission which was given to Israel. The True Church of God continues to carry out that commission even until this day. We will relate some of the messages and situations God used in an effort to turn the kings of Israel and the people back to Him before their final destruction.

DIMINISHING INFLUENCE

It took many years before God broke the "pride of the power" of the great nation of Israel. We have seen through archaeological evidence and the Bible that Israel's influence in the world was well known.

Following the break-up of the United Israel, domestic politics caused the nation to lose influence and ultimately all of her far-flung colonies which had been established during the days of King David and King Solomon.

Internal strife and a rejection of God and His way of living ultimately led to the decline of both the kingdoms of the divided Israel. As Israel declined in power and prestige, border skirmishes and territorial intrusions by Israel's enemies began to take their tolls on the country at a time when the national leadership and the religious institutions were being perverted.

Upon the death of Israel's first king, Jeroboam, his son Nadab reigned only two years before a conspiracy erupted by Baasha, ending with the death of Nadab. The scripture indicates that Nadab did not depart from his father's sins. (I Kings 15:28) The Bible shows that Baasha not only killed Nadab, but he also destroyed all possible heirs of the house of Jeroboam to make sure none of Jeroboam's offspring could rebel against him. Baasha became king of Israel circa 910 BC. King Baasha reigned in Israel for 24 years, continued in the sin of Jeroboam, and even added more religious perversion which contributed to a long, national, moral decline before the fall of the nation.

God took notice of Baasha's evil way and God sent Jehu, the prophet of God.

> Forasmuch as I exalted thee out of the dust, and made thee prince over my people Israel; and thou hast walked in the way of Jeroboam, and hast made my people Israel to sin, to provoke me to anger with their sins; Behold, I will take away the posterity of Baasha, and the posterity of his house; and will make thy house like the house of Jeroboam the son of Nebat. Him that dieth of Baasha in the city shall the dogs eat; and him that dieth of his in the fields shall the fowls of the air eat. (I Kings 16:2–4)

We can see from these few verses that God pronounced Baasha's punishment because of his sins; he would be murdered and his body desecrated.

OVERTHROWN KINGS

The fourth king of Israel was Tirzah, the son of Baasha, who only reigned two years before a conspiracy erupted and he was killed by the succeeding king, Zimri, who became the fifth king circa 886 BC. When Zimri took over as king of Israel, he made sure that no living descendants of Baasha survived who might rebel against him. However, a conspiracy formed against Zimri and he only reigned seven days. Zimri was overthrown and killed by Omri. Omri had been a military leader under Baasha in the army of Israel. Omri then became the sixth king and he took over circa 886 BC. However, Omri's reign was not without serious difficulty. Many did not see Omri as a legitimate heir to the throne since he was only a military man under King Baasha. Even so, the Bible reports that Omri did not depart from the "sins of Jeroboam" and continued to cause Israel to sin.

As a result of Omri proclaiming himself king and taking the kingdom by force, a division erupted among the people. Omri led one faction while Tibni, the son of Ginath, reigned jointly with him for a short period of time. Finally, Omri won out. Omri reigned from 886 to 875 BC. While reigning in Israel, Omri bought a hill with two talents of silver and built the capital city of Israel—Samaria. During his reign, he consolidated the power of his kingdom as much as possible. In prophetic writings in the Bible, God sometimes refers to Israel, the Northern Kingdom, as Samaria.

In 1868, F. A. Klein, a German missionary, discovered what has become commonly known as the Moabite Stone. This stone records the attempt of the second King Jeroboam to re-subdue Moab. In addition, the stone refers to "Omri, king of Israel" and Israel as "the land of Omri." In addition, the black obelisk of Shalmaneser III (860–825 BC) speaks of tribute from Jehu, the successor of Omri." The black obelisk now resides in the British Museum. A Harvard University expedition, while excavating the ruins of Samaria, discovered the foundations of Omri's palace. All of these archaeological findings verify the validity of the Biblical account of Omri's reign.

Omri, like his predecessors, continued to lead the nation away from God. While it seemed the nation was prospering, its morals were in decline. The Bible attests that Omri was, up until that time, the most evil king Israel had endured.

> But Omri wrought evil in the eyes of the LORD, and did worse than all that were before him. For he walked in all the way of Jeroboam the son of Nebat, and in his sin wherewith he made Israel to sin, to provoke the LORD God of Israel to anger with their vanities. (I Kings 16:25–26)

BAAL WORSHIP AND JEZEBEL

Ahab, the son of Omri, began to reign in Israel circa 875 BC. Up until this point, Israel continued to recognize the Eternal One as their God. In spite of the fact they had perverted their religious practices, they still looked to the God of Abraham, Isaac and Jacob as their God, and there were still those who refused to follow the perverted ways of Jeroboam in worshipping God.

Under the reign of Ahab, things took a dramatic, downward turn which would ultimately lead to the destruction of the nation. Ahab married a woman from Zidon named Jezebel. The name Jezebel has become synonymous with *prostitution* and *evil, loose women.* In fact, the name Jezebel is used in the book of Revelation when God is condemning the practices of the Thyatira Church.

> Notwithstanding I have a few things against thee, because thou sufferest that woman Jezebel, which calleth herself a prophetess, to teach and to seduce my servants to commit fornication, and to eat things sacrificed unto idols.... But unto you I say, and unto the rest in Thyatira, as many as have not this doctrine, and which have not known the depths of Satan, as

they speak; I will put upon you none other burden. (Revelation 2:20–24)

Jezebel was a very dominant, sun-worshipping, evil woman who had great influence over Ahab and the life of all Israel. It was she who brought *sun worship* to Israel.

Jezebel convinced her evil husband, King Ahab, to build churches to the Zidonian god, Baal. He also, under the influence of Jezebel, built many worship centers throughout the country that were identified by obelisk, phallic symbols. In an effort to please his wife, Ahab built a magnificent temple to Baal in the capital city of Samaria. It was during the reign of Ahab and Jezebel that the people began to totally reject the God of Israel and began worshipping the sun god, Baal. As a result of this idolatrous worship, the Bible says Ahab, with the influence of Jezebel, provoked God to anger more than all the other kings of Israel before him. I Kings 16:33, "And Ahab made a grove; and Ahab did more to provoke the LORD God of Israel to anger than all the kings of Israel that were before him."

ELIJAH

It was during this time when the moral decay and perversion of the people of Israel accelerated that God raised up a great prophet whom He sent directly to Ahab and the people of Israel to warn them against the idolatry of Baal. Elijah, the Tishbite from Gilead, was the man God selected.

God used one of His most effective weapons against the idolatry of Israel; He sent a drought that caused the nation to be plunged into great discomfort for three years. It came to the attention of Ahab that Elijah had announced this drought from God because of the evils of Ahab and his domineering co-ruler, Jezebel. After three years of drought, God told Elijah to visit Ahab because He (God) intended to end the drought.

Elijah was concerned about going to Ahab, because he knew that Jezebel had been responsible for killing many of the true prophets of God who remained in Israel. However, God encouraged Elijah and promised that no harm would come to him when he visited Ahab. I Kings 18:17, "And it came to pass, when Ahab saw Elijah, that Ahab said unto him, Art thou he that troubleth Israel?" Elijah answered Ahab that it was he, Ahab, who had caused the trouble in Israel because of Baal worship. Verse 18, "And he answered, I have not troubled Israel; but thou, and thy father's house, in that ye have forsaken the commandments of the LORD, and thou hast followed Baalim."

The people were used to following their leader and they had become confused. Who was the real God of Israel? Was it the Eternal God? Or was it Baal? Elijah intended to directly challenge Jezebel and the followers of Baal in a contest to determine who was the true God. Elijah proposed that Jezebel round up her top prophets—450 prophets of Baal and 400 prophets of the groves—and there would be a demonstration to identify without a shadow of a doubt who the true God of Israel really was! Jezebel agreed to this contest and Ahab sent out a decree inviting the Israelites to meet at a specific time at mount Carmel. Then the 450 prophets of Baal, the children of Israel and Elijah came together, "And Elijah came unto all the people, and said, How long halt ye between two opinions? if the LORD be God, follow him: but if Baal, then follow him. And the people answered him not a word."(I Kings 18:21)

The agreement was made among Jezebel, her preachers and Elijah for the preachers of Baal and Elijah to set up their altars for sacrificing. The contest was for each side to take a bullock for a sacrifice and place it upon their respective altars. However, the rules indicated that neither the prophets of Baal nor Elijah could light the fires under their sacrifices during the offering process. The contest between God and Baal would be resolved by whichever God/god sent fire from heaven to consume the sacrifice being offered. Would the fire come from Baal to consume the sacrifice of the prophets of Baal, or would the fire come from God to consume the sacrifice Elijah had prepared?

It was agreed that whichever sacrifice was consumed would identify the true Living God of Israel.

THE CONTEST

The contest began early in the morning and the prophets of Baal began dancing and singing and speaking in "unknown" tongues and calling upon the name of Baal to send fire from heaven and consume their burnt offerings to identify which God/god was the true GOD.

> Let them therefore give us two bullocks; and let them choose one bullock for themselves, and cut it in pieces, and lay it on wood, and put no fire under: and I will dress the other bullock, and lay it on wood, and put no fire under: And call ye on the name of your gods, and I will call on the name of the LORD: and the God that answereth by fire, let him be God. And all the people answered and said, It is well spoken. And Elijah said unto the prophets of Baal, Choose you one bullock for yourselves, and dress it first; for ye are many; and call on the name of your gods, but put no fire under. (I Kings 18:23–25)

The prophets of Baal cried out to their god to answer them and consume their sacrifice. They were probably yelling, screaming and wildly dancing to the point of total exhaustion in an effort to cause their god to react. At this point, Elijah mocked them because Baal would not answer. I Kings 18:27, "And it came to pass at noon, that Elijah mocked them, and said, 'Cry aloud: for he is a god; either he is talking, or he is pursuing, or he is in a journey, or peradventure he sleepeth, and must be awaked.'"

The priests of Baal became so frantic in their incantations, they began to cut themselves causing blood to gush out. These priests seemed to believe that, by inflicting pain upon themselves, Baal would answer their call. The priests of Baal continued all day long until late in the afternoon when it was time for the evening sacrifice to the God of Israel.

Elijah took twelve stones, according to the twelve tribes of Israel and set up an altar. He placed the wood and the cut-up bullock on the altar. To ensure there was no possibility that Baal worshippers could accuse Elijah of trickery, Elijah then called for four barrels of water to be poured on the sacrifice and the wood stacked at the altar. He then commanded that it be done a second and a third time until the altar was standing in water making it impossible for a fire to be lit by human hands. At this point, Elijah asked the following prayer.

> And it came to pass at the time of the offering of the evening sacrifice, that Elijah the prophet came near, and said, "LORD God of Abraham, Isaac, and of Israel, let it be known this day that thou art God in Israel, and that I am thy servant, and that I have done all these things at thy word. Hear me, O LORD, hear me, that this people may know that thou art the LORD God, and that thou hast turned their heart back again. (I Kings 18:36–37)

Immediately, God sent fire from heaven and consumed the offering, the wood, the stones, and the dust; it even licked up the water that had been surrounding the altar. When the people saw this, they fell on their faces and they truly had to admit that the Eternal God of Israel was the true God and that Baal was no god at all.

Then Elijah commanded that the 450 prophets of Baal be rounded up and taken to the Brook Kishon where Elijah slew them. Elijah announced to Ahab that *now* God would send rain on the land.

As soon as Jezebel heard what had happened, she vowed that she would kill Elijah for killing the 450 prophets of Baal. When Elijah heard this, his faith began to wane and he immediately fled Israel to save his life. Elijah fled south to Beersheba located in Judah. From the Brook Kishon at the foot of Mount Carmel to Beersheba is 90 miles, so you can see he was frightened of this evil sun-worshipping woman. From Beersheba, he continued into the wilderness a day's journey to hide from Jezebel and her soldiers. He rested, was rejuvenated and fed by God, then God instructed him to go to Horeb, the mount of God—Mount Sinai. (I Kings 19:3–8)

Obviously, God was disappointed with Elijah for fleeing from Jezebel because of her proclamation. God was also disappointed in Elijah because he was showing a lack of faith that God would protect him from this evil queen. Elijah's faith waned even after witnessing the power that God had shown him and all the people of Israel.

At this point, Elijah believed there were no followers of God left in Israel. Yet, God said that He still had 7000 who had not fallen for the perversions of Jeroboam or the Baal worship of Ahab and Jezebel. I Kings 19:18, "Yet I have left me seven thousand in Israel, all the knees which have not bowed unto Baal, and every mouth which hath not kissed him."

Soon after this, God decided to *pass the mantle* to another prophet whom He would also send to Israel to warn them of their evil ways. God showed Elijah that Elisha, the son of Shaphat, would now resume the mission to give a witness and a warning to the people of Israel.

GOD STILL LOVED ISRAEL

Even though Ahab and Jezebel continued as evil co-rulers, God continued to bless Israel.

An example of God's continuing support of Israel is found in I Kings 20, when the king of Syria threatened Ahab and the Israelites. In fact, Ahab, in an effort to avert a war with the Syrian king, tried the tactic of appeasement. Unfortunately, it did not work.

> And Ben-ha'dad the king of Syria gathered all his host together: and there were thirty and two kings with him, and horses, and chariots: and he went up

and besieged Samaria, and warred against it. And he sent messengers to Ahab king of Israel into the city, and said unto him, Thus saith Ben-ha'dad, Thy silver and thy gold is mine; thy wives also and thy children, even the goodliest, are mine. And the king of Israel answered and said, My lord, O king, according to thy saying, I am thine, and all that I have. And the messengers came again, and said, Thus speaketh Ben-ha'dad, saying, Although I have sent unto thee, saying, Thou shalt deliver me thy silver, and thy gold, and thy wives, and thy children; Yet I will send my servants unto thee to morrow about this time, and they shall search thine house, and the houses of thy servants; and it shall be, that whatsoever is pleasant in thine eyes, they shall put it in their hand, and take it away. (I Kings 20:1–6)

Ahab realized there was no satisfying the king of Syria, so he met with his top advisors and they decided that Israel had to fight the Syrians to protect themselves. God sent a prophet to Ahab and proclaimed that God was still on the side of Israel and that they would be triumphant in this war. I Kings 20:13, "And, behold, there came a prophet unto Ahab king of Israel, saying, Thus saith the LORD, Hast thou seen all this great multitude? behold, I will deliver it into thine hand this day; and thou shalt know that I am the LORD."

Sure enough, the battle played out as if it were a battle between the God of Israel and the gods of Syria. God used this battle to once again prove to the Israelites that He was their God and the gods of the Syrians and Jezebel were no gods at all.

And the prophet came to the king of Israel, and said unto him, Go, strengthen thyself, and mark, and see what thou doest: for at the return of the year the king of Syria will come up against thee. And the servants of the king of Syria said unto him, Their gods are gods of the hills; therefore they were stronger than we; but let us fight against them in the plain, and surely we shall be stronger than they. (I Kings 20:22–23) Verses 28–29, And there came a man of God, and spake unto the king of Israel, and said, Thus saith the LORD, Because the Syrians have said, The LORD is God of the hills, but he is not God of the valleys, therefore will I deliver all this great multitude into thine hand, and ye shall know that I am the LORD. And they pitched one over against the other seven days. And so it was, that in the seventh day the battle was joined: and the children of Israel slew of the Syrians an hundred thousand footmen in one day.

The battle was won and Israel enjoyed peace for three years with Syria. God allowed Ahab and Jezebel to continue in their evil rule which resulted in a continued decline in the moral character of the people of Israel. God records that Ahab was the worst king yet and that he continued to walk in the sins of Jeroboam. Ahab's persistent tolerance of Jezebel's Baal worship continued to plague Israel until the nation ultimately fell.

THE END WAS NEAR

Each successive king of Israel continued the Baal worship introduced by Jezebel and the perversion of the True Church of God started by Jeroboam. During these successive kings, Israel continued to be plagued with internal strife and conspiracies against the ruling kings. In spite of the decline of the national morality and the recurrence of kings who did not know God, the nation continued to rock along with a degree of prosperity and security.

Circa 748 BC, Peka began to reign over Israel and he reigned for 20 years. It was during his reign that Assyria began to grow in strength and to challenge Israel for power. In spite of all these threats from the Assyrians, Peka did not return to God, but he continued in the sins of Jeroboam and the idolatry of Baal worship. Tiglathpileser (II Kings 16:29) captured a section of land from Israel and carried the people of Naphtali into captivity under Assyrian rule. As a result of the turmoil, Hoshea conspired against Peka and killed him and began to reign circa 730 BC.

Hoshea was the final king of Israel; during his reign, God had seen enough. Unfortunately for Hoshea and Israel, a new king had come to power in Assyria and he was able to strengthen himself and his nation against Israel for the ultimate battle. The new king who assumed command in Assyria circa 730 BC was Shalmaneser who did not regard the King of Israel or the God of Israel. He demanded tribute from Hoshea and the Israelites with his newfound power. In an effort to appease Shalmaneser, Hoshea agreed to become his servant and gave him tribute.

However, Hoshea was very foolish and conspired with Egypt against Shalmaneser. When Shalmaneser learned of the conspiracy, he captured Hoshea, put him in prison and ultimately executed him. For the next three years, Shalmaneser and the Assyrian army besieged the land of Israel. After nine years of rule by Hoshea as king of Israel, Shalmaneser of Assyria captured the Israelite stronghold and began deporting the Israelites out of the land. The Assyrian method of treating its conquered peoples was to deport the captured people from their land to destroy their sense of nationalism and make them more easily subdued.

God plainly shows that He allowed Israel to fall and become the captives of the Assyrians. God's anger was so great against Israel and its idolatry that He removed the Israelites from their land. Notice God's indictment against Israel in the following verses.

> In the ninth year of Hoshea the king of Assyria took Samaria, and carried Israel away into Assyria, and placed them in Halah and in Habor by the river of Gozan, and in the cities of the Medes. For so it was, that the children of Israel had sinned against the LORD their God, which had brought them up out of the land of Egypt, from under the hand of Pharaoh king of Egypt, and had feared other gods, And walked in the statutes of the heathen, whom the LORD cast out from

before the children of Israel, and of the kings of Israel, which they had made. And the children of Israel did secretly those things that were not right against the LORD their God, and they built them high places in all their cities, from the tower of the watchmen to the fenced city. And they set them up images and groves in every high hill, and under every green tree: And there they burnt incense in all the high places, as did the heathen whom the LORD carried away before them; and wrought wicked things to provoke the LORD to anger: For they served idols, whereof the LORD had said unto them, Ye shall not do this thing. Yet the LORD testified against Israel, and against Judah, by all the prophets, and by all the seers, saying, Turn ye from your evil ways, and keep my commandments and my statutes, according to all the law which I commanded your fathers, and which I sent to you by my servants the prophets. Notwithstanding they would not hear, but hardened their necks, like to the neck of their fathers, that did not believe in the LORD their God. And they rejected his statutes, and his covenant that he made with their fathers, and his testimonies which he testified against them; and they followed vanity, and became vain, and went after the heathen that were round about them, concerning whom the LORD had charged them, that they should not do like them. And they left all the commandments of the LORD their God, and made them molten images, even two calves, and made a grove, and worshipped all the host of heaven, and served Baal. And they caused their sons and their daughters to pass through the fire, and used divination and enchantments, and sold themselves to do evil in the sight of the LORD, to provoke him to anger. Therefore the LORD was very angry with Israel, and removed them out of his sight: there was none left but the tribe of Judah only. Also Judah kept not the commandments of the LORD their God, but walked in the statutes of Israel which they made. (II Kings 17:6–18)

Verse 22, "For the children of Israel walked in all the sins of Jeroboam which he did; they departed not from them;"

Not only did God remove Israel from the land, but he allowed the Assyrians to repopulate the land with Gentiles from Babylon.

Israel lost her national greatness and also her *identity* because of idolatry and a perversion of the true Church of God. It took a little over 200 years during which time God constantly pleaded with the nation, through his prophets, to turn and come back to Him. Even though Israel enjoyed greatness and international stature during their existence independent of Judah, she ultimately fell. From that time on, the Ten Northern Tribes of Israel became known as the lost tribes of Israel.

PUNISHMENT BEGINS

After the Israelites were taken from bondage in Egypt, God gave the people His Laws and Commandments which carried with them blessings and curses. God promised that the people would be prosperous and enjoy the good life if they would live by his statutes and precepts as described in the Law. By the same token, He also uttered a strong warning if the people turned from the Law of God and what would happen if they did not follow Him.

But if ye will not hearken unto me, and will not do all these commandments; And if ye shall despise my statutes, or if your soul abhor my judgments, so that ye will not do all my commandments, but that ye break my covenant: I also will do this unto you; I will even appoint over you terror, consumption, and the burning ague, that shall consume the eyes, and cause sorrow of heart: and ye shall sow your seed in vain, for your enemies shall eat it. And I will set my face against you, and ye shall be slain before your enemies: they that hate you shall reign over you; and ye shall flee when none pursueth you. And if ye will not yet for all this hearken unto me, then I will punish you seven times more for your sins. And I will break the pride of your power; and I will make your heaven as iron, and your earth as brass: And your strength shall be spent in vain: for your land shall not yield her increase, neither shall the trees of the land yield their fruits. (Leviticus 26:14–20)

The history of Israel records the punishment which God levied against that idolatrous nation. In verse 18 where the term "seven times" is used, it describes the length of time God would punish the rebellious Israelites because of their sins.

"Seven times" is prophetically referring to seven years, where each year contains 360 days. Using the concept of "DAY for a YEAR," multiply seven years by 360 days; the answer is 2520 days. In this case, each day represented a year and therefore God would punish Israel for a period of 2520 years.

This punishment began with the fall of Israel circa 720 BC and lasted 2520 years. Therefore, the punishment was completed around 1800 AD.

Despite the punishment, God has not been false to His Promises made to the children of Israel during the time of Abraham, Isaac and Jacob. Remember, the promises were specifically given to Israel's two grandsons, Ephraim and Manasseh. (Genesis 48:11–16)

Israel said "his name" would now be the name of the two sons of Joseph—Ephraim and Manasseh. He also indicated what would happen to these sons and their descendants in the latter times. We all understand that the latter time refers to the time at the end of civilization as we know it and just before the Return of Jesus Christ. Notice the timing is mentioned in Genesis 49:1, "And Jacob called unto his sons, and said, Gather yourselves together, that I may tell you that which shall befall you in the last days."

Go back to Genesis 48:16. Notice that Israel said that Ephraim would grow into a multitude of people in the midst of the earth. We also know that it was prophesied that Ephraim would become a great nation. In fact, the prophecy indicates that Ephraim would become a grouping of states, united together as a powerful nation. The prophecy goes on to extend to his older brother Manasseh in Genesis 48:19, "And his father refused, and said, 'I know it, my son, I know it: he also shall become a people, and he also shall be great: but truly his younger brother shall be greater than he, and his seed shall become a multitude of nations.'"

Notice in this statement, Israel indicates that Manasseh would become a *great* nation, but that Ephraim, his younger brother, would be a nation made up of many states. This prophecy and promise was never fulfilled under the United Kingdom of Israel or the nation of Israel after the split-up. Therefore, since God cannot lie, it became necessary for Him to fulfill this prophecy after the 2520 years of punishment for Ephraim and Manasseh, the two brothers who became known as "Israel." That Punishment began circa 720 BC and ended circa 1800 AD.

KINGS OF ISRAEL
(After the split between Judah & Israel)

King	Reign - BC	Characters
Jeroboam	933–911	Idolatry
Nadab	911–910	Idolatry
Baasha	910–887	Idolatry
Elah	887–886	Idolatry
Zimri	886	Idolatry
Omri	886–875	Idolatry
Ahab	875–854	The Worst Idolator
Ahaziah	855–854	Idolatry
Joram	854–843	Idolatry
Jehu	843–816	Idolatry
Jehoahaz	820–804	Idolatry
Joash	806–790	Idolatry
Jeroboam II	790–749	Idolatry
Zechariah	748	Idolatry
Shallum	748	Idolatry
Menahem	748–738	Idolatry
Pekahiah	738–736	Idolatry
Pekah	748–730	Idolatry
Hoshea	730–721	Idolatry

THE SCATTERING

It is generally believed that all of Israel was taken captive with the fall of Samaria in circa 721 BC at the hand of the Assyrian king, Shalmaneser. The Bible indicates in II Kings 17 that in the ninth year of King Hoshea of Israel, Shalmaneser, king of Assyria, captured Samaria and transported the inhabitants into an area known as Halah and Habor by the River Gozan, located in the country of the Medes. Today, that area is Iraq. Even though this was the official ending of the Kingdom of Israel located in the ancient lands to which Israel migrated when they departed Egypt, this is not exactly the whole story.

THE DOOMED KINGDOM

At least a decade earlier, and probably more, many of the Israelites realized the nation was headed for disaster as king after king came into power and the moral corruption and degradation of the empire became more obvious. Israel found itself fighting many more wars and skirmishes which took their toll on the great empire. In fact, many Israelites received a wakeup call when, during the reign of King Pekah, the Assyrian king, Tiglathpileser attacked the region occupied by Naphtali and conquered that tribe completely. This happened circa 734 BC, more than a decade before the fall of Samaria.

At that time, the Assyrian king removed all of the tribe of Naphtali into the land of Assyria. The tribe of Naphtali had occupied the areas of Galilee and Gilead in Israel.

It was at this point that the tribe of Dan and others began a voluntary migration from Israel because of the desperate times they were facing.

It was not until 721 BC that Samaria fell at the hands of a new leader of Assyria, King Shalmaneser. With the defeat of Samaria, Shalmaneser transported the remaining Israelites in Samaria into the land of the Medes, as mentioned in II Kings 17:6. The land of the Medes was located south and west of the Caspian Sea.

This marked the official end of the Kingdom of Israel, leaving only the Kingdom of Judah and the tribes making up that kingdom, Judah, Benjamin and Levi, plus some of the Israelites who had fled south to Judah when they saw the end of their nation was near.

Thanks to the tribe of Dan, we are able to able to trace the northwesterly migration of the Israelites as they were forcibly removed or voluntarily left their land at the eastern end of the Mediterranean Sea.

The historian Thomas Moore, writing *The History of Ireland* in three volumes, helps us identify the north and western migration of the Israelites. Notice the statement made about the descendants of Dan by Israel just before his death. Genesis 49:17, "Dan shall be a serpent by the way, an adder in the path, that biteth the horse heels, so that his rider shall fall backward."

This coded language of the Bible shows us that God would use the tribe of Dan to leave their identifying mark as they traveled away from Israel. Much like a snake crawling in soft sand will leave a telltale design indicating it has been there, so God uses the tribe of Dan to leave their mark wherever they migrate. God intended that Dan would set up way marks and identifying points to help us trace the Israelites as they journeyed from their own homeland. God did not intend that the "Lost Tribes" would be lost forever.

In fact, God addresses Ephraim.

Is Ephraim my dear son? is he a pleasant child? for

since I spake against him, I do earnestly remember him still: therefore my bowels are troubled for him; I will surely have mercy upon him, saith the LORD. Set thee up way marks, make thee high heaps: set thine heart toward the highway, even the way which thou wentest: turn again, O virgin of Israel, turn again to these thy cities. (Jeremiah 31:20–21)

In Genesis 49:17, Israel is foretelling the future of the different tribes of Israel and it is a significant fact to note that the tribe of Dan, no matter where they traveled, would name that area after their father, Dan.

The tribe of Dan originally occupied a strip of coastal country along the Mediterranean Sea just west of Jerusalem. However, Dan outgrew that area and we read in Joshua 19:47, "And the coast of the children of Dan went out too little for them: therefore the children of Dan went up to fight against Leshem, and took it, and smote it with the edge of the sword, and possessed it, and dwelt therein, and called Leshem, Dan, after the name of Dan their father."

Also, in Judges 18:11–12, it is recorded that "Dan took Kirjath-Jearim and called the place Mahaneh-Dan unto this day." A little later, 600 armed Danites came to Laish and occupied it and they named the city Dan after their father. (Verse 29) These verses help us to see that the Danites left their name as they traveled, fulfilling their prophesied destiny of "marking the trail."

We now understand that Dan occupied two different territories in the land of Israel before the Assyrian overthrow. One colony lived on the seacoast of the Mediterranean Sea and these were principally sailors who manned the ships of Solomon during the United Kingdom period. After the split between Judah and Israel, the Danites continued to sail the seas and, in many cases, manned the Phoenician ships as crew members. Notice the statement made in Judges 5:17 about Dan. "...and why did Dan remain in ships?"

When it became obvious that Assyria was going to conquer Israel, the Danites sailed west through the Mediterranean Sea toward the ancient colonies Israel had established along the

Mediterranean seacoast and westward. Not only were Danites on the ships, but they also carried members of the other tribes. Moses prophesied about Dan just before his death in Deuteronomy 33:22, "And of Dan he said, Dan is a lion's whelp: he shall leap from Bashan." This leap from Bashan was referring to Dan and his ships escaping the Assyrian onslaught. Bashan was east of the northern colony of Dan, thus in the path of the Assyrian armies. True to form, the Danites left their names along the Mediterranean coast spelled "Den," "Don," and "Din." It is also important to remember that, in the ancient Hebrew language, vowels were not written. The sound of these vowels had to be supplied by speaking or markings. Thus, the word "Dan" in its English equivalent, would be spelled "Dn." The word might be pronounced "Den" or "Din" or "Don" or "Dun" and still could be the same original Hebrew.

Irish history, according to Thomas Moore, indicates the early arrival of settlers in Ireland circa 720 BC were known as the *Tuatha de Danaans.* This is translated as the "Tribe of Dan," and sometimes appears simply as *Tuathe De,* meaning the "people of God." Throughout Ireland, we find many of these Danish way marks. Notice Dans-Laugh, Dan-Sower, Dun-Dalk, Dun-drum, Don-egal Bay, Don-egal City, Dun-gloe, Din-gele, Dunsmor (meaning "more Dan"). "More" with the name "Dun" in the Irish language means the same as Dan in the Hebrew. The northern colonies of Dan, as well as Naphtali, were taken captive by the Assyrians. However, the coastal areas of Dan were not taken captive because of their ability to escape in ships.

The Northern Kingdom of Israel became scattered and some were taken captive and traveled north with the Assyrians, while others voluntarily left by going south to Judah and westward in the ships of Dan to escape the captivity. Those taken captive by the Assyrians and migrating north also left their mark as they began to travel away from their homeland of Israel, northward between the Caspian and the Black Seas and northwesterly. There, we find the rivers Dnieper, Dniester and the Don.

In a study of ancient and later geography, we also find these same way marks as: Dan-Au, the Dan-Inn, the Dan-Aster, the Dan-Dari, the Dan-Ez, the Don, the Dan, and the U-Don; the Eri-Don to the Danes. Denmark means "Dan's Mark."

As the Danish seamen traveled to what is known today as the British Isles, they set up way marks, using such names as Dun-Dee, Dun-Raven, Lon-Don; and in Scotland, the Dans, Dons and Duns are as prolific as in Ireland. Now we can see that the serpent's tail, leaving its mark, has taken the Danites by way of the sea to Ireland, Scotland and England.

Not only did the ships of Dan travel throughout the Mediterranean, they also established settlements in Spain, Marseilles in France, across North Africa and other locations. Any of these lands could serve as homelands for the Israelites voluntarily leaving Israel just before its collapse. In fact, one of those colonies was Carthage which played host to many of the refugees leaving Israel.

Carthage, founded by the Phoenicians and Danites during the time of Solomon as a station for taking on new supplies as their ships went all over the world, probably received many of the Israelites as a stop-over en route to the Israelite colonies. Many of these people likely had relatives in these mostly Israelite colonies and could start afresh with very little culture shock as the language, custom and religions of these colonies were essentially the same as those of Israel. The fact that Carthage rose to such great power in the centuries after the fall of Israel also indicates that it received a major infusion of people. After the Assyrians took over the area of the Northern Kingdom of Israel, the Phoenicians were also pushed out of their coastal home on the eastern end of the Mediterranean Sea. The Phoenicians, with Israelites most likely among them, were looking for a place to resettle.

Some might easily conclude that the Israelites would flee to Judah. After all, Judah had 620,000 Israelites in its army who had fled to Judah during King Ahab's wicked rule. However, at that early time, Judah was ruled by good kings and Israel and Judah were allied nations. At the time of Israel's demise, Judah also had wicked kings and Israel and Judah were again enemies. Going to Judah was not an option because Judah was in close proximity to the very area that Assyria's troops were going to invade, so it offered no real security. Those fleeing Israel needed to find places far away from the conquering Assyrian armies.

The *History of Ireland* details the battles of the Danaans to establish a new homeland in Ireland between 700–900 BC. The book *Ireland,* by Emily Lawless (pgs. 8–9), an Irish historian, cites these historical records that the "Danaans fought a three-day battle against the Firbolg which centered around the hill called 'Ben-levy' after which they built many stone forts." Ben-Levy is of obvious Hebrew origin, as it includes the name of the Israelite tribe of LEVI. The Firbolg were the aborigines of Ireland.

J. H. Allen's book, *Judah's Scepter and Joseph's Birthright,* records that the greatest influx of the Tuatha De Danaan to Ireland occurred around 720 BC, just after the fall of Samaria!

The Irish Islands called the *Arans* still have remains of old forts bearing the name of the tribe of Dan. Two forts on the Arans are called Dun Aonghasa and Dun Chonchuir. Remember, ancient Hebrew does not write vowels, so the vowel "U" in these words was added later. The consonants D-N preserve the name of "Dan." These forts have an antiquity predating Christ, and had been crumbling for centuries before the Arans entered recorded history. They have been attributed to the Firbolg at the time of the "legendary invasion of Ireland." The name D-N attached to the castles indicates they may have been constructed or conquered by the Danaans or the tribe of Dan. Since the tribe of Dan had the habit of renaming existing geographic features after their own tribal names when they came to an area, it is possible that these forts were indeed built by the Firbolg and renamed after the Danites conquered them.

History has no record that the Danites ever moved again after their arrival in Ireland. Ancient records indicate that only the tribe of Dan arrived in Ireland at the time of the fall of Samaria. At the same time, a large portion of the Israelite tribe of Simeon chose a maritime escape from the Assyrians. Coinciding with the arrival of the Tuatha de Danaan in Ireland, the Simonii landed in Wales and Southern England circa 720 BC. This date is also just after the fall of Samaria and likely that the simultaneous arrival of the Danaan and the Simonii indicates that the tribes of Dan and Simeon sailed together for the British Isles.

Britain had long been a Phoenician colony and port of call, and had been settled by the name of the *covenant B-R-T people* centuries before the fall of Israel. Of course the covenant B-R-T people were there because the Danites sailed on the same ships as the Phoenicians. It is logical that the Israelites would seek refuge there in time of crisis. Notice what J.H. Allen has to say about the people of Wales, "The people of Wales call themselves in ancient Welch 'Bryth Y Brithan' or 'Briths Briton' which means 'the covenanters of the land of the covenant.' The first form of this phrase is also vernacular Hebrew."

The fact that these Brythonic Celts who migrated to the British Isles bore the Hebrew B-R-T, root word for covenant, confirmed their Israelite origin. These Israelite immigrants furnished much of the racial stock of early Celtic Britain. The Danaan and Simonii were only part of the waves of Celtic immigrants which arrived in Britain from Spain (early Israelite colonies) and several other countries. Celtic tribes had settled throughout Europe for centuries, and some of these tribes continued to migrate westward toward Britain.

THE CELTS

According to the *Encyclopedia Americana,* the Celts of Spain and Portugal began their migration as early as 1000 BC and continued through 600 BC. This period of the Celtic migration coincides with the rise and fall of the united kingdoms of Israel and Judah, under King David and King Solomon. It was during this time that Israel began to colonize both west and east of their homeland. This migration through 600 BC includes the time of the Fall of Israel in 721 BC.

Gerard Herm's book *The Celts* indicates the first Celtic-speaking tribes came to Ireland as far back as the Hallstatt era or what we would refer to as the beginning of the Iron Age. The Hallstatt period in central Europe is said to have begun circa 1000 BC to 500 BC, and the people were clearly Celts. The timing of the Celtic migration coincides with the rise of greatness of Israel with kings David and Solomon and ends with the fall of Jerusalem circa 586 BC. After the beginning of the Tene (Tin) era, the Celts were followed (by way of Britain) by other wandering hoards who spoke a Brythonic, pre-Celtic dialect. The Celtic migration took place over several centuries. Some were slow, overland migrations instead of the maritime migrations of the Danaan and Simonii. However, one cannot say that all Celts were descended from Israelites. It is a common fact that a conquered nation tends to intermarry with the conquerors, and therefore this could have been a mixture of Assyrian and Israelite immigrants.

However, it is significant that large masses of Celtic people still bore in their names the Hebrew word for *covenant,* the B-R-T or B-T-TH root word of Britain and Brythonic. It is significant to note the land of Britain still bears the same Hebrew name taken from the Brythonic Celts which migrated to their land and shared their tribal heritage.

As refugees, the Celts who were Israelites would naturally migrate toward a land bearing their tribal name in the hopes of finding a hospitable homeland. It is notable that sizeable contingents of the tribes of Dan and Simeon fled by sea to the British Isles and that other Israelites became Celtic migrants after the fall of Samaria. There is historical evidence in archaeological finds such as Hallstatt, Austria, (*Encyclopedia Britannica,* Eleventh Ed.) that the main body of the Israelites fleeing the kingdom of Israel took an overland route to their new homeland. Obviously, they could not go east because of the Assyrian threat, and there were not enough vessels of the Danites to transport all of the Israelites to their new location. The Egyptian forces were dominant to the south which also cut off their migration, leaving only the north and west as the land route out of Palestine, and that is the route historical evidence indicates they took.

Colonel J.C. Grawler, a British government official during Queen Victoria's reign in the Nineteenth Century, researched the fate of the Northern Ten Tribes of Israel after the fall of Samaria and he cites both Jewish and Armenian sources who record that a mass of refugees from the Ten Tribes of Israel migrated through Armenia into the region north of the Black Sea, then known generally as the area of Tartary. Col. Grawler also cited the following observation about Tartary by Abraham Ortellius, the famous Sixteenth Century geographer. His description of Tartary notes the kingdom of Arzareth, where the Ten Tribes "retiring... took the name of *Gauthei* because, he says they were very jealous of the glory of God." Col. Grawler also called attention to a passage in the Apocryphal Book of II Esdras which asserts that the refugees of the Ten Tribes did, indeed, "migrate to a new place called Arzareth." In the passage from II Esdras 13:40–45,

> These are the Ten Tribes that in the days of Hoshea were carried away from their own land into captivity, whom Shalmaneser, king of Assyria, made captives and carried beyond the river... but they formed this plan among themselves, to leave the heathen population and go to a more distant region... so that there perhaps they might keep their statutes which they had NOT kept in their own country. And they went in the narrow passages of the Euphrates River for the Most High then did wonders for them, for He held back the sources of the river until they had passed over. But it was a long journey of a year and a half to that country.... called Arzareth.

This account of the Israelite migration parallels II Kings 17:1–6. The account in II Esdras indicates that there was a mass of Israelites who escaped an impending Assyrian captivity and fled to "Arzareth" in the Black Sea region. Also noteworthy is the contention of II Esdras that a group of Israelites actually repented of their sins and they were determined to obey God in their new homeland. Such a repentant attitude on the part of the Ten Tribes was foreshadowed in II Chronicles 28:5–15. During the reign of King Pekah of Israel, just a few years before the fall of Samaria and the flight of many of the Israelites from their homeland, the Ten Tribes heeded a warning from a prophet of God to release 200,000 Jewish captives taken in war with Judah. II Chronicles 28:12–13 records that the leaders of the tribe of Ephraim directed that the people obey God as instructed by the prophet. This came after many years of disregarding God and His prophets. It is remarkable that the Israelite people were again responding to God's direction just before Samaria fell.

The willingness of the people of Israel to respond to a prophet of God, in spite of the fact that their corrupt kings continued to disobey God, also proved that the Israelites at this point had little allegiance to the corrupt kings of Israel just before the fall of Samaria. The fact that many of the people recognized the corruption of their government and their leaders probably accounts for a large migration of Israelites from their land just prior to the Assyrian invasion. Perhaps the king, his reduced military forces and loyalists who stayed in Samaria to resist the Assyrians were so totally weakened that their cause was hopeless.

PROPHESIED TO BE LOST

The Bible clearly indicates that Israel would lose their identity, their land, their language, their religion and their name, and that they would be lost to themselves and to the world. Deuteronomy 32:26, "I said, I would scatter them into corners, I would make the remembrance of them to cease from among men:"

Notice also in Isaiah 28:11 that God stated that He would no longer speak to Israel in their native tongue, but in a new tongue. "For with stammering lips and another tongue will he speak to this people." God also indicated that He would call Israel by a new name. Isaiah 62:2, "And the Gentiles shall see thy righteousness, and all kings thy glory: and thou shalt be called by a new name, which the mouth of the LORD shall name."

The book of Hosea is a dual prophecy about Israel and Judah. In this book of the prophet Hosea, God uses a prostitute as a symbol for Israel. Notice Hosea 1:2–3,

> The beginning of the word of the LORD by Hosea. And LORD said to Hosea, 'Go, take unto thee a wife of whoredoms and children of whoredoms: for the land hath commited great whoredom, departing from the LORD.' So he went and took Gomer the daughter of Diblaim; which conceived, and bare him a son.

God had a prostitute bear two children to Hosea. One child would represent Israel; the other would represent Judah. Notice the child that represented Israel is mentioned in Verse 6, "And she conceived again, and bare a daughter. And God said unto him, Call her name Loruhamah: for I will no more have mercy upon the house of Israel; but I will utterly take them away."

God does make the statement in verse 7 that He would have mercy on the House of Judah, while at the same time, He intended to scatter the Northern tribes and cause them to even lose the knowledge of their own identity. "But I will have mercy upon the house of Judah, and will save them by the LORD their God, and will not save them by bow, nor by sword, nor by battle, by horses, nor by horsemen."

In spite of God punishing Israel and causing them to lose their identity, He also promised that He would not destroy them. Notice Hosea 1:10, "Yet the number of the children of Israel shall be as the sand of the sea, which cannot be measured nor numbered; and it shall come to pass, that in the place where was said unto them, Ye are not my people, there it shall be said unto them, Ye are the sons of the living God."

God promised that He would *not* make an end of Israel, but for a short period of time they would not know who they were or where they came from. Isaiah 54:7, "For a small moment have I forsaken thee; but with great mercies will I gather thee."

This prophecy has not yet been completed as the identity of the modern-day Israelites is not known to the general public. God has not yet set about to recover Israel and Judah into a single great nation. God promised Israel that, if they disobeyed Him, He would displace them from their land and take them to a *new land* which they had not previously known. Deuteronomy 28:36, "The LORD shall bring thee, and thy king which thou shalt set over thee, unto a nation which neither thou nor thy fathers have known; and there shalt thou serve other gods, wood and stone."

God precisely fulfilled this prophecy with the fall of Israel in 721 BC, and yet that prophecy will once again be fulfilled in the very near future with the modern-day Israelites—Ephraim and Manasseh. Notice again, God also prophesied through Hosea 3:4 that Israel would be without a king or royal line for many days, "For the children of Israel shall abide many days without a king, and without a prince, and without a sacrifice, and without an image, and without an ephod, and without teraphim:"

THE SIFTING

The Prophet Amos reveals what God intended to do with the nation of Israel after they were taken captive by the Assyrians. Amos 9:9, "For, lo, I will command, and I will sift the house of Israel among all nations, like as corn is sifted in a sieve, yet shall not the least grain fall upon the earth."

Fortunately for us, God intended for those who have "ears to hear and eyes to see" to be able to know with assurance where the Israelites were sifted.

DAN LEAVES THE SERPENT'S TRAIL

Believe it or not, God intended that the location of the Lost Tribes of Israel would be discovered in the last days. In order for this to be accomplished, it became necessary for God to leave way markers to follow the migration of the Israelites as they left their homeland in the Middle East. These way marks can be easily found today by noticing the names of localities which bear the name of Dan.

Notice when the Eternal spoke of Ephraim in Jeremiah 31:20–21, "Is Ephraim my dear son? ... for since I spake against him, I do earnestly remember him still: ... I will surely have mercy upon him, saith the Lord. Set thee up waymarks, make thee high heaps: set thine heart toward the highway, even the way which thou wentest: turn again, O virgin of Israel, turn again to these thy cities."

OTHER WAY MARKS

Not only did God use names other than Dan, but He also used a derivative of Isaac to make doubly sure that the identity of the Lost Tribes could be known.

As the Israelites, along with the Assyrian captors, began to migrate north and west, the historian Flavius Josephus stated concerning the Ten Tribes of Israel during his day, "Wherefore, there are but two tribes [Judah and Benjamin] in Asia and Europe subject to the Romans, while the Ten Tribes are beyond Euphrates till now and are an immense multitude, not to be estimated by numbers." (*Josephus Antiquities* Vol. 11, 5)

Josephus, who lived in the First Century AD (eight centuries after the Israelites were taken captive), indicates that their population had become too numerous to count, and that the Euphrates River served as their western border of habitation. Josephus also states that the population that lived in Judea during the Roman occupation was made up only of two tribes that returned from Babylonian captivity. Ezra 4:1 indicates Judah and Benjamin, "Now when the adversaries of Judah and Benjamin heard that the children of the captivity builded the temple unto the LORD God of Israel;" Ezra 1:5 indicates that the Levites also accompanied the Jews on the return. These were the three tribes that made up the southern kingdom of Judah.

It is important to recognize that the Northern Ten Tribes did not return to the land of Judea, but Josephus clearly states that some were still living in the area across the Tigris River. Josephus makes a very important point—the Ten Tribes of Israel did not simply disappear, but migrated from the land of their captors after they were taken from the land of Israel. In time, the Israelites migrated to the Black Sea and they became known as the *Scythians*. *The Encyclopedia Britannica* (Vol. 20, page 237) records that the

Scythians were present in Eurasian locations from the Seventh Century BC because of tombs which have been located dating back to that time. *The Encyclopedia Americana* (Vol. 24, p.471) also states "The Scythians...are those tribes that occupied this territory (the region north of the Black Sea) from about 700 BC and formed a single cohesive political entity until the Fourth Century BC, when the nation was splintered into several groups."

These dates coincide with the 721 BC collapse and capture of the Israelite Kingdom by the Assyrians. Another historian, Sharon Turner, makes this statement about the Scythians, "The Anglo-Saxons, low-land Scots, Germans, Danes, Norwegians, Swedes, Dutch, Belgians, Lombards and Franks have all sprung from the great fountain of the human race which we have distinguished by the term 'Scythian' or 'Gothic.'" He goes on to state, "The first appearance of the Scythian tribes may be placed according to Strabo and Homer about the Eighth or, according to Herodotus, in the Seventh Century BC. "(*The Anglo Saxon Race*, W.H. Poole, p. 113) He records further, "The first scenes of their civil existence and of their progressive power were in Asia. There they multiplied and extended their territorial limits for several centuries unknown to Europe."

We will show later that the descendants of Israel also became known as Saxons. The inner regions of Europe were essentially unpopulated and could be considered a wilderness area. During the seventh and later centuries, the population of Europe was basically confined to the large seacoast areas, leaving central Europe unsettled. In time, the Israelites looked to the west because the area west of the Ural Mountains to the Atlantic Ocean was a vast wilderness territory and essentially unpopulated. The area of central Europe was called the "wilderness," which accounts for the fact that God said, "I will bring you [Israel] into the wilderness." (Ezekiel 20:35)

The settlements in the Seventh to Fifth Centuries BC were basically confined to the seacoasts and peninsulas. Very little was known of the territory of that great tract of land or its resources we know as Europe today. To this territory named Germania is the direction that the Tribes of Israel began to move in their westward trek. They named the first area in which they settled after their great lawgiver—the land of Moses, now Moesia. The two great rivers of that country were named the Danube and the Dnieper, names that are still used today. These people have written their names upon monuments and enduring marble throughout the ages.

ASSYRIA FALLS

Nineveh was destroyed by the Babylonians circa 621 BC. The Assyrian monarchy was then divided between them. A large portion of Israel took advantage of this opportunity, asserted its independence and escaped, moving to the area we now know as Armenia, to the north of ancient Assyria. During these several war-like situations, added to by the conquest of Alexander the Great and his immediate successors, the Israelites resumed a nomadic state and moved northward and westward to escape the power of the Greek Empire.

Sharon Turner also states, "Although the Saxon name became on the continent the appellation of a confederacy of nations, yet, at first, it denoted a single state and it appears they were so much isolated that the Romans did not come in contact with them though continually devastating by fire and sword the people intervened between them and the Saxons."

It is quite obvious that God intended to preserve the Israelites and not allow them to be destroyed by the Romans, the Greeks or any other later empires. Even though God had displaced Israel from the land, He still maintained a watchful eye over them as they moved northwest away from the Middle East.

Turner states,

> The Saxons were one of the obscure tribes whom providence was training up to establish more just government, more improving institutions and more virtuous, though fierce, manners in the corruption and incorruptible population of imperial Rome and they

advanced with steady and unreceding progress to the distinguished destiny which they were conducted.

Providence has destined them to be the stock of a nation whose colonies, commerce, arts and knowledge are pervading every part of the world; it cherished them by a succession of those propitious circumstances which gradually conformed and conducted them to that great enterprise for which they were principally destined. (Vol. 1, p. 165)

When these people completed their trek through the wilderness of Europe in a westerly direction, the time came for them to emerge as a people to reckon with; this corresponded to the time when the Roman Empire began to dissolve.

DACIANS

The Dacians were a large group of people who settled north of the Danube. They later founded a powerful Republic anciently called Dacia, the people of Davi. They found their surroundings to be favorable; they prospered until they were attacked by the Romans who not only made Moesia a Roman province, but also attacked the Israelites in Dacia and drove them still farther into the wilderness. History records that the king of Dacia, rather than submit to the Roman yoke, killed himself stating that "death was preferable to bondage."

The Dacians had adopted a motto concerning the Roman attack of "no surrender," and they made it so hot for the Romans that they ultimately withdrew and resigned all claim to the territory north of the Danube. The Dacians, however, in an attempt to avoid war, decided to move farther west into the wilderness, at which time they were called the Gaetae or *Gothic,* which means the people of God.

ANGLES AND JUTES

Those who were referred to as the "Angles" and the "Jutes" got their names simply from the territories in which they lived. Angles got their name from Angulus (the angle, the shape of the land in which they had been living). The Jutes got their name from the land jutting out into the sea. The fact is the Angles, Saxons, and the Jutes were actually the same people, racially speaking. It is quite clear from the identity of their languages and ethnic backgrounds they were branches of the same stock with some dialect differences.

Many ancient historians agree that the Jutes were Hebrews of the tribe of Dan and that the Jutes, Angles and Saxons were all related one to another. (*Vestus Chronicol Holsatiae,* 54). It is important to notice that the tribe of Dan, as we have said before, was divided into two parts in the land of Israel—one that lived on the seacoast, and the other inland near Lebanon. Therefore, it would follow that the tribe of Dan would certainly appear with the rest of their Israelite brethren as they traveled cross country through Europe, while the other half came to Ireland by sea, known as the Tuatha de Danaan.

According to Brewer's historical atlas, "They came, they said, of the three stouter people of Germany, viz. the Saxons, Angles and Jutes." Gratten, in his *History of the Netherlands,* states, "The Saxons were all driven from Germany; Coltaire II exterminated any who were left behind; he caused all of them to be beheaded who exceeded the height of his sword and thus drove them out of Europe." This also coincides with the declaration of R.G. Latham in the *Ethnology of the British Isles,* "Throughout the whole length and breadth of Germany, there is not one village, hamlet or family which can show any definite signs of descent from the continental ancestors of the Angles of England; there is not a man, woman, or child who can say 'I have pure Angle blood in my veins ...'" (p 30)

To sum up these three historians, the Angles—who were the Israelites—were all compelled to leave the country of the eastern area and move toward western Europe.

THE SAXON NAME

In 1723, Dr. Abbadie Amsterdam stated, "Unless the Ten Tribes have flown into the air or have plunged into the center of the earth, they must be sought for in the north and west and in the British Isles."

The name "Saxon" in the dictionary claims it comes from "Seaxe," meaning a short sword. However, short swords or long knives were used thousands of years before we hear any such word as Saxon. The term *Saxon* is improperly identified as meaning "a short sword," therefore, we must continue to look for the derivative of this name. God proclaimed through Isaiah the prophet that the Israelites would live under a new name. Notice Isaiah 62:2, "And the Gentiles shall see thy righteousness, and all kings thy glory: and thou shalt be called by a new name, which the mouth of the LORD shall name." This name would continue to be a derivative of one of the patriarchs of Israel, *Isaac.*

Originally the people from whom Abraham descended were called *Hebrews.* After Abraham, they were then referred to as the *children of Abraham,* later the *sons of Jacob,* and finally the *children of Israel* after God changed Jacob's name to Israel. With the destruction of Israel, the Israelites actually lost their name, their language, and much of their culture as they were sifted through the nations. Notice that God revealed the new name in Amos 7:16, "Now therefore hear thou the word of the LORD: Thou sayest, 'Prophesy not against Israel, and drop not thy word against the house of Isaac.'" Notice that God referred to Israel as the *house of Isaac.*

Dr. W. Holt Yates says "The word 'Saxon' comes from 'son of Isaac,' by dropping the prefix 'I' and adding the suffix 'ons' we are able to identify these people as 'Saac,' 'Saak,' 'Saach,' 'Saax,' 'Sach-Sen,' 'Sak-Sen,' and 'Saxon.'" He also shows that in most eastern languages "son of" is written "sunnia." Dr. Yates indicates that in many languages, a prefix or suffix is added to indicate "son of" (Mac, Fitz, O, Ben, Bar, Ebu); therefore "Saxon" has its derivative as "the sons of Isaac."

The great British writer, John Milton, in his *History of Britain,* speaks of the Saxons. "They were a people thought by writers to be descended of the Sacae, a kind of Scythian in the north of Asia, called Sacasons, or 'Sons of Sacae,' who with a flood of other northern nations came into Europe toward the decline of the Roman Empire." (Vol. 5, 248) John Milton indicated that the racial significance of the Saxons, from his extensive research proved that they were descendants of the ancient "Sacae" and were of Scythian origin.

According to the father of modern historians, Herodotus, "The first scenes of their civilization's existence and of their progressive power is in Asia to the east of the Araxes. Here they multiplied and extended their territory limits for some centuries unknown to Europe." (*History of the Anglo-Saxons,* Vol. 1, book 2, 110) He also said "To this judicious and probable account of Herodotus, we add the information collected from Diodorus. He says that 'the Scythians formerly inconsiderable and few, possessed a narrow region on the Araxes; but, by degrees, they became more powerful in numbers and in courage. They extended their boundaries on all sides, till at last they raised their nation to great empire and glory.' The Persians call all the Scythians 'Sacae.'" (Herodotus, Vol. 7, 64) The historians Milton, Turner, Strabo and Herodotus all regard the Sacae as Scythians.

You have seen ample evidence from recognized world class historians that the Scythians, the Moesians, and the Sacae were all the ancestors of the Saxons who we now know made their way out of Israel in an effort to flee the captivity of the ancient Assyrians. There can be no doubt that our Anglo-Saxon ancestors were in fact the sons of Isaac, being under a new name as they were dispersed out of the land of Israel. Genesis 21:12, "In Isaac shall thy seed be called."

The great Greek historian and map maker, Strabo, who lived in 19 AD stated that most ancient Greek writers called the people who lived beyond the Caspian Sea 'Sacae' or 'Messegatae. In modern understanding, Saxons and Goths lived in the fertile valleys of Armenia.

Another excellent method of tracing the movement of the Israelites is to look at the forms of government they established as the tribes were dispersed out of Israel. It is obvious that their form of government was different from the rest of the world's governments because it was based on and resembled the original pattern that they had received from Moses.

In the setting up of these new political areas, they always used a system of twelve governing bodies. This, of course, comes from the twelve tribes of Israel as Moses originally set them up, with each tribe under its father's name. Herodotus says "Their having the number twelve was a matter of deliberation and choice, and not chance." (*The Histories*, Vol. 1)

The Ionians possessed many of the strongest characteristics of the Israelites. They were remarkable for personal beauty, for mental vigor and for love of liberty. The city of Phila-del-phia or of "brotherly love," mentioned in Revelation 3, was built by them and the temple called "Didymus" was located there. They were several times reduced by the Persians and they were driven by them into the wilderness to the north and farther west. (*The Histories*, Vol. 1)

We now know that in the northern part of Italy, between the Arno and the Tiber, there was another colony of the Israelites. It was called the Tyr-sennia and can be translated "sons of Tyre," or "sons of the second Tyre." Here we find the same model of state government, breaking it down into twelve divisions or twelve provinces. They were called "Lu-cu-mo-nin," a Hebrew word meaning *twelve states*. Each state or province had a measure of independence of its own and was united as one for the general good. (*Etruscans*, wikipedia)

Historian, Dr. Friedman, writes, "In the area on the other side of the Apennines the Etrurians [Etruscans], a band or group of the same people, founded a colony and established a commonwealth of twelve provinces. The language of the Etrurians was largely Hebrew. They believed in 'one God,' the Supreme Eternal God and also believed in future rewards and punishments by God for a person's actions."

William Pinnock said, "The Etrurians were Scyths, wanderers from the east and of the arts they obtained a good degree of power. They possessed a strong naval force and knew well how to use it. At one time, they claimed to be masters of the seas."

Friedman and Pinnock both agree that "It was from the Etrurians, the Romans received most everything valuable which they possessed both in arts and in armament." (Pinnock's *Improved Edition of Dr. Goldsmith's History of Rome*) It is also agreed that the Etrurians and the Saxons came from the same original stock and were, no doubt, the same people.

In Germany, the Saxons were greatly strengthened by the Etrurians. Their origin was for a long time a puzzle. We have seen that the Germans, who in fact were the ancient Assyrians, continued to drive their Israelite captives out of their land after they too were dispersed from their land by the ancient Babylonians. When the Israelites or Angles from Germany moved on, they settled on the western coast of Europe and the east coast of Britain and founded the kingdom of East Anglia, placing it under the government of twelve chiefs, or kings. A man by the name of Uffa was the first to be placed in command.

When the Saxons came across the channel to England to the assistance of England under Hengist, their territory was divided into twelve provinces, each having a head or governor, and each with its own constitutional law. When England changed its institutions, laws, and language upon the settlement of the Saxons, Angles and Jutes, they formed a "heptarchy" somewhat analogous to that of the twelve provinces, only the number was seven instead of twelve. It is interesting to note that in all these Israelite colonies, we find the same form of constitutional law and representation according to the population, or a representative government, efficient police and trial by a jury of twelve.

Both history and archaeology are full of information available to the truly inquisitive student to locate the travels of the ancient

Israelites as they made their way across Europe and westward through the Mediterranean Sea. True, much history was lost during the book-burnings of the Dark Ages, but God has fulfilled His commitment to continue watching over the House of Israel and has left many identifying trails to follow the travels of the sons of Isaac, whom God calls Israel in the pages of prophecy in your Bible.

JUDAH FOLLOWS ISRAEL INTO CAPTIVITY

The history of the Jews is well known, even up to the present date. However, the history of Israel has been harder to trace since their captivity by the Assyrians circa 720 BC. While we began tracing its history in the last chapter, we can get additional clues by studying specific prophecies dealing with the House of Israel and the House of Judah. We believe that a careful study of these prophetic words will coincide with the secular history, enabling us to trace the movements of the House of Israel as they were removed from their land circa 720 BC.

We will continue to look at historical and archaeological proofs of the travels of the Israelites in the light of Biblical prophecy to prove the modern-day whereabouts of the people who make up the descendants of the ancient Northern Ten Tribes of Israel.

PROPHECIES

Prophecy is nothing more than history written in advance of the act or event. Since the Christian world ignores the vast majority of prophecy in their Bibles, it is easy to understand why the modern-day identity of Israel appears to be lost.

Believe it or not, the Bible clearly indicates that Israel would lose their identity, land, language and religion if they refused to obey God. Notice Deuteronomy 32:26, "I said, I would scatter them into corners, I would make the remembrance of them to cease from among men:"

In another prophetic statement, it indicates that God would no longer speak to the Israelites, using their Hebrew tongue, but that He would use another tongue, which they had not known. Isaiah 28:11, "For with stammering lips and another tongue will he speak to this people."

As stated earlier, the prophecies of Isaiah also indicate that Israel will be given a new name. Isaiah 62:2, "… and thou shalt be called by a new name, which the mouth of the LORD shall name." Notice also Isaiah 65:15, "… for the Lord GOD shall slay thee, and call his servants by another name:"

God also uses the prophet Ezekiel to help us understand that He scattered the Israelites to all parts of the world. Ezekiel 34:6, "My sheep wandered through all the mountains, and upon every high hill: yea, my flock was scattered upon all the face of the earth, and none did search or seek after them." The term "through all the mountains" is referring to the vast relocation of the Israelites throughout the world. This verse also indicates that, once they were taken captive, no one searched for their whereabouts.

Notice also the statement in Hosea concerning the dispersal of the Israelites. Hosea 8:8–9, "Israel is swallowed up: now shall they be among the Gentiles as a vessel wherein is no pleasure. For they are gone up to Assyria, a wild ass alone by himself: Ephraim hath hired lovers." Also, look in Hosea 9:1, which indicates that the Israelites began worshipping other gods.

ISRAEL'S LOCATION PROPHESIED

Notice that God uses Jeremiah to help identify the location of the scattered Israelites.

Go and proclaim these words toward the north, and

> say, 'Return, thou backsliding Israel, saith the LORD; and I will not cause mine anger to fall upon you: for I am merciful, saith the LORD, and I will not keep anger for ever. Only acknowledge thine iniquity, that thou hast transgressed against the LORD thy God, and hast scattered thy ways to the strangers under every green tree, and ye have not obeyed my voice, saith the LORD. Turn, O backsliding children, saith the LORD; for I am married unto you: and I will take you one of a city, and two of a family, and I will bring you to Zion: And I will give you pastors according to mine heart, which shall feed you with knowledge and understanding.' (Jeremiah 3:12–15)

Notice also Jeremiah 31:8, which indicates from where God will gather Israel to once again form a great nation after the return of Jesus Christ.

The prophet Jeremiah also tells us of a future experience that the children of Israel will have at the return of Jesus Christ and the re-establishment of the knowledge of the Israelites.

> Therefore will I cast you out of this land into a land that ye know not, neither ye nor your fathers; and there shall ye serve other gods day and night; where I will not shew you favour. Therefore, behold, the days come, saith the LORD, that it shall no more be said, The LORD liveth, that brought up the children of Israel out of the land of Egypt; But, The LORD liveth, that brought up the children of Israel from the land of the north, and from all the lands whither he had driven them: and I will bring them again into their land that I gave unto their fathers. (Jeremiah 16:13–15)

Notice that God says He will retrieve Israel from the land of the north, which includes not only Europe, but also from the lands where the Israelites have made their homes for many centuries.

HISTORICAL TESTIMONY

According to Moore's *History of Ireland*, the "Scythea of Europe came from the northern parts of Persia and this seems to be the opinion of most inquirers on the subject, hence the near affinity which is found between the Germans and the Persian languages." Castle's *History of England* also says, "The Saxons were a tribe of Scythians, and the similarity of the Saxon language, in some respects, to that of Persian, seems to be more sufficient reason for believing that the Saxons were originally of oriental origin."

The Saxon language is very much like the German language; there is no doubt that the Saxons, the Germans and/or the Dutch were all of an Assyrian origin. The Hebrew (Israelite) captives, on regaining their freedom, would seek a land in which to settle and in the only part of the continent of Europe which was not already thickly populated. Thus, according to Castle, the different peoples were supposed to be of the same race, although the Saxons might be a Hebrew people and the other Scythic peoples were Assyrians.

The historian Ortellius says, "The Ten Tribes of Israel took the name of 'Gauthei,' which means 'the people of God.' The name "Gauthei,' afterwards was changed to 'Goth.'" Anastasius also wrote in the Sixth Century, "Scythea, as it is called by the ancients, is the region of the north inhabited by the Gothi." (*Lectures on Ancient Israel, J. Wilson*, #7, 125)

According to the historian William F. Collier in his work *The Great Events of History*, "Europe was gradually peopled from Asia. Four great tides of migration may be noted. First came the wave which peopled Greece and Italy; then the Celts and the Simbri who occupied Spain, France and Britain; in the third place, the Germans who fled central Europe; and lastly Samaritan or Slavi tribes who peopled the northeast and upon whom pressed the Huns from Mount Ural and Tartas from beyond the Caspian. The continuous flowing of these barbaric tribes west and south, under the ceaseless pressure of new immigrants from the East, there mingling and blending with each other, and with the old populations of the land into which they poured–formed the power by which fragments of the fallen Roman Empire were wrought into the variegated Mosaic of Medieval and Modern Europe." According to Collier, the chief Germanic tribes were from the Goths, the Franks, the Vandals, the Lombards, the Saxons and the Scandinavians. He goes on to state that "the earliest home of the Goths was Scandinavia, where we could still mark their dwelling places by such words as 'Godaland,' 'Godes-con-zia' (castle of the Goths), and plainer still 'Gothland.'" But, again, according to Collier, these people began a southwest-ward push by 200 AD. He notes that soon these people were found in central Europe in great divisions—the Visigoths (west Goths), Ostrogoths (east Goths) and Gepidae (Lagards). These people were found to be most of the civilized German tribes and are fur-ther remarkable for having adopted Christianity, not only earlier than their brother wanderers, but even earlier than the Greeks and Romans. Dr. Collier indicates that the Saxons at first occupied the hosting area and soon spread over the basin in a westerly direc-tion. Two kindred tribes—Angles and Jutes—filled the peninsula of Denmark. All were of the Teutonic type—blue-eyed, red or yel-low hair, and pink-cheeked. The invasion of Britain by these three tribes is one of the most remarkable facts in the history of Western European civilization.

> In the interior of Europe, the wandering light began to decline and the populations became much more fixed and estates and possessions began to be settled. As these people settled, the interior part of Europe began to jell and fixed character traits began to develop among the people who settled in various areas. These people began to be very attached to places in which they dwelled and the society began to be fixed in the very geographic locations which remain until this day. (Vol.I. 27)

JUDAH'S CAPTIVITY

When the Israelites were cast out of their land, they were busy try-ing to re-establish their daily lives and, in the process, re-establish themselves as a nation. However, from 721 BC until the fall of Judah, circa 586 BC, the Jews continued on the path which would ulti-mately lead them into captivity, just as their brothers in Northern Israel had done. It is important for us to take a short detour and go back and look at the nation of Judah, because the prophet Jeremiah not only plays an important part in the nation of Judah, but he has an essential part in helping us to identify and locate the travels of Israel after they departed the promised land.

JEREMIAH

The prophet Jeremiah prophesied for almost 40 years—from 620 BC to circa 590 BC. Remember, Israel went into captivity circa 721 BC and Judah did not officially go into captivity until the kingdom came to an end circa 586 BC. Jeremiah was a prophet to Israel and Judah. He continued to speak out against the *idolatry* of the Jews and the continued idolatry of the dispersed Israelites, even though they had gone into captivity many years before.

Jeremiah was given a unique commission to fulfill as a prophet. Jeremiah 1:10, "See, I have this day set thee over the nations and over the kingdoms, to root out, and to pull down, and to destroy, and to throw down, to build, and to plant." This commission has several parts to be fulfilled. The first one is to "root out." As we con-tinue to identify the travels of the so-called Lost Israelites, we find that Jeremiah's commission is very fascinating and will help us to further understand the connecting link between history, prophecy and the present day.

When the Northern Tribes of Israel went into captivity, Judah had not yet rejected the religion of God; they continued to keep the covenant God had made with Israel. The dynasty of David contin-ued to rule on the throne in the southern three tribes making up the nation of Judah.

The promise God made to David that he would always have an heir sitting on the throne in the House of Israel, required God to intervene and work out some miraculous events, involving Jeremiah the prophet. Notice God restates this promise to Jeremiah for all who will hear.

> For thus saith the LORD; David shall never want a man to sit upon the throne of the house of Israel; Neither shall the priests the Levites want a man before me to offer burnt offerings, and to kindle meat offerings, and to do sacrifice continually. And the word of the LORD came unto Jeremiah, saying, Thus saith the LORD; If ye can break my covenant of the day, and my covenant of the night, and that there should not be day and night in their season; Then may also my covenant be broken with David my servant, that he should not have a son to reign upon his throne; and with the Levites the priests, my ministers. (Jeremiah 33:17–21)

Jeremiah was well aware that God was placing upon his shoulders the implementation of this promise. It is very important that we understand the historic thread that ties Israel of the Middle East with Israel now dispersed. In order for us to understand this, we must now look at the history of the scepter and how Jeremiah played a part in making sure that it was preserved for the descendants of David.

Jeremiah was called by God after Israel had gone into captivity. God used Jeremiah to warn and witness to the nation of Judah because she was now playing the same idolatrous game of the "harlot" as Israel had done before her captivity. (Jeremiah 3:6–11) In these verses, God is using Jeremiah to cry out to the Jews in an effort to cause them to repent and escape the same destruction that Israel had faced 130 years earlier. This leads us to the commission that God gave Jeremiah in Jeremiah 1:10. God raised up Jeremiah as a very special prophet who played a major, yet covert, role in the captivity of Judah.

Something of the importance of his mission may be gleaned from the significant fact that the Bible mentions only a few men who were set aside for their respective offices before they were born. Jeremiah was one of these men. Jeremiah 1:5, "Before I formed thee in the belly I knew thee; and before thou camest forth out of the womb I sanctified thee, and I ordained thee a prophet unto the nations." When God told Jeremiah this news, he was overwhelmed. Notice Jeremiah 1:6, "Then said I, Ah, Lord GOD! behold, I cannot speak: for I am a child."

At this point, Bible scholars believe that Jeremiah was about seventeen years old. God gave Jeremiah his commission mentioned in verse 10, "See, I have this day set thee over the nations and over the kingdoms, to root out, and to pull down, and to destroy, and to throw down, to build, and to plant." Notice that Jeremiah was to be set over nations, meaning more than one kingdom. Yet, he was a young Jewish boy who lived in Judah whom God was setting aside to be a prophet to Judah and to other nations and kingdoms! Jeremiah was given the commission over these two kingdoms of Judah and Israel to do two things: first, to pluck up or root out; second, to pull down or to overthrow. The next part of his commission was to build and to plant.

JEREMIAH THE SPOKESMAN

Jeremiah was a prophet called by God to warn the nation of Judah of their transgressions against God and His Laws. He was sent to warn Judah of the impending punishment—the invasion and captivity at the hands of the Chaldean armed forces, unless they acknowledged their sins and changed their ways. He was then used as a go-between or an intermediary between the kings of Judah and Nebuchadnezzar the king of Babylon.

The scripture in the book of Jeremiah and other places well document Jeremiah's warning to Judah about the impending captivity, the pulling down of the Kingdom of Judah, and the overthrowing of the throne of David in the Kingdom of Judah. It is generally recognized that the House of Judah was invaded by the armies of King Nebuchadnezzar and that the Jews were taken captive into Babylon circa 585 BC. At that point, they ceased being a kingdom and were no longer under the rule of King David's dynasty, with King Zedekiah being the last formal king of the Jews. The first and second parts of Jeremiah's commission were fulfilled at this time.

At this point, many people believe that the throne came to an end and, in effect, they think that God was not true to His Word when He promised David that his throne would continue throughout all generations. Does this mean that God actually forgot His covenant and the promise He made to David? Or, would the throne of David be established in some other location to continue until Christ Himself came back to claim that throne? Let's examine Jeremiah's commission to pull down and to overthrow the throne of David in Judah. Notice also, the second half of the commission has to do with building and planting something!

Jeremiah was used to root out the throne of David from Judah and transport it to a new location in order to preserve it, according to God's promise many years before. In the sight of the world, the last king to sit on the throne of David was Zedekiah of Judah. He was overthrown and the throne rooted out of the land of Judah circa 585 BC, nearly 600 years before Christ.

What happened to that throne, and Jeremiah's part in it, is the thread that helps us identify the location of the throne today. We know for sure that Jeremiah did not plant or rebuild the throne of David in Babylon. God had promised that David's descendants would rule over the Israelites for all generations, not over the Gentiles. Since the Babylonians were Gentiles, we must look elsewhere to see where God moved that throne to preserve it over the Israelites, and how God continues to fulfill his promise to David.

From 585 BC on, the throne of David has *never* been located among the Jews! In fact, the throne of David was not reigning over the Jews at the time of Christ. The Jews were under Roman rule, with a king who could not trace his lineage to David. When you read the statement about the birth of Christ in Luke 1:32, we see that Christ will be given the throne of His father, David. For God to give that throne to Christ, it **must be in existence!**

The work of Jeremiah, as revealed in the Bible, is a most fascinating story. The first chapters of the book of Jeremiah are devoted to history, warning of the impending captivity of the Jews. He warned the kings, priests, prophets and the people of Judah. For his efforts, they threw him in prison and refused to heed his words or obey God. As a result, God allowed the Jews to be taken captives. History reveals that Babylon took Judah captive in different stages. The first stage was in 604 BC, a date about two years later than the reckoned date now recognized by most historians. The land did not completely pass to these Gentile Babylonians, however, until circa 585 BC.

Notice that the last and final king, recorded in the Bible or secular history, who sat on the throne of David was King Zedekiah of Judah. Zedekiah was 21 years old when he began to reign and he reigned eleven years in Jerusalem. Notice briefly, the description of the final tearing down and rooting out of the throne of David, "In the ninth year of Zedekiah, king of Judah, in the tenth month, came Nebuchadnezzar, king of Babylon and all of his army against Jerusalem, and they besieged it. And in the eleventh year of Zedekiah, in the fourth month the ninth day of the month, the city was broken up." As Zedekiah realized that his kingdom was about to fall, he and his warriors tried to flee, but the Babylonian army pursued them and captured Zedekiah in the plains of Jericho. When he was captured, they brought him before Nebuchadnezzar, king of Babylon, where he passed sentence upon Zedekiah. The king of Babylon then slew the sons of Zedekiah before his own eyes and the nobles of Judah. He put out Zedekiah's eyes and bound him in chains to carry him to Babylon. (Jeremiah 39:1–7)

In Jeremiah 52:11, we find almost the same word description of these events, with the added phrases "... and put him [Zedekiah] in prison till the day of his death." These passages bring out the points:

1. The king of Babylon slew all the sons of Zedekiah who were heirs to the throne of David.

2. He also slew all the nobles of Judah so as to leave no possible heirs to the throne.

3. After putting out Zedekiah's eyes, the last king who sat on David's throne was taken to Babylon where he was imprisoned.

4. As it appears and as the whole world believes, the throne of David ceased with no possible heirs or sons to keep the dynasty alive.

From that day on, the throne never again existed in Judah, in Jerusalem or among the Jews. Jeremiah's commission was essentially to overthrow the kingdom of Judah and tear down the throne of David as it had existed in Judah from the time of David. It is from this point that we see the thread which helps locate the northern Ten Tribes. Jeremiah was to root out the branch of the royal family and descendants of David and move it to a new location where it would be planted.

In accomplishing Jeremiah's commission, we must understand that the kingdom in Judah had come to an end. The scepter—which signified the rulership of the king—and a very special stone were to be removed. The stone, which dated back to the time of Jacob, was the stone that every ruler of Israel was crowned upon. When the northern Ten Tribes left the United Kingdom, the stone remained with the Southern Tribes.

JEREMIAH'S WORK

According to the object of Jeremiah's call and work, the first king on David's throne to be deposed was Josiah, for it was the thirteenth year of his reign that God called Jeremiah. (Jeremiah 1:1–2) Jeremiah himself gives no account of the downfall of Judah, but it is recorded in II Kings 23 and II Chronicles 35. It took place in the days of Pharaoh Necho, king of Egypt and Carchemish, king of Assyria.

Josiah, the king of Judah, was a good king; he did all that he could possibly do to restore the people to the worship of God. Josiah had all the wizards, soothsayers, idol makers and the sodomites put out of the land in order to bring the people to repentance and to rely upon God as their leader. However, God would not withhold his prophesied punishment of the kingdom of Judah, whose sins had become worse than Israel's. Even though Josiah was a good king, he could not prevent the impending calamity rapidly coming upon the nation of Judah. The Bible states that there was no king like him and that he "loved the Lord with all of his heart and all of his might to follow the law of Moses and to teach the people to obey God." However, God remembered all of the provocations of Manasseh, son of Hezekiah, encouraging the people to do evil; because of King Manasseh, God said He would remove Judah (the Jews) out of His sight as he had removed Israel two hundred years earlier. (II Kings 23:25–27)

The Bible reveals that Josiah was the best king that the Jews had ever had. Not only did he put away those abominations, he also kept the greatest Passover that was ever held in Israel or Judah since the days of Samuel the prophet. Because of Josiah's faithfulness and commitment to God, He postponed the destruction of Judah until Josiah died. Unfortunately for the Jews, God had made up His mind—the nation of Judah was to fall and the kingdom of David was to be removed.

The events which led to Josiah's and Judah's downfall began when Pharaoh Necho, the king of Egypt, came up to fight against Carchemish, the king of Assyria. Josiah, without any provocation, decided to stick his nose into the fight where he should not have been. He took up arms against Pharaoh Necho, in spite of Necho urging Josiah to stay out of the fight. The Bible states that, nevertheless, Josiah would not turn his face from this battle against the King of Egypt. Unfortunately, the archers shot at King Josiah and the king said to his servants, "Have me away for I am sore wounded." His servants then took him out of the chariot and put him in the second chariot he had brought with him to Jerusalem; he died and was buried in one of the sepulchers of his fathers. All of Judah and Jerusalem mourned for Josiah and Jeremiah lamented for him. (II Chronicles 35:21–25)

Jeremiah was witness to the good king being pulled down and he lamented for him together with the whole nation. As a result of Josiah's death, Shallum, the son of Josiah, ascended the throne.

> Weep ye not for the dead, neither bemoan him: but weep sore for him that goeth away: for he shall return no more, nor see his native country. For thus saith the LORD touching Shallum the son of Josiah king of Judah, which reigned instead of Josiah his father, which went forth out of this place; He shall not return thither any more: But he shall die in the place whither they have led him captive, and shall see this land no more. (Jeremiah 22:10–12)

Jeremiah records the fact that another overthrow was about to take place and yet Jeremiah's work continued!

The next son of Josiah, Jehoiakim, was to take the throne. When Jehoiakim took the throne, God made a proclamation against him.

> Therefore thus saith the LORD concerning Jehoiakim the son of Josiah king of Judah; They shall not lament for him, saying, Ah my brother! or, Ah sister! they shall not lament for him, saying, Ah lord! or, Ah his glory! He shall be buried with the burial of an ass, drawn and cast forth beyond the gates of Jerusalem. (Jeremiah 22:18–19)

Another king was deposed. Coniah the son of Jehoiakim, was the next to reign.

> As I live, saith the LORD, though Coniah the son of Jehoiakim king of Judah were the signet upon my right

hand, yet would I pluck thee thence; And I will give thee into the hand of them that seek thy life, and into the hand of them whose face thou fearest, even into the hand of Nebuchadnezzar king of Babylon, and into the hand of the Chaldeans. And I will cast thee out, and thy mother that bare thee, into another country, where ye were not born; and there shall ye die. But to the land whereunto they desire to return, thither shall they not return. Is this man Coniah a despised broken idol? is he a vessel wherein is no pleasure? wherefore are they cast out, he and his seed, and are cast into a land which they know not? O earth, earth, earth, hear the word of the LORD. Thus saith the LORD, Write ye this man childless, a man that shall not prosper in his days: for no man of his seed shall prosper, sitting upon the throne of David, and ruling any more in Judah. (Jeremiah 22:24–30)

Coniah makes the fourth king deposed since the Lord gave the commission to Jeremiah. But, there is still another as recorded by the prophet. Jeremiah 37:1, "And king Zedekiah the son of Josiah reigned instead of Coniah the son of Jehoiakim, whom Nebuchadnezzar king of Babylon made king in the land of Judah." Zedekiah now became the successor to Coniah and ascended the throne circa 600 BC. His reign lasted only eleven years and he is the last king of the Jewish kingdom of the Davidic line who was to reign in Jerusalem.

Remember, in all of this, God had said He would tear down, but He would also build up David's throne for all generations, and that the scepter would never depart from Judah. Notice this promise that was made in Genesis 49:10, "The sceptre shall not depart from Judah, nor a lawgiver from between his feet, until Shiloh come; and unto him shall the gathering of the people be." With all of these kings being torn down, it becomes especially important for us to look more closely at Zedekiah and learn of his fate and also that of his family—sons and daughters!!

During the reign of Coniah, the king of Babylon subdued Judah and carried away the king, his mother, his wives and others into Babylon. But, then the tolerant Nebuchadnezzar, king of Babylon, took Mattaniah, the third son of Josiah, who was the brother of Jehoiakim, Coniah's father, and *changed his name to Zedekiah* and made him king instead of Coniah. Consequently, at that time, when Zedekiah ascended the throne, the country of Judah was a province of Babylon.

For those who may wonder about Zedekiah and just whose son he was, we must research genealogy from the Bible and history. In Josiah's family, there were at least two Zedekiahs appearing among the family line for centuries. There were also Shallums, and even Coniah's name was spelled three different ways. We will also say for the more critical students that often the man is said to be the son of another, when in fact he is the grandson or even further removed. Christ is the son of David, and yet David is his great-grandfather 28 generations back. "From David unto the carrying away into Babylon are 14 generations and the carrying away into Babylon unto Christ are 14 generations." (Matthew 1:17) This Zedekiah was the third son of Josiah. II Kings 24: 17–19, "And he did that which was evil in the sight of the LORD, according to all that Jehoiakim had done."

We can see Zedediah was the fifth to occupy the throne of David since Jeremiah had received his commission. The first part of Jeremiah's commission, which included the tearing down and rooting out of the throne of David was about to come to an end. Zedekiah was the last king to sit on the throne in Judah. Jeremiah records the downfall of Zedekiah and his sons, the royal princes.

> In the ninth year of Zedekiah king of Judah, in the tenth month, came Nebuchadnezzar king of Babylon and all his army against Jerusalem, and they besieged it. And in the eleventh year of Zedekiah, in the fourth month, the ninth day of the month, the city was broken up. And all the princes of the king of Babylon came in, and sat in the middle gate, even Nergalsharezer,

Samgarnebo, Sarsechim, Rabsaris, Nergalsharezer, Rabmag, with all the residue of the princes of the king of Babylon. And it came to pass, that when Zedekiah the king of Judah saw them, and all the men of war, then they fled, and went forth out of the city by night, by the way of the king's garden, by the gate betwixt the two walls: and he went out the way of the plain. But the Chaldeans' army pursued after them, and overtook Zedekiah in the plains of Jericho: and when they had taken him, they brought him up to Nebuchadnezzar king of Babylon to Riblah in the land of Hamath, where he gave judgment upon him. Then the king of Babylon slew the sons of Zedekiah in Riblah before his eyes: also the king of Babylon slew all the nobles of Judah. Moreover he put out Zedekiah's eyes, and bound him with chains, to carry him to Babylon. And the Chaldeans burned the king's house, and the houses of the people, with fire, and brake down the walls of Jerusalem. (Jeremiah 39:1–8)

With Zedekiah, we find the end of the history of the last prince of the House of David who has ever reigned over the Jewish people from that time until the present. We now know that the Jews re-established their nation, but they did not have a king or a royal family ruling over them, even until this day. With the resulting overthrow of Zedekiah, we find the Pharez branch of the house of Judah, to which David belonged, came to an end.

But, this climax which was the ending of the Kingdom of Judah was only the completion of the first part of Jeremiah's mission. The first part of his commission mainly dealt with the plucking up, throwing down and afflicting to bring to an end the Kingdom in Judah. Indeed, it was so well done, that most Biblical authorities believe that the Kingdom of David came to an end with the capture and death of King Zedekiah. This, of course, ignores the remaining mission of Jeremiah in fulfilling the commission God had assigned him.

THE TWO LINES OF JUDAH:PHAREZ AND ZARAH LINES

If you will recall, previously we discussed the birth of Judah's two sons, Pharez and Zarah. Pharez became the genealogical line from which King David came. This Pharez line of kings remained on the throne of Judah until its final collapse circa 580 BC. However, the Zarah line, the one which descended from the brother who had the red ribbon tied around his hand just before his birth, did not inherit the throne in Israel or Judah. In spite of the fact that they were Jews, they chose to align themselves with the Ten Northern Tribes of Israel at the split between Israel and Judah. They realized they would never ascend the throne in Judah. However, by aligning themselves with the Ten Northern Tribes, there existed the possibility that they could attain it in Israel.

At this point, we need to stop and consider a riddle God gave to the Prophet Ezekiel almost two hundred years after Israel went into captivity.

> And the word of the LORD came unto me, saying, 'Son of man, put forth a riddle, and speak a parable unto the house of Israel; And say, Thus saith the Lord GOD; A

great eagle with great wings, longwinged, full of feathers, which had divers colours, came unto Lebanon, and
took the highest branch of the cedar: He cropped off
the top of his young twigs, and carried it into a land
of traffick; he set it in a city of merchants. He took
also of the seed of the land, and planted it in a fruitful
field; he placed it by great waters, and set it as a willow tree. And it grew, and became a spreading vine of
low stature, whose branches turned toward him, and
the roots thereof were under him: so it became a vine,
and brought forth branches, and shot forth sprigs.
There was also another great eagle with great wings
and many feathers: and, behold, this vine did bend her
roots toward him, and shot forth her branches toward
him, that he might water it by the furrows of her plantation. It was planted in a good soil by great waters,
that it might bring forth branches, and that it might
bear fruit, that it might be a goodly vine.' (Ezekiel
17:1–8)

God gave us this piece of information as another clue to help us
identify the modern-day location of the tribes of Israel. The "eagle"
spoken of here is actually referring to a sailing ship. It also helps to
identify the owners of the ship and its seamen. God gave four dis-
tinctive marks, or ensigns, which would identify the leading tribes in
Israel. The *lion* ensign was reserved for Judah, the *bull* for Ephraim,
the *man* for Reuben and the *eagle* for the tribe of Dan. The Danites
were seafaring people, indicated in Judges 5:17, "Gilead abode
beyond Jordan: and why did Dan remain in ships? Asher continued
on the sea shore, and abode in his breaches." The question is being
asked regarding why Dan seemed to be so committed to ships. Of
course, the ships of Dan plied the Mediterranean Sea and all parts
of the world, beginning with King David and King Solomon.

This is a *vital key* to understand the meaning of this riddle.
The eagle is referring to the great ships of Dan. The riddle goes
on to indicate a very high dignitary, as symbolized by the highest

branch of the cedar tree, was taken from the top of this tree and was carried in the ships of Dan to a new location. The individuals spoken of here were members of the tribe of Judah of the Zarah line. Even before the fall of Israel in 721 BC, these descendants of Zarah were developing new colonies, especially on an island near the "great waters." Notice verse 5 , " … he placed it by great waters." It would be up to the Prophet Jeremiah in 581 BC to complete the fulfillment of this prophecy. We now know that the island home which was selected for the descendants of Zarah was located in none other than what we know today as Northern Ireland, near Ulster Plantation.

ZARAH TRIBE ESCAPES

Even though the Zarah branch of the tribe of Judah were not of the royal line, they had great influence and recognition in the Northern Kingdom. After it became evident that Israel was going to fall, the Zarah line of Jews fled with many of the Israelites on the ships of Dan to be relocated in their new land. This was prophesied to occur in the riddle, which we discussed earlier in Ezekiel 17:1–8.

The eagle was used as the standard (flag) of the tribe of Dan. These ships were essentially manned by Phoenicians and the men of Dan. The sailing ships with overlapping sails are pictured as a great eagle with its feathers. In verse 4, God states that He chopped off the top of the young twigs and carried them to a new location. In this case, He is referring to the most noble ones of the Zarah branch of Jews who were living in Israel just before the Assyrian invasion. Verse 5 shows that these young high ranking individuals were taken to a new land and planted where they grew and produced a kingly ruling line, as pictured by the "willow tree." Verse 6 confirms this. This event took place prior to 721 BC. According to Edmund Curtis, University of Dublin, in his book *A History of Ireland,* the three sons of Mildeah of Spain, namely Heremon, Heber and Ir, came to Erin (Ireland) and conquered the land from the Tuatha de Danaan. He states that from these three sons descended all the royal clans of later Ireland.

The new land where the young tender branch was taken—the leader of the Zarah line—was Northern Ireland by way of Spain. Northern Ireland was the land placed in the great waters where the kingdom would survive. Verse 7 speaks of another event which occurred after circa 585 BC. Once again, ships were used to save the dynasty of Judah, but this time it was to save the royal dynasty of the Pharez line—the descendants of King David. Notice in verse 7 that this individual is referred to as a female rather than male. This young maiden was, it turns out, one of the daughters of the last king of Judah, King Zedekiah.

JEREMIAH IS INVOLVED

Jeremiah, the prophet, was given the task of saving the king's daughters when Nebuchadnezzar captured and slew Zedekiah and his sons. (Jeremiah 43:6–7) His first stop was Egypt; then they escaped Egypt. Jeremiah 44:14, "…none shall return but such as shall escape." Jeremiah was given the responsibility of transporting the king's daughter, Tea Tephi, to Northern Ireland where she married King Heremon (called Eochaidh the Heremon in the Royal British genealogy charts), who was of the Zarah line; his ancestors had established a new kingdom after the fall of Israel in 721 BC. Tea Tephi married Heremon which *healed the breach* that had been prophesied at the time the twins, Pharez and Zarah, were born to Judah.

> And it came to pass in the time of her travail, that, behold, twins were in her womb. And it came to pass, when she travailed, that the one put out his hand: and the midwife took and bound upon his hand a scarlet thread, saying, This came out first. And it came to pass, as he drew back his hand, that, behold, his brother came out: and she said, How hast thou broken forth? this breach be upon thee: therefore his

name was called Pharez. And afterward came out his brother, that had the scarlet thread upon his hand: and his name was called Zarah. (Genesis 38:27–30)

According to Irish history, circa 585 BC, a notable man, came to Ulster, the most northern province of Ireland, accompanied by a princess, the daughter of an eastern king; with him came a man called Brach (Baruch, Jeremiah's secretary). It is said that this royal party brought with them remarkable effects: a harp, an ark and a stone. On the royal arms of Ireland is the harp of David. In shops in Ireland today, one can purchase jewelry in the shape of David's harp. I purchased a brooch in the shape of David's harp for my wife when we were in Ireland years ago.

According to J. A. Allen, (*Joseph's Birthright....*) Jeremiah agreed to allow Heremon to marry Tea Tephi if he would build a college for the prophets. He agreed and named the school Mur-Ollam (pronounced the same in both Hebrew and Irish). He changed the name of his capital city (Lothair or Cothair Croffin) to that of Tarah, named for Tea Tephi, meaning "one banished" or "flight." Tarah was the hill on which the ancient kings of Ireland were crowned. Tara was also the capital of the Tuatha De Danaan. Today, on Tarah hill, located between Dublin and Belfast, there are monuments and a church or abbey. According to tradition, Jeremiah was martyred. I have climbed a hill in Ireland on which is a burial mound said to be Jeremiah's tomb.

SAVING A ROYAL REMNANT

Jeremiah the Prophet had become very well-known during the waning days of the Kings of Judah. He was imprisoned until the day the Babylonian forces captured the city and ended the reign of the kings of Judah circa 586 BC. Nebuchadnezzar was aware that Jeremiah had warned the kings of Judah that God was against them and they would be delivered into his hands. Nebuchadnezzar may have understood he was actually fulfilling God's punishment upon the Jews. The fact that Jeremiah seemed to take sides against Judah must have pleased King Nebuchadnezzar. Notice the message Jeremiah gave the king of Judah from God.

> But I will deliver thee in that day, saith the LORD: and thou shalt not be given into the hand of the men of whom thou art afraid. For I will surely deliver thee, and thou shalt not fall by the sword, but thy life shall be for a prey unto thee: because thou hast put thy trust in me, saith the LORD. (Jeremiah 39:17–17)

With the capture of Jerusalem and Judea, Nebuchadnezzar issued orders to his captain of the guard, Nebuzaradan, concerning Jeremiah during the capture of the city.

> Now Nebuchadnezzar king of Babylon gave charge
> concerning Jeremiah to Nebuzaradan the captain of
> the guard, saying, Take him, and look well to him, and
> do him no harm; but do unto him even as he shall say
> unto thee. So Nebuzaradan the captain of the guard
> sent, and Nebushasban, Rabsaris, and Nergalsharezer,
> Rabmag, and all the king of Babylon's princes; Even
> they sent, and took Jeremiah out of the court of the
> prison, and committed him unto Gedaliah the son
> of Ahikam the son of Shaphan, that he should carry
> him home: so he dwelt among the people. (Jeremiah
> 39:11–14)

This scripture further details the good treatment Jeremiah
received from Nebuzaradan.

> And now, behold, I loose thee this day from the chains
> which were upon thine hand. If it seem good unto thee
> to come with me into Babylon, come; and I will look
> well unto thee: but if it seem ill unto thee to come with
> me into Babylon, forbear: behold, all the land is before
> thee: whither it seemeth good and convenient for thee
> to go, thither go. Now while he was not yet gone back,
> he said, Go back also to Gedaliah the son of Ahikam
> the son of Shaphan, whom the king of Babylon hath
> made governor over the cities of Judah, and dwell with
> him among the people: or go wheresoever it seemeth
> convenient unto thee to go. So the captain of the
> guard gave him victuals and a reward, and let him go.
> (Jeremiah 40:4–5)

This is a good example of how God will protect His servants
in the face of danger. God protected Jeremiah because he was obedient to God. In fact, Nebuzaradan extended to Jeremiah many
privileges to go wherever he pleased and provided him with all that
he needed for the journey he was soon to undertake. Jeremiah 40:6,

"Then went Jeremiah unto Gedaliah the son of Ahikam to Mizpah; and dwelt with him among the people that were left in the land."

THE POOR LEFT BEHIND

After the fall of Jerusalem and the taking of Zedediah and most of the citizens, Nebuchadnezzar's army left behind the poor and down-trodden of the nation of Judah.

> Now when all the captains of the forces which were in the fields, even they and their men, heard that the king of Babylon had made Gedaliah the son of Ahikam governor in the land, and had committed unto him men, and women, and children, and of the poor of the land, of them that were not carried away captive to Babylon; (Jeremiah 40:7)

Essentially, Jerusalem had been destroyed. The Babylonians compelled Gedaliah to set up a provincial government in a city other than Jerusalem. Gedaliah chose the city of Mizpah and many of the remaining Jews gathered around the appointed governor. Some of the captives who remained became leaders of the remnant of Jews and they came together as a single unit under the governor.

It wasn't long until the king of Ammon and other Judean neighbors began to cast longing eyes upon these remaining Jews and determined to attack the small force of Jews and carry away captive the remainder. The king of Ammon entered into a plot with Ishmael, the son of Nethaniah, to assassinate the new governor. Johanan, the son of Kereah, discovered the plot and told Gedaliah. At the same time, Johanan offered to slay Ishmael, but Gedaliah would not permit it, nor would he believe Johanan's story and accused him of speaking falsely. However, it was only a short time until the plot was successfully carried out by Ishmael and nine of his confederates. The object of this assassination was to make it easier for the Ammonites to make captives of the rest of the Jews who were unarmed, and carry them away into Ammon to increase and strengthen the kingdom of the Ammonites. (Jeremiah 41:1–9)

During this conspiracy against the governor, another event is mentioned that virtually the whole religious world overlooks. Most believe that all of the descendants and children of King Zedekiah were put to death. However, this is not true.

> Then Ishmael carried away captive all the residue of the people that were in Mizpah, even the king's daughters, and all the people that remained in Mizpah, whom Nebuzaradan the captain of the guard had committed to Gedaliah the son of Ahikam: and Ishmael the son of Nethaniah carried them away captive, and departed to go over to the Ammonites. (Jeremiah 41:10)

The daughters of King Zedekiah had not been slaughtered by Nebuchadnezzar at the fall of the kingdom of Judah. The term "daughters" obviously means two or more, but history seems to indicate that there were only two girls surviving as the daughters of King Zedekiah.

When Johanan and his captains heard of Ishmael's action, they set about to recover the captives. When Ishmael saw the approaching forces of Johanan, he became frightened and fled and left the Jewish captives behind. Then Johanan and his forces took the remnant of people whom he had recovered from Ishmael and dwelt in the area of Chimham, near Bethlehem. Johanan determined that it would be better for the Jews to go to Egypt. At this point, Johanan asked Jeremiah, who was among those Jews, to petition God to tell them whether they should go to Egypt or remain.

> And said unto Jeremiah the prophet, Let, we beseech thee, our supplication be accepted before thee, and pray for us unto the LORD thy God, even for all this remnant; (for we are left but a few of many, as thine eyes do behold us:) That the LORD thy God may shew us the way wherein we may walk, and the thing that we may do. (Jeremiah 42:2–3)

Jeremiah did as Johanan asked and, after ten days, God answered Jeremiah.

> If ye will still abide in this land, then will I build you, and not pull you down, and I will plant you, and not pluck you up: for I repent me of the evil that I have done unto you. Be not afraid of the king of Babylon, of whom ye are afraid; be not afraid of him, saith the LORD: for I am with you to save you, and to deliver you from his hand. And I will shew mercies unto you, that he may have mercy upon you, and cause you to return to your own land. (Jeremiah 42:10–12)

At the same time, God warned them that, if they did decide to migrate into Egypt, all the evil they were trying to escape would in fact overtake them in Egypt. (Jeremiah 42:13–22) Unfortunately for the remnant, Johanan decided to do exactly the opposite of what God had said. In fact, he accused Jeremiah of speaking a lie, that the Lord had not said what Jeremiah had delivered. (Jeremiah 43:1) Johanan accused Jeremiah and Baruch of actually setting them up so that the Chaldeans would come in and take them captive. (Jeremiah 43:3–4) Johanan and the remnant of the Jews, which included women, children and the king's daughters, as well as Jeremiah and the scribe Baruch, were all taken to the land of Egypt.

> Even men, and women, and children, and the king's daughters, and every person that Nebuzaradan the captain of the guard had left with Gedaliah the son of Ahikam the son of Shaphan, and Jeremiah the prophet, and Baruch the son of Neriah. So they came into the land of Egypt: for they obeyed not the voice of the LORD: thus came they even to Tahpanhes. (Jeremiah 43:6–7)

JEREMIAH PROPHESIES THE END OF THE JEWISH REMNANT IN EGYPT

As soon as the Jews made their way into Egypt, the Eternal came to Jeremiah in Tahpanhes.

> Take great stones in thine hand, and hide them in the clay in the brick kiln, which is at the entry of Pharaoh's house in Tahpanhes, in the sight of the men of Judah; And say unto them, Thus saith the LORD of hosts, the God of Israel; Behold, I will send and take Nebuchadnezzar the king of Babylon, my servant, and will set his throne upon these stones that I have hid; and he shall spread his royal pavilion over them. And when he cometh, he shall smite the land of Egypt, and deliver such as are for death to death; and such as are for captivity to captivity; and such as are for the sword to the sword. And I will kindle a fire in the houses of the gods of Egypt; and he shall burn them, and carry them away captives: and he shall array himself with the land of Egypt, as a shepherd putteth on his garment; and he shall go forth from thence in peace. He shall break also the images of Beth-she'mesh, that is in the land of Egypt; and the houses of the gods of the Egyptians shall he burn with fire. (Jeremiah 43:9-13)

This Word from God plainly told of what He intended to do with the Jews now dwelling in Egypt. God indicated that, because of their failure to obey and their continued wickedness, they had provoked Him and, as a result, He intended to destroy all of them except a few who would escape. Jeremiah 44:14, "So that none of the remnant of Judah, which are gone into the land of Egypt to sojourn there, shall escape or remain, that they should return into the land of Judah, to the which they have a desire to return to dwell there: for none shall return but such as shall escape."

QUEEN OF HEAVEN WORSHIP

Not only had the Jews disobeyed God's direct command, but after they came to Egypt they began to sink deeper into idolatry as they burned incense and worshipped the Queen of Heaven. The Queen of Heaven is none other than the ancient Babylonian/Chaldean goddess, whose name in modern English is "Easter." As a result of this open rebellion against God and idolatrous worship of Ishtar, the "queen of heaven," Jeremiah informed the people their end was at hand.

In spite of all of this, God continued to remember His promise to King David and He made sure that a small number would escape from Egypt, in order to carry on the kingly line of David. Jeremiah 44:28, "Yet a small number that escape the sword shall return out of the land of Egypt into the land of Judah, and all the remnant of Judah, that are gone into the land of Egypt to sojourn there, shall know whose words shall stand, mine, or theirs." God now pronounced the end of this remnant. He instructed Jeremiah's companion, Baruch, to write these words.

> Thus saith the LORD, the God of Israel, unto thee, O Baruch; Thou didst say, Woe is me now! for the LORD hath added grief to my sorrow; I fainted in my sighing, and I find no rest. Thus shalt thou say unto him, The LORD saith thus; 'Behold, that which I have built will I break down, and that which I have planted I will pluck up, even this whole land. And seekest thou great things for thyself? Seek them not: for, behold, I will bring evil upon all flesh,' saith the LORD: but thy life will I give unto thee for a prey in all places whither thou goest. (Jeremiah 45:2–5)

Baruch had been Jeremiah's companion and scribe and he had suffered much of the same persecution, affliction and accusations that had been levied against Jeremiah. This small, rag-tag bunch of Jews that came into Egypt were of the poorest of the poor and essentially unable to defend themselves. And yet, God was watching over the descendants of David, the daughters of King Zedekiah, because God never forgot the promise He made to King David concerning the perpetuation of his throne.

To recap what the scriptures have just told us:

1. There was a small company of people who had gone into Egypt from Judea, which included the king's daughters. These girls were of the royal seed of the house of David who were fleeing from the slayers of their father Zedekiah, the last king of the house of Judah, and the slayers of their brothers, the sons of Zedekiah and the princes of Judah.

2. In this small group of Jews, with these princesses, was Jeremiah whom the Lord had chosen to do the work of tearing down, building and planting the kingdom. Jeremiah was the principal individual who now would transport the royal material with which to build and plant a new kingdom.

3. In this same company with Jeremiah and his royal charge was also Baruch, his faithful scribe whom some genealogists believe to have been the uncle of the daughters of King Zedekiah.

4. God had promised that the lives of this small number would be protected and given a reward in all lands where they would go.

At this point, the Biblical account of Jeremiah and this small remnant, including the daughters of Zedekiah, falls silent. However, folklore and other historical evidence will pick up the story so that we may know how Jeremiah fulfilled his mission.

THE PRINCE OF THE SCARLET THREAD

While we leave the royal remnant to make their escape, it is time for us to look into the fields of history to see if we can locate a royal prince to whom a wedding would be appropriate for one of these daughters of King Zedekiah. Remember that God promised Jeremiah that he would root out, but also once again plant the line of David in a new land.

While we are searching for the evidence, remember that God gave the kingdom of Israel to David forever and that Israel was *never* the name of the ancient Jewish nation. In the Bible, the name Israel was only applied to the Ten Northern Tribes that had gone into captivity circa 721 BC. We notice from the scriptures that God drove Israel to an unknown land after they were forced out of their homeland in the Middle East. We have traced that group across Europe to Ireland.

Several facts are important to remember. First, the *scepter,* which kings use to symbolize their rule, would always belong to the descendants of Judah, the family of David, and *not* to the kingdom over which he and his descendants ruled. Secondly, Judah was only one of the tribes that made up the United Israel, under Kings David and Solomon. Finally, God intended to drive the Israelites out of their land and they would even be called by another name when they settled in a new land. The fact that they were not known by the name of Israel after their removal *does not,* in any way, suspend any of the prophecies regarding David's descendants and the plight of the Israelites.

After the fall of both Israel and Judah, God directly intervened to heal the breach that was created at the birth of the twin boys of Judah, Pharez and Zarah, hundreds of years earlier. It was at this point in history, circa 586 BC, that God intended to heal that breach, using the royal remnant (the daughters of Zedekiah) of the tribe of Judah. When you study the prophet Jeremiah, you realize that his prophecies ultimately dealt with Judah and its kings, while Ezekiel, Jeremiah's contemporary, primarily prophesied concerning Israel. Notice, however, what Ezekiel does say concerning the destroying of the commonwealth of Judah, the removal of the *scepter* and the overthrow of the throne of the royal family. God intended to transplant David's throne from Judah to a safe haven in the house of Israel thousands of miles away. (Ezekiel 17)

PHAREZ AND ZARAH

While it is easy to trace through Biblical chronology, the fact that Pharez was the line of David, you have to look in the kingdom of Israel to determine what happened to the Zarah line. The Zarah line came to rule in Israel through one of his descendants by the name of Zimri, who overthrew Baasha, the third king of Israel. Zimri was, in fact, a descendant of Zarah. Since Israel went into captivity before Judah, we now know that the kingly line of Zarah also was taken captive and was actually transported to its new island home on the ships of Dan, as shown previously. (Ezekiel 17:1–8) The first ship took the royal line of Zarah and the second ship, some 140 years later, took the royal line of Pharez, the daughters of King Zedekiah, and Jeremiah to the same location for a royal wedding between the daughter of Zedekiah of the Pharez line and the prince of Zarah, also of a royal line.

IRISH HISTORY

In order to establish the destination of Jeremiah and the royal remnant, it is necessary to have a quick review of Irish history. Roderick O'Flaherty, a credible Irish historian, wrote two volumes entitled *Ogygia,* or a *Chronological Account of Irish Events.* While introducing his book, he says, "In Ogygia, or Ireland, that the Irish date their history from the first eras of the world; and indeed in comparison with them the antiquity of most other countries is modern and almost in their infancy."

Ireland was also called "Erwin" from "Eran," who is named in Numbers 26:36, "And these are the sons of Shuthelah: of Eran, the family of the Eranites." It is believed that the island was named and came from the following Hebrew translations: Eirin, Eir-Ne, Eib-Heir, Eib-Er, Eib-Eir from the word Heber. The Greeks called

Ireland Hieron, "holy island, the land of saints." By this name it was known to Ptolemy. Aristotle called it Ierne; Strabo called it Ierni; other Greek writers called it Iernidae, Juverna. "Badonicus," says Gildas, "went to Iernis that he might be instructed in philosophy and divinity."

Irenses, Iri, Ire, Irelandi, Irlandia, Vernia, Overnia, Bernia, Iberia, Hiberione are different forms of the names given above. The great British historian Bede called the inhabitants of Ireland "Dalreadinians." The island was for a long time called Scotia-Major. It is now known as the *Emerald Isle*. On Ptolemy's map, the Clanna or "sons of Eib-heir" take the whole of Ireland north of Asgeir-Riada, with the exception of the extreme west, occupied by the Olnegmacht. He identifies these Eib-Heir with the Iberni, who left their mark in the name of a town and river at the extreme southwestern peninsula where a portion of the clan entered the land; and these Iberni further identified with the sons of Heber.

Subsequent waves of people who came to the land, now known as Yarish Land, were people who were called "Baal-Goi." They were worshippers of Baal, the sun god, They were of the old Hebrew stock who had fled from the wars of the East. Their leader's name was Nemedh, and they came through Europe from the Black Sea and the "great wilderness" which was the name by which Europe was known before it was settled. This great wilderness was the area from the Baltic to the land of the "setting sun." They cleared twelve plains of wood, built two royal forts, established Baal worship and exterminated the previous settlers. These people were called "Dir" or "Firbolg" or by others, "Diri-Pelgic" which means Belgic-men. Dr. Thomas Moore, the historian, derived the name from Baal-Goi. The rounded towers in Ireland and other monuments prove most plainly that, at one time, Baal was worshipped as the god of these people.

Another wave of strangers from the East came to Ireland. These people came from Meosiae or sometimes Moetia near Thrace. These people were called Kimmerii by the Greeks who pressed them sorely in war when 5000 of the Kimmerri seized the Grecian fleet and set sail at once to join their brethren in the "farthest off isles." These men were of small stature, dark hair, of great energy; they were well skilled in metals, blasting and smelting operations. They had operations in both Ireland and Wales. In Wales, they were often called "Iceni" and "Sueveni." It was about this time that Ireland was divided into five provinces.

The area of Moetia was populated by those who followed the ways of Moses; in other words, the displaced children of Israel after 720 BC. The term Moetia actually is from these people who followed the ways of Moses as part of their religious beliefs.

SPAIN

One cannot consider the history of Ireland without also including a short statement about Spain. An expedition from Spain with eight sons of Milesius landed in the southwest of Ireland. Five of the sons were lost in a terrible storm; Heber, father of the Eiberites, fell in battle on Greashill, Kings County. Heremon, his brother, fixed his residence at Teamore (now Tara) in Meath. A race of 20 kings of the same family came and went under the crown descended to Ollav Fola, of the family of Ir who commenced his reign circa 900 BC and organized a grand triennial meeting of the chiefs which he named Fez. This meeting was composed of chiefs, priests and bards who met at his castle in Tara. He caused a record to be made of the national events in a volume which was named "Psalter of Tara." Some of these poetic records are still in existence. He reigned for forty years with great honor and died a natural death, a very unusual circumstance in those times. His son reigned seventeen years and died in the same manner. During the next 260 years, thirty-one kings wore the honors of royalty; all but three fell in battle or died a violent death. Those Eiberites claim to be from Asia (Middle East) and were among the escaped of Israel, of the tribe of Asher. They found their home near the River Shannon and they are named on an ancient map, Eib-heir or Heber. (*The History of Ireland*, Moore)

THE DANES' PART

The next wave of newcomers was the Tuatha de Danaan, or the Tribe of Dan. For 1200 years before Christ, Dan had a large fleet in the waters lying between the Baltic and Mediterranean Sea in Palestine. They were spoken of as accomplished soothsayers, necromancers who could quell storms, cure diseases, work in metals, foretell events, forge magical weapons, and were mighty in war. The first company of the Danaans settled near Londonderry and later they went to England and also settled in Scotland. They returned to Ireland and Danaans controlled the country for a period of 197 years.

About or during this time, there came another company of the Tuatha de Danaan, bringing with them a prophet from Jerusalem and a man by the name of Simon Barach and a goodly company of the royal household. This, of course, is describing Jeremiah, Baruch and the daughters of King Zedekiah.

THE TENDER BRANCH

As we have seen in Ezekiel's prophecy (Ezekiel 17:1–8), a tender branch would be transported by the ships of Dan to their new location. God had prepared for this event for several centuries to move the throne of David from Jerusalem to its new location. In working out the necessary events, God made sure that a descendant of the Zarah line had well established his kingdom in the new land of Ireland before Jeremiah, Baruch and the king's daughters made their way there more than 150 years later.

In effect, God planted His tree, which is symbolic of the throne in the islands of the West, which we now understand is the land of Ireland. Historically, there was a large and prosperous colony of Hebrews who lived in Ireland long before Jeremiah was even born. They had been preparing the way to carry out these prophecies for several centuries. They had already gained a great commercial enterprise with the Tuatha de Danaan and their merchant ships.

The merchant princes found a home there and were prepared to give a wonderful royal welcome to the tender branch—the young daughter of King Zedekiah who was to be planted on this high mountain in a land of commerce and prosperity. The Bible does not actually name the location, but it does indicate it is in the isles of the West surrounded by the great oceans. (Ezekiel 17:5)

The Bible does not tell us how long Jeremiah, the king's daughters and Baruch remained in Egypt before they ultimately left on the final stage of Jeremiah's mission. Some historians mistakenly believed that these daughters were actually the daughters of the Pharaoh, but, in fact, they were the daughters of Zedekiah, coming through Egypt from Jerusalem. Jeremiah did not go straight to Ireland, but he first stopped off in Spain where a descendant of Zarah was ruling. This would explain why Spain opened its arms to the Jews after 70 AD because of their ancient heritage and association with Israel. The reason for the stop in Spain was so that the other daughter of King Zedekiah, Scotia, could marry a royal in Spain. After accomplishing this feat, Jeremiah and the remaining daughter, Tea Tephi, journeyed to Ireland.

The Irish do not always call Jeremiah by his proper name; in some cases he is called Ollan-Fodla. Their history indicates that he was a revealer or prophet, one divinely commissioned and a teacher from God; with him was a scribe, Simon Barach, which helps us to identify this person as Jeremiah. They introduced many new things into Ireland—The Tables of the Law, the Mur-Olla-Main or school of the prophets, a system of civil jurisprudence with a chief priest or head and he was called Jodhan-Morain. They appointed a rectaire, a Hebrew word for judge. They brought with them a very special stone. It is the same stone that rested in Westminster Abbey until recently when it was returned to Scotland. This was the stone upon which all kings and queens of Britain for 2300 years have been crowned. This group, led by Ollan Fodla (Jeremiah) also brought a harp and other musical instruments and the grand old melodies, which as Milton says, "might create a soul under the ribs of death."

THE MARRIAGE

Dr. W. H. Poole, in his book *Anglo-Israel,* describes the wedding of the Heremon and Tea Tephi. The King of Ulster was dressed in royal robes. He was tall and slender of form with a broad forehead, sparkling, blue, laughing eyes, thin red lips, and pearly, shiny teeth. He wore a skirt of white kingly linen, called byssus, with golden clasps for buttons. A red and white cloak fluttered about him, fastened in front with a clasp of gold and golden fastenings. The description of this striking young man was on the day of his wedding where the man from the East and his secretary were in attendance with the bride, the princess, the daughter of King Zedekiah. It was said "to see her, the tender branch, was to love her" for she was of all virgins the most beautiful. Tephi was her name, a pure Hebrew name; a pet name like a flower denoting fragrance and beauty. The king or chief made proposals to her and she consulted her guardian as she was duty bound.

The prophet consented to the union on three conditions.

1. The worship of Baal must be renounced and the worship of the true God established.
2. The nation must accept the moral laws contained in the two tablets–the Ten Commandments.
3. He must provide a school for the Ollams. The school for the Ollams was to purge out Baal and to establish the Law of God in place of the Law of Baal.

We now see that God, through the Princess Tephi and her marriage to Eochaidh, the Heremon, a descendant of the Zarah line, now healed the breach between the descendants of Zarah and the descendants of Pharez. This occurred circa 580 BC according to English Heritage documents.

Today, two emblems identifying the nation of Ireland include a red hand, which symbolized the red thread that was tied around the hand of the twin Zarah and the harp, which symbolized the harp of David, the house of Pharez, now combining to make one great kingdom of Ireland. God moved the throne from Jerusalem to Ulster in Northern Ireland. It is truly amazing how God worked out all the circumstances over many hundreds of years to ensure the continuation of the throne of David even though Israel and Judah had been driven from their lands in the Middle East.

THE STONE OF DESTINY

efore we can proceed further with the investigation of
the whereabouts of the so-called Lost Tribes of Israel, we
need to take a step backwards and discover the history of
an artifact that further proves the modern-day whereabouts of the
descendants of the ancient Israelites. Our investigation will take us
thousands of years back in history to the time of Isaac's younger
son, Jacob.

As you recall from previous chapters, Jacob, the younger son of
Isaac, managed to claim the blessings of his father over his older
brother Esau. As a result of this subterfuge, Jacob was forced to
leave home, never to see his father and mother alive again. No
doubt, Jacob had some guilty feelings about deceiving Isaac into
giving him the birthright blessing.

Jacob knew that Esau was angry with him and had vowed
revenge. As a result, Jacob was constantly on the move to avoid
coming in contact with Esau. It was during one of these times that
he found and used a stone to remind him and his descendants of a
very special time in his life and how it would affect his descendants.
During the Old Testament times, stones were used instead of metals, monuments or written documents as witnesses of memorable
events, to preserve the remembrance or promises made and their
binding future.

JACOB'S DREAM

According to Genesis 28, after he had received the birthright blessing from Isaac, Jacob left Beersheba and traveled toward Haran. As
he approached the city of Luz, the sun was setting, the gates had
been closed and Jacob realized he would be sleeping outside in the
open, awaiting the morning when the city would once again open
its gate. As he was looking around, he noticed a stone which had
been hewn as a building stone by the stone cutters doing construction work in the city. Apparently the stone was not needed and was
thrown outside the city gates. Jacob saw the stone could be used for
a pillow while he slept in the open that night. While sleeping, Jacob
had an unusual dream. (Genesis 28:11–15) The most important
part of this dream was that Jacob understood God was in it and that
He was making a covenant with him. Genesis 28:14, "And thy seed
shall be as the dust of the earth, and thou shalt spread abroad to the
west, and to the east, and to the north, and to the south: and in thee
and in thy seed shall all the families of the earth be blessed."

When Jacob awoke, he knew without a shadow of a doubt that
God had certainly been in that place where he was sleeping and had
given him a message. (Verse 16) As a result of this promise and his
dream, Jacob rose up early and anointed this pillow stone to com-
memorate the covenant God made with him and his future generations. Verse 18, "And Jacob rose up early in the morning, and took
the stone that he had put for his pillows, and set it up for a pillar,
and poured oil upon the top of it."

Not only did God promise to give him tremendous material
blessings and the longevity of his descendants, but he also blessed
Jacob; Jacob, in return, vowed that he would follow God. To com-
memorate this event, he promised to give God a tenth of all that he
would ever possess.

> And he called the name of that place Bethel: but the
> name of that city was called Luz at the first. And Jacob
> vowed a vow, saying, If God will be with me, and will
> keep me in this way that I go, and will give me bread

to eat, and raiment to put on, So that I come again to my father's house in peace; then shall the LORD be my God: And this stone, which I have set for a pillar, shall be God's house: and of all that thou shalt give me I will surely give the tenth unto thee. (Verses 19–22)

From this point forward, Jacob walked and followed God to the best of his ability. Over time, God informed Jacob of his glorious future and that of his children. He was also told that his descendants would ultimately be ejected from the land of Canaan, but they would be as numerous as the dust of the earth and would spread abroad in the four directions of the compass. In addition, God also promised that He would be with Jacob in all of his and his descendants' wanderings throughout all history. No doubt, Jacob clearly understood the promises God was making which prompted him to say "This stone which I have set up for a pillar shall be God's House [Beth-El]." You might wonder what he meant by this statement. It is to be understood that (God's house) God will always be found where this stone is located. Jacob then set up this stone as a witness to his belief that God would be with him and his seed according to this promise forever. Jacob established the importance of this particular stone by pouring a portion of oil upon it. The stone then became a consecrated or "set apart" stone to remain with the descendants of Jacob.

This stone became known as the Stone of Israel, which we will see played a big part in the nation's history, and continues to play an important part in the nations of the modern-day descendants of Israel.

IN THE LAST DAYS

By reading the forty-ninth chapter of Genesis, we see Jacob, the father of the twelve sons that would make up the Israelite nation, telling his sons what their descendants would be facing in the last days before the Return of Jesus Christ. Remember, all of this activity concerning the stone started with Jacob, long before his family grew to twelve sons and daughters. Genesis 49:1, "And Jacob called unto his sons, and said, Gather yourselves together, that I may tell you that which shall befall you in the last days." Jacob is telling his sons what their descendants would be like. The proclivity of each son helps us identify those peoples in our modern times.

Notice the prophecies Jacob made regarding his son, Joseph.

> Joseph is a fruitful bough, even a fruitful bough by a well; whose branches run over the wall: The archers have sorely grieved him, and shot at him, and hated him: But his bow abode in strength, and the arms of his hands were made strong by the hands of the mighty God of Jacob; (from thence is the shepherd, the stone of Israel:) Even by the God of thy father, who shall help thee; and by the Almighty, who shall bless thee with blessings of heaven above, blessings of the deep that lieth under, blessings of the breasts, and of the womb: The blessings of thy father have prevailed above the blessings of my progenitors unto the utmost bound of the everlasting hills: they shall be on the head of Joseph, and on the crown of the head of him that was separate from his brethren. (Genesis 49:22–26)

Jacob makes the statement in verse 24 that Joseph would shepherd, or take care of the stone of Israel, the same stone that Jacob had anointed. In this statement, Jacob, whose name was changed by God to Israel, gives to this stone a far wider and deeper significance than realized up to this point. It is this stone, which he anointed for a special purpose a "pillar of witness" and the "stone of testimony." These blessings and prophecies were coming at the end of Jacob's life; at this point, he was entrusting to Joseph and his descendants, Ephraim and Manasseh, the stone of Israel for safekeeping and preserving.

The word "shepherd" in this verse is exactly as you would expect—a shepherd is to take care of his sheep, so were the descendants of Joseph to "shepherd" or take care of the stone of Israel. From that time forth, Joseph and his descendants would shepherd or take care of this stone of Israel, even until this day.

KING DAVID AND THE STONE

David refers to this stone the builders chose not to use which became the stone for Jacob's *pillow* and *pillar*. Psalms 118:22–23, "The stone which the builders refused is become the head stone of the corner. This is the LORD's doing; it is marvellous in our eyes." The stone that David was referring to was none other than Jacob's *pillow*, then *pillar*, the stone which was brought into Jerusalem when David conquered the city and made it his capital. Jesus quoted from this very Psalm in referencing Himself, using the words which referred to the stone in Psalms 118. Matthew 21:41, "Jesus saith unto them, Did ye never read in the scriptures, The stone which the builders rejected, the same is become the head of the corner: this is the Lord's doing, and it is marvellous in our eyes?"

After this, Jesus made another astounding statement concerning the true Church taken from the Jews and installed in the other nations of Israel. In this case, Jesus was essentially saying to the Jews and the head of the church in Jerusalem that the good news about the coming Kingdom of God, originally given to Judah, would now be taken away from them, and it would prosper in the nation of Israel. Verses 43–44, "Therefore say I unto you, The kingdom of God shall be taken from you, and given to a nation bringing forth the fruits thereof. And whosoever shall fall on this stone shall be broken: but on whomsoever it shall fall, it will grind him to powder."

Peter uses this same stone to reference Christ in Acts 4:11 when he refers to both Christ and Jacob's pillar stone. He is using the pillar stone of Jacob as a representation of the stone of our salvation —Jesus Christ! "This is the stone which was set at nought of you builders, which is become the head of the corner."

Peter again refers to this stone of Jacob and compares it to Jesus Christ, the *corner stone.*

> To whom coming, as unto a living stone, disallowed indeed of men, but chosen of God, and precious, Ye also, as lively stones, are built up a spiritual house, an holy priesthood, to offer up spiritual sacrifices, acceptable to God by Jesus Christ. Wherefore also it is contained in the scripture, Behold, I lay in Sion a chief corner stone, elect, precious: and he that believeth on him shall not be confounded. Unto you therefore which believe he is precious: but unto them which be disobedient, the stone which the builders disallowed, the same is made the head of the corner, And a stone of stumbling, and a rock of offence, even to them which stumble at the word, being disobedient: whereunto also they were appointed. (I Peter 2:4–8)

Notice Peter's phraseology is exactly the same as David used when speaking of the stone as being rejected by the builders. No truer words have been spoken, because the stone of Jacob has been essentially overlooked by the churches and history. While teaching His disciples and the people around Him, Jesus never used things as examples that did not exist. It would have been false and untrue. To talk of a "rejected stone" that had no existence and never was rejected would be very unlike the teaching of Jesus. We find in all of his parables and teachings, He used things that *are* to illustrate things that *are to be.* The "stone rejected," had to Him and to all the inspired writers a real existence and a true and well known history.

THE CROWNING STONE

The historian W. H. Poole, in his Lectures on *Anglo Israel or the Saxon Race,* makes the following observation in his Sixth Lecture concerning the use of Jacob's Pillar in the crowning of the Israelite kings. "Note, the king, when chosen, was brought to the altar, and he stood on a stone or pillar, literally mat-za-bah—a stone—pillars were made of stone. They were placed on a stone, elevated, raised so that they might be seen."

We find an example of this when King Joash was crowned in the presence of the guards of honor and the priests in ancient Judah.

> And to the captains over hundreds did the priest give king David's spears and shields, that were in the temple of the LORD. And the guard stood, every man with his weapons in his hand, round about the king, from the right corner of the temple to the left corner of the temple, along by the altar and the temple. And he brought forth the king's son, and put the crown upon him, and gave him the testimony; and they made him king, and anointed him; and they clapped their hands, and said, 'God save the king.' (II Kings 11:10–12)

Did you notice this final statement? "God save the king." This is exactly the same phrase used by the British when referring to their monarch in their salutation. Even now, their national anthem repeats the words "God save the king or queen!" Notice also, further confirmation of this coronation upon the stone, when Athaliah heard the noise, how she responded.

> And when Athaliah heard the noise of the guard and of the people, she came to the people into the temple of the LORD. And when she looked, behold, the king stood by a pillar, as the manner was, and the princes and the trumpeters by the king, and all the people of the land rejoiced, and blew with trumpets: and Athaliah rent her clothes, and cried, Treason, Treason. (Verses 13–14)

As a result of this outburst against the newly crowned king, the leaders of Judah cast her out from the city to be slain. (Verses 15–16) The coronation of the king took place while he stood upon the pillar of stone and made a covenant with the people and the

Eternal God. We can see upon this pillar of witness that the most solemn and binding transactions were made.

> And the king stood by a pillar, and made a covenant before the LORD, to walk after the LORD, and to keep his commandments and his testimonies and his statutes with all their heart and all their soul, to perform the words of this covenant that were written in this book. And all the people stood to the covenant. (II King 23:3)

Clearly, the Bible has recorded that the king stood on the stone, as was the manner of all previous kings in the usual way of crowning kings. It was their custom to have him stand upon the stone, take the "oath of office," and receive the crown. The custom continued until Judah fell in approximately 585 BC. The crowning ceremony included the people and the lords of the state who stood around the newly crowned kings and the guards of honor blew with trumpets and clapped their hands and greeted the new king, crying aloud, "God save the king!"

The coronation of all kings from Ireland, Scotland, and ultimately England follows this same pattern, according to the historian Sharon Turner, when describing the ancient ceremonies relating to the Anglo-Saxon government and the crowning of each of its kings. This can be seen as further proof that the ancient Israelites settled these lands.

THE COVENANT STONE

Approximately 31 years after the coronation of King Joash, we find another good king making a covenant between himself and God. Notice that King Josiah rededicated himself to follow God; a commitment was made by the people to rededicate themselves to live according to God's Laws.

> And the king sent, and they gathered unto him all the elders of Judah and of Jerusalem. And the king went

up into the house of the LORD, and all the men of
Judah and all the inhabitants of Jerusalem with him,
and the priests, and the prophets, and all the people,
both small and great: and he read in their ears all the
words of the book of the covenant which was found in
the house of the LORD. And the king stood by a pillar,
and made a covenant before the LORD, to walk after
the LORD, and to keep his commandments and his
testimonies and his statutes with all their heart and all
their soul, to perform the words of this covenant that
were written in this book. And all the people stood to
the covenant. (II Kings 23:1–3)

And the king stood in his place, and made a covenant before the LORD, to walk after the LORD, and
to keep his commandments, and his testimonies, and
his statutes, with all his heart, and with all his soul, to
perform the words of the covenant which are written
in this book. And he caused all that were present in
Jerusalem and Benjamin to stand to it. And the inhabitants of Jerusalem did according to the covenant of
God, the God of their fathers. And Josiah took away
all the abominations out of all the countries that per-
tained to the children of Israel, and made all that were
present in Israel to serve, even to serve the LORD their
God. And all his days they departed not from following the LORD, the God of their fathers. (II Chronicles
34:31–33)

The pillar spoken of was the same pillar over which he was
crowned and was Jacob's pillar stone. The king and the people
pledged themselves to once again unite under the name of the
Eternal God, to do His will and walk in His Commandments.

JEREMIAH'S COMMISSION

As we said earlier, Jeremiah was commissioned by God not only to oversee the downfall of the nation of Judah, but he was also the one whom God chose to transplant the kingly line from Jerusalem to the new land which we now know was Ireland. He brought with him and his small band of followers, along with the daughters of the slain king Zedekiah, the *stone of destiny*—Jacob's pillar—the stone over which all of the kings of Judah had been crowned.

LIA-FAIL STONE

The term "Lia-Fail" is a word that is derived from the Irish or Celtic language and Hebrew. It means "the stone of destiny, the stone wonderful, the coronation stone, the stone of the witness, the stone of the testimony, the stone of Tara, the stone of Scone, the royal stone." This stone is the same stone brought to Ireland with the collapse of Judah in circa 585 BC by Jeremiah.

Jacob's pillar, the stone of destiny, is an oblong stone about 22 inches in length, 13 inches broad and 11 inches deep. Its color is similar to that of granite with veins of red in the stone. According to geologists, this stone that is picked up in Irish history is the one and the same stone, Jacob's pillar.

Professor A.C. Ramsey LL.D, Fr. S., Director of the Royal Survey of England, inspected this stone on June 19, 1865, to determine its origin. The Professor and his group examined the stone while it was resting in Westminster Abbey. He makes the following statement,

> The coronation stone consists of a dull reddish or purple sandstone with a few small imbedded pebbles; one of these is quartz; the others are of a dark material the nature of which I was unable to ascertain. They may be Lydian stone. The rock is calcareous and is of the kind which masons call free stone. Chisel marks are visible on one or more of its sides. It bears evidence of

having been prepared for some place in a building, but rejected or never used.

After the examination, Professor Ramsey's associates determined "there was no rock or stone to match this rock in Scone, or indeed, in England, Ireland or Scotland. They have gone all the way to Bethel, near Luz, before they found the strata from which it was taken." According to Canon Tristan, in his work on the Land of Moab, he says, "There is such a strata of reddish sandstone existing near the Dead Sea. It is a strata of that very rock from which the Lia-Fail stone is composed." Tristan said that by simply placing the stone under the microscope, the resemblance is easily seen, and the identity of the location of the source of the stone is settled.

Another noted British historian, in his book, *Neil's History of Westminster Abbey,* states the stone is primarily quartz with light and red colored felspar, light and dark mica, with probably some green horn-blended intermixed; some fragments of a reddish gray clay slate. According to the *Encyclopedia Britannica,* "The Danaans carried into Ireland several necromantic curiosities, the most remarkable of which was the Lia-Fail Stone or Stone of Destiny, to which tradition tends to believe that sovereignty would remain with the nation whose kings were crowned upon it."

The late Dean Stanley, D.D, who was chief guardian of Westminster Abbey says, in his work *Historical Memorials of the Abbey,* "We learned that this stone was taken to Egypt. I have shown you how in the previous chapters and how it was in Jerusalem and that, at the time of the captivity, Jeremiah and his party took not only the king's daughters, but also the stone of destiny to be deposited in the new land by the sea which is modern-day Ireland." Stanley also provides us additional information about the journeys of the stone, indicating that King Gathelus from Greece brought an Egyptian princess (not Egyptian, but the Judean princess, who traveled by way of Egypt with Jeremiah and was the daughter of slain King Zedekiah of Judah) to Spain and married her. He states that Simon Burch and a prophet or revealer brought the stone to Spain, and that King Gathelus was crowned upon this stone and that he determined to keep it in Spain. This was in spite of the fact that Jeremiah intended to carry the stone to its next destination in Ireland. Jeremiah, realizing his commission, seized the stone and, with his assistant Burch (Baruch) conveyed it away to the appointed place called Lothaire-Groffin, afterwards later called Tara—a Hebrew word meaning *two tablets*. On this sacred hill, in Tara's hall, the sacred stone found a quiet resting place for nearly 1000 years. Eochaidh the Heremon married Tea Tephi, the Hebrew princess, daughter of Zedekiah, and was crowned the new ruler while they were upon the stone of destiny, and 54 successive kings were also crowned upon the stone.

THE STONE IS MOVED

About the time Rome began sending missions into Ireland, when Palatus was sent from Rome and St. Patrick sent from Gaul, the stone was sent to the Isle of Iona where it remained for many hundreds of years. While on the Isle of Iona, a religious man by the name of Columba, born in 532 AD, became the honored Bishop of the area and founded a monastery in the Field of Oaks to preach the Roman Catholic version of Christianity to the Picts.

Columba founded a school of the prophets called by the historians a monastery, though not of the typical monastical life, habits, or manners as we think of today. He had twelve disciples, students of the Bible, who translated the scriptures; he sent missionaries among the English and Scottish people and to Anglo-Saxons everywhere. The churches that he formed were called "Culdees" which some say is from the Gaelic word "Cuil," "Ceal," or "Cylle," and means a cell or sheltered place for worshippers of God. The interesting point about why these churches were founded, according to Stanley, is that Bishop Columba received the sacred trust to take care of the "Lia-Fail" stone which came from Tara, Ireland. Bishop Columba fully believed this was the stone of Jacob's pillar over which many kings had been crowned in Israel, and now Ireland.

ADRIAN

When Adrian was crowned king over the Scots in 574 AD, he resolved to ask a blessing on the coronation at the hands of the Bishop at Iona. Columba was the bishop and he laid his hands upon Adrian's head and crowned him king. The stone upon which he stood was called the *stone of fate.* The stone was then carried to Dunstaffnage Castle, then to Scone Abbey, near Perth.

About 840 AD, Kenneth I of Scotland was the first Scot king who took the stone from Dunstaffnage Castle to Scone, the capital of his kingdom, and here it received its name "The Stone of Scone." Kenneth I made it the official coronation seat of all the Scottish kings. From that time forward, no Scottish king could rule in Scotland who was not crowned over the "Stone of Scone," so the stone became the greatest treasure of the Scotsmen.

In 1296 AD, Edward I of England, one of the most war-like of the feudal monarchs, invaded and conquered Scotland. Edward I was a very soldierly king who spent most of his life in warfare, fighting sometimes against the French, sometimes against the Welch, sometimes against the Scots. Hearing the "Stone of Scone" was held in such high reverence by the Scots and believing that they could never have another king if the stone were removed, Edward I ordered that the stone be taken to Westminster Abbey in London, England. By defeating the Scots, he proclaimed that the King of England was now the overlord of the King of Scotland and he hoped that, by having English kings crowned and seated upon the "Stone of Scone," the Scotsmen would recognize the King of England as their king also. The Scots, however, fiercely resisted the union with the English crown for many centuries afterwards. It was this same Edward I, after returning to London, who ordered a chair be made which would contain the stone. This became the official coronation chair and a platform was built for the stone underneath the seat. The man commissioned to make the chair was named Walter the Painter. He was paid 5£ for his work to produce the chair that would hold the "Stone of Scone."

THE STONE IS MOVED AGAIN

During World War II, the stone was moved to Scotland during the Battle of Britain in 1940 when the invasion seemed only a matter of time. The British government initiated a secret meeting with the Privy Council to determine how to protect this great Stone of Destiny.

The discussion centered around the question to which there was no easy answer. What should be done with the age-old, tradition-embellished coronation stone in Westminster Abbey? This was the stone on which Scottish and later British kings were crowned, so it seemed, since time immemorial. Some advised shipping it out of the country—advice that was rejected outright—since the chance of sinking the ship or shooting down the aircraft carrying the precious cargo was too great. A worse fate for the stone than falling into enemy hands would be for it to rest forever at the bottom of the sea. It was finally decided to hide the stone somewhere on the island. The Dean of Westminster Abbey was delighted when the Abbey itself was chosen for the stone's hiding place and recorded, "Digging in the cellars was commenced immediately, but the workmen were unaware of the purpose for it all."

When finished, a plan was successfully drawn up showing the location where the stone could be found. The plan was sent immediately to the Prime Minister of Canada, the safest place across the ocean just in case the invasion occurred. As you can see, no effort was spared in safeguarding this very special stone to hide its location from the enemy. On Christmas Eve 1950, an elaborate plan was successfully executed by some influential Scottish nationals to take the stone home to Scotland. The coronation stone was smuggled out of the Abbey and taken to Scotland. After the theft was discovered, ports and airports were watched, cars stopped and searched, but all in vain. King George VI, knowing he had but a short time to live, became increasingly alarmed. If the coronation stone could not be found, soon his daughter would have to be crowned without the historical stone.

Two letters were sent to the Glasgow Daily Record by those responsible for the stone's disappearance, one to be given to the authorities. They had intentionally left behind a wristwatch and the letters were sent identifying the watch in detail. The authorities were now sure they had made contact with the correct people. After a 109 day hunt, the stone was found at the Abbey of Arbroath, where King Bruce (Robert the Bruce) and the Scottish Barons drew up the famous declaration of independence. The coronation stone was carefully wrapped in a Scottish flag with the request that the stone remain in Scotland, with the provision that English kings could continue to be crowned upon it either in Scotland or the stone could be taken to England for that purpose, but it was to be left in Scotland.

It was taken to England for the coronation of Queen Elizabeth II where it remained until, finally in 1996, the stone was returned to Scotland, where it now rests.

JESUS' EARLY YEARS

A fter the fall of the Kingdom of Judah and the removal of the coronation stone and the two daughters of King Zedekiah by Jeremiah, we are able to continue reading the history and the plight of the Jews as documented in the Bible.

When Nebuchadnezzar took the Jews captive, the Bible speaks of one of the captives—a young man of noble blood. This man was none other than the prophet Daniel, whom God used to save the Jews in captivity and to pen one of the most complete books of Prophecy, starting with the time of Nebuchadnezzar and ending in our future at the return of Jesus Christ. The Books of Ezra and Nehemiah provide additional insight as to the plight of the Jews following the downfall of the Babylonian Empire which was conquered by the Medes and Persians. The Books of Ezra and Nehemiah deal with the point in history when the Jews were allowed to return to Jerusalem and rebuild the city and temple. In fact, it was Artaxerxes, one of the kings under whom the Jews lived when in Babylonian captivity, who facilitated the beginning of the major return of the Jews to Judea.

> And it came to pass in the month Nisan, in the twentieth year of Artaxerxes the king, that wine was before him: and I took up the wine, and gave it unto the king.

Now I had not been beforetime sad in his presence. Wherefore the king said unto me, Why is thy countenance sad, seeing thou art not sick? this is nothing else but sorrow of heart. Then I was very sore afraid, And said unto the king, Let the king live for ever: why should not my countenance be sad, when the city, the place of my fathers' sepulchres, lieth waste, and the gates thereof are consumed with fire? Then the king said unto me, For what dost thou make request? So I prayed to the God of heaven. And I said unto the king, If it please the king, and if thy servant have found favour in thy sight, that thou wouldest send me unto Judah, unto the city of my fathers' sepulchres, that I may build it. (Nehemiah 2:1–5)

In this case, we see Nehemiah, a servant to King Artaxerxes, requesting permission to return to Jerusalem with the necessary papers and implements to rebuild the city and the temple. This event occurred in the month of Nisan (or Abib) circa 445 BC. The month of Nisan falls in the spring near the vernal equinox, during the time frame of our present day March or April.

There are reams of historical data documenting the return of the Jews to Jerusalem and the rebuilding of the nation prior to the time of the Roman occupation. Not all of the Jews wanted to return to Judah; some stayed and mixed with the Babylonian populace. However, at no time were the Jews ever allowed to re-establish the Davidic kingly line which had come to an end with Zedekiah and his sons. In fact, the rulers over the Jews were usually puppets of the Romans. This is evidenced in the New Testament speaking of King Herod who was, in fact, a puppet king of the Roman Empire. King Herod was not of the Davidic line, nor was he a pure-blooded Jew.

While Judah was returning to her homeland, God was prospering and protecting the Davidic kingship in Ireland where Jeremiah took Zedekiah's daughter Tea Tephi to marry the Irish king Eochaidh the Heremon. In the previous chapter, we showed that Jeremiah also transported Jacob's pillar for the specific purpose of crowning the new Davidic kingly line and to show where God intended to carry on the House of Israel.

For the next 500 years, the kingdom prospered through Ireland, Scotland, and ultimately ended up in England. Between 6 and 4 BC, an event occurred which would impact the whole world. Christ, the one who will eventually claim the throne of David, was born.

THE BIRTH OF CHRIST

The Christian world has mistakenly placed the birth of Christ at 1 AD and His death in 33 AD. However, Biblical historians know this is not correct and place His birth between 4 and 6 BC. This apparent conflict between what is taught and the actual fact developed when a Catholic monk named Dionysius Exiguus, circa 530 AD, devised a new calendar dating it from the birth of Christ. He made at least a four-year error in his calculations; Christ was actually born four to six years earlier than Dionysius had calculated. Unfortunately, that Roman calendar has remained in effect until this day, and most religious leaders teach and believe that Christ was born in 1 AD.

TRADITIONS REGARDING JESUS

We find an unusual statement about Christ's life from about age 12 to age 30. "And there are also many other things which Jesus did, the which, if they should be written every one, I suppose that even the world itself could not contain the books that should be written. Amen." (John 21:25) The Bible falls silent concerning the life of Jesus between the ages of 12 and 30. Notice Luke 2:42, "And when he was twelve years old, they went up to Jerusalem after the custom of the feast;" and Luke 2:51–52, "And he went down with them, and came to Nazareth, and was subject unto them: but his mother kept all these sayings in her heart. And Jesus increased in wisdom and stature, and in favour with God and man."

Tradition holds, and with good reason, that Joseph the husband of Mary, the mother of Christ, was a good deal older than Mary. In fact, many Biblical scholars believe that Joseph had a family from a previous wife who had died. Mary was much younger than Joseph, and most scholars believe that Joseph died soon after the event mentioned in Luke 2 when Jesus was approximately twelve years old. It is at this point that we must revert to oral chronicles and stories, coupled with the historical facts in order to get a complete picture. A British musician, William Blake, produced a famous hymn by the name of "Jerusalem" which included the words of a poem that has been handed down in English culture for many years. The words of the hymn include the following:

> And did those feet in ancient time Walk upon
> England's mountains green? And was the Holy Lamb
> of God In England's pleasant pastures seen?

The question the poem raises is whether Jesus actually visited England and, if so, for what purpose? The scripture only speaks of Christ's life prior to twelve years of age and after thirty years until his death.

There is nothing in the Bible to suggest that Jesus could not have visited any foreign areas prior to His ministry. Indeed, it states that He spent time in Egypt with His family shortly after His birth. (Matthew 2:13) Too many people make the wrong assumption that Jesus only became a world famous figure after His death and that His human life was lived out in obscurity in Galilee and Judea.

History, however, records that Jesus was more well-known, even in the remote regions of the world, than previously thought. The historian, Eusebius, writing in the early Fourth Century, records that the fame of Jesus and the knowledge of His healing miracles spread beyond the borders of His own nation. Eusebius was a bishop of the Catholic Church and historian of considerable reputation. During his lifetime, he had access to official archives and records of the original First Century documents that were still available. Eusebius relates that the resurrection of Jesus Christ was not just an obscure event mentioned only by the gospel writers, but he records that the event was well-known to the Roman Emperor

Tiberius and the Senate. Eusebius reports that Tiberius was so impressed with the report of the resurrection that he tried to have Jesus ranked among the Roman gods. However, the pagan Roman senate rejected his proposition.

The Bible reports that, at the time of His crucifixion, there was darkness on the earth until the ninth hour. (Luke 23:44) In Ireland, Conor Macnessa, king of Ulster who died in 48 AD is said to have inquired of his Chief Druid priest as to the meaning of the darkness. The Druid, after consulting the Druidic prophecies relating to the Messiah, gave the king a correct explanation of the darkness. One might think it strange that the Irish Druids should have prophetic knowledge of Christ until we realize the Druids were closely related to the "magi" or wise men who visited Jesus just after His birth. The word *magi* is really the Latin equivalent of druid. In many Celtic records, the word druid is used instead of magi. In some early Irish histories, Simon Magus (Acts 8:9) is known as "Simon the Druid."

The modern depiction of Druidism is quite different from the actual practice of the religion during the time of Christ. As a result, the impact that Druidism had on the ancient world is often not fully realized. Druidism was the outgrowth of the perversion of the true Old Testament Church during the time of ancient Israel which started with Jeroboam and continued with the Israelites as they were taken captive by the Assyrians. This would explain why the Druids had some knowledge of the coming Christ because of their studies and understanding of the Old Testament prior to the separation of Israel and Judah.

CHRIST–HIS TEENAGE YEARS

If Jesus Christ had spent His teenage years in Galilee, one would certainly expect the people of the area to have retained some information relating to this local young man who later became famous. The fact that there are no historical records relating to Christ's teenage years in Galilee or Judea establishes the possibility that Christ did not spend His early years there after his twelfth birthday.

Ancient traditions of England indicate that several sites claim that Jesus was there during His teenage years; among these are St. Michael's Mount, St. Justin–Roseland, Redruth, Glastonbury, and Priddy. The tradition appears to have been the inspiration for naming districts of Jesus' Well in Cornwall and Paradise in Somerset, England. Across the English Channel in Brittany, the same tradition has lingered for many years. The source of the French version is not difficult to trace. Following the Saxon invasion of Britain from the Fifth Century onward, many Britons fled from the western parts of Britain to nearby Brittany, taking much of their history in written and spoken form with them. The stories relating to Jesus appear to have been of considerable antiquity.

According to these stories, Christ was storm bound on the western coast of England throughout the winter. The location of the visit is given as "the summer land," a name often used in ancient times for the modern-day area of Somerset. The district associated with this visit to Somerset is known as Paradise. This place is sometimes found on old maps of the area.

In Isaiah 41, we find that one of the major themes deals with the Second coming of Christ. As you read this section, you will notice that there are no fewer than seven references that are made to "the isles" and "the isles afar off." Other ancient writers used similar terminology when writing of Britain. They used such terms as "isles of the west" and "isles of the sea." Historians of Roman times report that some of the Jews were speaking not of "isles" in general, but of a specific group of islands, i.e. Britain.

It has been a well established fact that Phoenician trading vessels visited Britain in ancient times and this is taught in college history by L.S. Stabrianos in his *History of the World to 1500*, page 78. He refers to the Phoenicians as a Semitic-speaking people who traveled throughout the Mediterranean coastal area and were frequent traders to the British Isles in the area of Cornwall, where they traded for valuable tin.

The British tin mines were regularly visited by ships of the Romans and Phoenicians during the time of Christ. The historian Herodotus, writing in 445 BC, speaks of Britain as the "Tin Lands," and the major supplier for tin among the nations along the Mediterranean Sea. Some authorities believe that trade existed as early as 1500 BC, and that the tin mines of Britain mainly supplied the gorgeous adornments that were found in Solomon's Temple.

Ancient "pigs of lead" bearing official Roman seals have been discovered in the west of England dating from the time of the First Century Emperors Claudius and Nero. An interesting point indicated by the Gospel writers is that Jesus was very much relaxed and confident on the sea. The fact that Christ was so relaxed on the sea would not have come naturally to a man who had spent most of his life in the vocation of carpentry. The fact is, there is only one place in the Bible which seems to indicate that Jesus was a carpenter, and this verse could be subject to interpretation as Christ being the "son" of a carpenter. Notice Matthew 13:55 which indicates Jesus was the son of a carpenter and Mark 6:3 where He is called a carpenter. On the other hand, Jesus Christ knew much about fishing and the sea as indicated by His spending many hours either in a boat or along the seashore. This indicates that Christ was an experienced man of the sea and that He had sailed the oceans prior to beginning his ministry at age 30.

A man who had experienced sailing the Mediterranean Sea and the Atlantic Ocean would have considered a storm on a mere lake to be a matter of no great consequence, as described in the event of His calming the storm. (Mark 4:37; Luke 8:23)

JOSEPH OF ARIMATHEA

In the many traditions relating to Jesus coming to Britain, it is believed that He was brought there by Joseph of Arimathea who was the uncle of Mary, Jesus' mother. The gospel record of Joseph of Arimathea burying the body of Jesus in his own sepulcher strongly supports that tradition. A casual reading of the account would cause one to believe that Joseph claimed the body of his friend from Pilate, using only the grounds of being a friend or follower of the dead man.

This is far from being the case because the Chief Priest, with the permission of Pilate, made special arrangements for guarding the security of the body of Jesus for the express purpose of keeping it out of the hands of His followers. (Matthew 27:62–66)

The Bible also indicates that Joseph did not reveal, at that time, that he was a follower of Jesus. He was a disciple secretly "for fear of the Jews." (John 19:38) Therefore, we must assume that Joseph did not approach Pilate on the grounds of being a disciple. What exactly was his status? Based on Jewish traditions and teachings, the only grounds he could have used to request the body that would have been in agreement with Jewish law and Roman law, without giving offense to the Chief Priest, would have been as the nearest adult, male relative of Jesus. Under both Jewish and Roman law, it was the responsibility of the nearest relative to dispose of the dead, regardless of the circumstances of the death.

The mother of Jesus, Mary, clearly would have been in no fit emotional state to take on such a task as removing her son from the stake and carting Him to a burial place. The brothers of Jesus, if they were Mary's sons, would have been younger than Christ, and therefore the duty would have fallen to the elder member of the family, the uncle of Mary—Joseph. If the brothers and sisters of Jesus were Joseph's (Mary's husband) children, then Joseph of Arimathea would have been the nearest male blood kin through Mary. Ultimately, unless Joseph had strong grounds for claiming the body, the Jews would have resisted the idea of a non-relative taking the body of Jesus away because they feared they might concoct some story about the resurrection of Christ.

In all of this, you may wonder why Mary's legal husband, Joseph, who was the legal father of Jesus, did not claim the body. As mentioned earlier, the last time the scripture speaks of Jesus, Joseph and Mary together is in Luke 2:44–52. From then on, the Bible speaks of His mother and His brothers and sisters. This is a very clear indication that Joseph died when Jesus was a young man or teenager. This explains why the people in His hometown of Nazareth asked the question, "Is not this the carpenter's son? Is not his mother called Mary?" (Matthew 13:55) If Jesus had grown up His entire life in Nazareth, no such question would have been asked by his fellow townsmen.

In the Latin Vulgate translations of the Bible, Joseph of Arimathea is described as "Decurio" and in Jerome's translation as "Nobilis Decurio"—the noble decurio. The term Decurio was commonly used to designate an official under Roman authority who was in charge of metal mining. The office seems to have been very lucrative for Joseph and one that was much coveted. Cicero remarked that it was easier to become a senator of Rome than a Decurio in Pompeii. The office is also known to have existed under the Roman administration in Britain.

In Mark 15:43, we read that Joseph of Arimathea had the rank of "honorable counselor," which further indicates that he had an office under the Romans. The ability of Joseph to go boldly before Pilate also indicates that he had great authority in the land, and that he had a position of influence in the Roman government.

JOSEPH IN CORNWALL

There are many records and traditions associating Joseph of Arimathea with the mining activities of Cornwall and the Mendips. Mendips was in the district where Somerset and Glastonbury were located. It is not surprising that, as an authority in the Roman government, he would have many commercial interests in all parts of the world! History records and ample evidence proves that the British mines were a major source of tin and lead. In Roman times, because tin was used in the making of alloys, the metal was in great demand. It is highly probable that Joseph obtained his wealth from trading in these valuable metals.

Because of the trade between Rome and Britain, there was a large community of Judeans living in Cornwall during the time of

Christ called the Saracens. These Judeans were engaged in the trade of extracting and exporting metals from the Cornwall area. The historian Dr. William Pryce published a work in 1790 on the origin of the Cornish language and he states that "Cornish and Breton were almost the same dialect of a Syrian or Phoenician root."

Even some modern historians who tend to be skeptical of this story will readily admit that wealthy merchants could more easily have traveled from Palestine to Glastonbury during the years following the crucifixion than at any later time until well into the Ninth Century. It should also be noted that trading links between the two areas existed long before the Roman invasion of Britain in 43 AD.

THE EDUCATION OF JESUS

If, in fact, Joseph did assist the family of Jesus after the death of Mary's husband, and with the education of Jesus, he could have provided a fine education for the young man, including much foreign travel.

According to local tradition, Joseph of Arimathea taught the boy Jesus how to extract Cornish tin and purge it of its wolfram. For Jesus to have learned this process, He would have had to visit the mining area near Cornwall where this process took place. In almost all of the west country sites which involved the tradition of the metal mining industry, there is a quaint proverb about Priddy, which says, "As sure as our Lord was at Priddy..." referencing the mining center of the Mendips mining district in the Roman times and even before.

It should be emphasized that there was extensive use of tin to make various other metal forms in the construction of both buildings and ships during the time of Christ. Archaeological digs have shown that, in the houses of the wealthy, plumbing involving the use of pipes and valves was commonplace and made from metals extracted from southwestern England.

The gospel makes it very plain that Jesus did not begin His

ministry as a penniless vagabond. He conducted His ministry on a full-time basis. His disciples, too, were for the most part, full time students. The cost of maintaining thirteen people for this period of time must have been considerable. Although the disciples and probably some of His other followers contributed to the common fund from time to time, it is likely that Jesus Himself provided the bulk of the funds. Although Judas was the treasurer for the group, Jesus was the one who determined how the money was to be spent.

If Jesus had been a penniless vagabond, He would not have paid taxes, but the scriptures indicate that He did pay taxes. He attended banquets along with the social elite of His day. One of His parables shows the necessity for the wearing of apparel appropriate for such occasions. The robe He wore on the day of His crucifixion was made of a very expensive, seamless, piece of material. Only those who could afford expensive clothing could possess a robe without a seam. Robes with seams were of much lesser value and cheaper to purchase. The soldiers at Christ's crucifixion gambled for His fine robe.

It would appear that Jesus must have been a successful and prosperous young man prior to entering the Ministry. He certainly was more than an ordinary tradesman. The occupation of "carpenter" given only one place in the scripture obscures the fact that He was not necessarily a carpenter of homes, but, in fact, His trade may have been linked to that of a ship's carpenter rather than a homebuilder. While traveling with His uncle, He may have performed carpentry duties which are numerous on the wooden ships used in the merchant trade of those days.

Eusebius states that, during the First Century AD, Britain had many schools of learning for a young man to study and develop skills in various aspects of commerce during His day. He states that British architects were in great demand on the continent. The process of enameling metal was invented in Britain just prior to the time of Christ. A good example of a local "La Tenne" art is the famous Glastonbury bowl which was produced about the time of

Christ. There is little doubt that Jesus could have developed skills from the British institutions.

We know, from the Biblical accounts, that Jesus was a superb public speaker who had a tremendous impact on the crowds that gathered around Him. The primary reason for His impact was clearly the content of the material about which He was speaking. Another important factor was His style of public speaking. In the Greek rendering of Mark 1:22 it reads: "And they were struck with awe at his mode of instruction."

No doubt Jesus was a well educated speaker and learned this from teachers who were experienced in public speaking. The Bible records that the people of his hometown of Nazareth were astonished at His speaking. "And all bare Him witness and wondered at the gracious words which proceedeth out of His mouth. And they said, Is not this Joseph's son?" (Luke 4:22)

From this statement, it is obvious that Christ got very little of His formal education and training in the village of Nazareth. If His training had merely been the product of a local school or educator, then the people would not have been astonished at His speaking ability. In fact, if He had been trained in Nazareth, His teachers would have made themselves known to the people. Therefore, it is highly unlikely that Christ received a higher education in the Middle East, but somewhere away from Nazareth and Galilee. In fact, a statement was made in John 1:46 about what would come from the small town of Nazareth, "And Nathanael said unto him, Can there any good thing come out of Nazareth? Philip saith unto him, Come and see."

Jerusalem, not Nazareth, was the academic center of the nation where speakers and the educated were trained in the temple schools. Mark relates in Mark 1:22, "And they were astonished at his doctrine: for he taught them as one that had authority, and not as the scribes." Notice that the Jews were puzzled by the fact that Jesus seemed to be so well educated, and they asked in John 7:15, "How knoweth this man letters, having never learned?"

The term "letters" refers to a degree such as a Bachelor of Science

(BS) or MA (Master's degree) or PhD (Doctor of Philosophy). According to the Weymouth translation, it renders the scripture in John 7:15, "How does this man know everything of books, although He has never been at any of our schools?" Obviously the Jews in Judea wondered how this superbly educated man and public speaker came to be without any formal education at any institution in Galilee or Judea. If such training had been received, they would have known about it and would not have made the remark "…never having learned." We must conclude that Jesus received his education outside of Judea and Galilee, and this leaves Britain as the place He most likely spent much of His teenage years. In fact, during the time of Christ, there were 40 colleges or universities on British soil training Romans and others throughout the empire. The educational standards were such that students came not only from the British nobility, but also from many foreign nations. It is said that even Pontus Pilate as a young man studied in Britain.

The studies included public speaking and architectural design. Many of the buildings that stand in Rome today are the products of British educated architects. In fact, the historian Tacticus has recorded many speeches word for word of several high-ranking Britons of Christ's day. Such speeches were very often colorful, stirring and inspiring, much like the ones Jesus gave to his followers.

Greek was the language of the educated in Britain and therefore Greek would have been the language learned by Christ. We know that Jesus read and understood Greek because, in the account of His reading from the scriptures in the Jewish synagogue, He read from the Greek Septuagint Bible, which was the only available complete Bible used by the Jews during Christ's time. Since Greek would not have been taught by His mother, Mary, or the locals of Nazareth, this is further evidence that Christ was educated in England. Therefore, He spoke Greek in addition to the Aramaic language He learned as a child. In the Greek manuscripts, John 7:35 makes the following statement, "Is He about to go to the dispersion of the Greeks? And to teach the Greeks?"

The Jews obviously would not have made this statement unless they heard Him speak in the Greek language fluently. Mark also relates a conversation Jesus had with a woman in the region of Tyre and Sidon, adding the point that "the woman was a Greek." (Mark 7:26) Julius Caesar stated that Britons used Greek in commercial transactions. Many of the educated classes in Briton spoke the language fluently. A few, such as Pomponia Graecina were among Europe's leading scholars in the Greek language.

People often think that, because Jesus was the Son of God, everything was already in his mind and intellect. Of course, He did have God's Spirit to the full, but He was born into this world as a human baby, having to learn everything just as any other human baby has to learn. He was given abilities, but He had to be taught skills regarding speaking, etiquette, etc.

JESUS MEETS JOHN THE BAPTIST

A final indication that Jesus may well have spent His teenage and young adult years abroad prior to the beginning of His ministry is the curious relationship that He had with John the Baptist, His cousin, who was six months older. In comparison to the intimate rapport that Jesus had with His own disciples, His relationship with John the Baptist was somewhat formal and distant. A clue to the reason for this is given by John when he mentioned "and I did not know him." (John 1:33)

Although the two men were linked and their mothers seemed to have been close friends, they appeared to have had little or no contact with each other as adults. If Christ had lived in the Galilean region where John the Baptist also lived, they would have surely been close friends and would have known each other intimately. This is a clear indication that Jesus had been absent from the area for many years prior to the beginning of His ministry.

There can be no doubt that Jesus spent His teenage formative years up until age 30 away from Galilee and the Middle East. Just as young people go away to college to learn their particular study of choice which may not be available in their local areas, so did people of means in Jesus' time. And remember, he was a human being who was to be the epitome of human kind—so it is not likely that he worked in a carpentry shop in Nazareth all of his youth and young adult years and just learned what he picked up from among the locals.

The scripture in Luke shows that Jesus was subject to his parents, meaning that they were responsible for teaching Him things He did not already know. Just as any human being must learn through teaching or experience, the Bible plainly says that Jesus Christ learned through His experiences and sufferings. (Hebrews 5:8) His heavenly Father saw to it that Jesus had the parents God chose because of what they could give to Jesus, and God the Father also made the way for Jesus to have the opportunity to learn and grow as much as possible because He had a great job ahead of Him. It is sad that some movies have portrayed Jesus as a poor itinerant man who through extraordinary methods received scholarly training from God the Father with no outside help. God works in an orderly fashion and Jesus had to learn just as we do, through study.

When Jesus returned to Judea, He was an educated man who received His education much the same way as any other human being. Christ had to learn everything just as all human beings are taught. The only difference was that Christ had more Holy Spirit and was able to discern more quickly, separating the truth from falsehoods.

GLASTONBURY

According to the learned historian Archbishop Ussher, "The mother church of the British Isles is the church in Insula Avallonia called by the Saxons 'Glaston' which we now know is the small English town by the name of Glastonbury." According to Sir Henry Spellman in his work *The Concilia*, "It is certain that Britain received the faith in the first age from the first sowers of the Word. Of all the churches of whose origins I have investigated in Britain, the church of Glastonbury is the most ancient." Spellman continues, "We have abundant evidence that this Britain of ours received the faith and that, from the disciples of Christ Himself, soon after the crucifixion of Christ." (Spellman, 1)

Robert Parsons, the Jesuit in his *Three Conversations of England*, admits that "The Christian religion began in Britain within 50 years of Christ's ascension." His contemporary, Alfred in his *Regia Fides* says, "It is perfectly certain that before St. Paul had come to Rome, Aristobulus was in Britain." The historian Fuller also makes this statement: "If credit be given to these ancient authors, this church without competition would be senior to all Christian churches in the world." (Fuller, 14)

According to Erudite, Polydore Vergil, "Partly through Joseph of Arimathea, partly through Fugatus and Damien's, [Britain] was of all kingdoms the first that received the gospel." Polydore Vergil had special access to sources of the Glastonbury story and he was Prebendary of Brent in Wells Cathedral and Archdeacon of Wells, six miles from Glastonbury. In 1504, he was enthroned as Bishop of Bath and Wells as proxy for his foreign non-resident kinsmen, Adrian D. Castello and acted for him. Vergil was an avid believer in the story of Joseph of Arimathea and his activities in Glastonbury.

I have personally visited the museum book store in Wells, next to the cathedral. The curator I talked with stated that as long as he has been old enough to be aware of it, the tradition of Jesus living in Glastonbury as a child was taught as fact. While there, and later in Glastonbury, I purchased several books on related subjects.

The Roman Catholics, and specifically Cardinal Pole, during the time of the coronation of Queen Mary, admitted that Britain was the first outpost to be converted to Christianity; therefore, making the British church the elder sister and not a daughter of the modern Roman Catholic church.

The acceptance of Christianity under a good British king is dated prior to 170 AD. The king who made it the national religion was known as the good King Lucius, whom the British titled "Our most religious king." History records that the British had forgotten much of their great inheritance of Christianity which later was firmly defended by the British Archbishops and Bishops in the days of St. Augustine. "How many Britons realize that the superior dignity and antiquity of their national church was decided by church councils? The question was never disputed until 1409 when, for political purposes, it was called into question by the ambassadors of France and Spain. Four times the British asserted their claim at the Council of Pisa, in 1409; Constance, in 1417; Sienna, in 1424; and Basel, in 1434," said Nicholas Frome, Avid of Glastonbury. "It was there contended that the churches of France and Spain must yield in points to the antiquity and precedence to that of Britain as the latter church was founded by Joseph of Arimathea immediately after the crucifixion of Christ. There is a rare quarto given the pleading at the Council of Constance."

The date of formation of the church in Glastonbury is somewhat obscured. However, there are two dates that are claimed for the founding of the Glastonbury church—37 AD and 63 AD. Probably both dates really point to some special event in Glastonbury. We believe that the earlier date is the correct one, as also believed by Gildas the Wise, the earliest British historian who lived in 425–512 AD. He distinctly says that the light of Christ was shown here in the last year of the reign of Tiberius Caesar, which was in 37 AD. This fits with the claim recorded above, which gave precedent to British bishops at the church council on the grounds that Britain was converted immediately after the crucifixion of Christ. It also fits with the statements of Fuller and Polydore Vergil in their historical works about the church of Glastonbury being the senior church outside of the Jewish homeland. According to Spellman's words, "The British received the faith soon after the crucifixion," and Alfred's statement that "Aristobulus was in Britain before the Apostle Paul went to Rome," many years after the crucifixion of Christ.

It suffices to say there is ample evidence that the first truly Christian Church to be formed in the world outside of Judea was none other than the church built by Joseph of Arimathea in the small town of Glastonbury.

THE FIRST CHURCH BUILDING

I have personally visited the location where historians believe the first church in England was constructed by Joseph of Arimathea. In fact, the foundation points of the church have been located and are now preserved as a national monument. This church is located in Glastonbury, at St. Mary's church yard, near the present ruins of the Norman abbey, which stands on a site near what is called the "wattle" church built by Joseph of Arimathea and the disciples of Christ. The building was built in the same dimensions of the temple in Jerusalem and faced the same direction. History does not record another church facility in Rome until the time of Constantine when the empire followed him in becoming "Christian" circa 325 AD. Up until that time, Christians were required to meet secretly in homes, hiding from the Roman authorities.

The fact is, the site in Glastonbury where the church once stood is the earliest known "above ground" church in the world, outside of Jerusalem. It is also interesting to note that the ancient British Royal Family was intimately connected with the earliest apostolic church, both in exile in Rome and in Britain where they fostered it. There is an interesting relic depicting the friendship between the Apostle Paul and the British ruling king by the name of Caractacus and his family; contemporary portraits of Paul and Linus engraved in two glass plates exist in the Vatican Museum.

The remains of mud and wattle houses, which were of similar construction as the church built by Joseph of Arimathea, are on display in the Glastonbury Museum.

THE TRADITION—FACT OR LEGEND?

There is a strong tradition that has been handed down for centuries that is common among the hill people of Somerset, Gloucestershire, and in the west of Ireland that Joseph of Arimathea came to Britain, first as a metal merchant seeking tin from the Scillies and Cornwall, that he also traded in lead, copper and other metals from the hills of Somerset and that Jesus Christ, as a boy, came with him. This tradition comes from Walter Farrer, the late Archdeacon of Wells, and the Rev. Canon A. B. R. Young, Prebendary of Clogher from the *Traditions of Ireland.*

In recent history, an archaeological dig at Ostia, the seaport of Rome, found an ancient Roman drainpipe below the chariot road. It was bonded in some special way with tin. A section was cut off the drainpipe and sent to England for analysis. The verdict was that the metal came from the Mendips mines near Glastonbury. The British Museum has two very early exhibits of Roman-British lead from the Mendips hill district near Glastonbury. One is dated 49 AD and has the name of Britannicus, son of the Emperor Claudius on it. The other, dated 60 AD, bears the inscription, "British lead, the property of the Emperor Nero." It is also said that in the wonderful aqueduct in Jerusalem attributed to King Solomon, the particular type of lead found was mined in the Mendips and nowhere else was it found. This, of course, was brought to Jerusalem circa 1000 BC. The historian E.B. Duff, Court of the Holy Roman Empire, stated that in Maronite and Catluei villages in upper Galilee, there lingers a tradition that, as a youth, Christ went to Britain as a shipwright aboard a trading vessel of Tyre and that He was storm bound on the shores of the west of England throughout the winter. A Mr. Henry Jenner, F.S.A., late of the British Museum, son of the late Bishop Jenner, narrates that some years back in north London during the making of tin sheets for organ pipes, before the molten tin was poured, a man said every time, "Joseph was in the tin trade." (Jenner, 135–136) And, from all historical documents we could find, including the Bible, was a wealthy tin merchant.

It is also interesting that the fabled King Arthur, whom we now know was a real person, claimed descent from Joseph of Arimathea, whom he claimed was his uncle, and also King David. It was said that he was kinsman to the Virgin Mary. (Hearne 56–57)

Except for the fact that reputable historians support the concept of Joseph of Arimathea and Christ being in Glastonbury, the first impulse by modern-day people is to consider the tradition as ridiculous and reject it.

As the years have gone on and research has improved, a wider knowledge has been made available about the spectacular story of Christ living and visiting Somerset and Cornwall during his years of twelve to thirty. No doubt he accompanied His uncle Joseph on many voyages back and forth between Jerusalem, Rome and England during his formative years.

The Rev. C.C. Dobson, Vicar of St. Mary in the Castle Hastings definitely believes that Jesus actually stayed some time in Glastonbury and built a wattle house to live in. He bases this mainly on the letter quoted by himself in his former editions of his book, *From St. Augustine to Pope Gregory the Great,* and claims that the first followers of Christ visited Britain, "God beforehand acquainting them, found a church constructed by no human art, but by the hands of Christ Himself for the salvation of His people." (Capt, 43)

Naturally, the first impulse is to regard this statement as simply an absurd exaggeration. But in view of Dobson's suggestion, there might lurk a lingering tradition that Christ Himself built it or took part in the construction of a building in Britain during a visit as a youth, which tallies with Christ being brought up in the home of a carpenter. Dobson also thinks that the very strange name of Glastonbury, which means "The secret of the Lord," supports his theory. He goes on to state that it would further support the tradition that Christ and Joseph of Arimathea came in a ship of Tarsus to the Summer Land, which is Glastonbury (Somerset), and sojourned in Paradise. Remember, Somerset is often called by the name of Summer Land. Dobson has also discovered that at a seaside place called Burham, 17 miles from Glastonbury, there is a farm called the Paradise Farm in a district around Burham called Paradise in the old ordinance of survey maps; he links that name with Christ's traditional visits.

Several authors have written books about Joseph of Arimathea and Christ in Glastonbury, which should still be in print: Lionel

Smithett Lewis, an English writer; American archaeologist and historian, E. Raymond Capt; Mr. Ray Gibbs. When one considers the traditions of Glastonbury, they cannot be dismissed as mere fables or legends of fiction. In fact, the legends and traditions are generally rooted in a basis of truth. In the absence of positive proof to the contrary, there is no reason why one should not accept the traditions as having a foundation in fact.

TO THE LOST SHEEP
OF ISRAEL

J esus made a much overlooked statement to His disciples in the form of a command, "These twelve Jesus sent forth, and commanded them, saying, Go not into the way of the Gentiles, and into any city of the Samaritans enter ye not: But go rather to the lost sheep of the house of Israel. And as ye go, preach, saying, The kingdom of heaven is at hand." (Matthew 10:5–7)

Jesus was telling His twelve disciples their mission was to go to the Lost Sheep of the House of Israel rather than to the Gentile world. This concept is the exact opposite of what is taught in churches today. Essentially, most professing Christians believe that, soon after the death of Christ, the disciples and followers of Christ gave up on the Jews and turned all of their attention to the conversion of the Gentiles. One might argue that most of the New Testament seems to be written to the Gentiles from the pen of Paul. In addition, one might also argue that Peter, one of the twelve original disciples also went to the Gentiles. A careful study of the scriptures will reveal that Peter essentially had only one mission to carry Christ's message to the Gentiles when he was sent by Christ directly to the first Gentile convert, Cornelius. This story is found in Acts 10 which concludes with Peter baptizing Cornelius and his family. Not until the Apostle Paul was fully prepared did Christ intend that His message would be delivered to the Gentiles.

The important fact of Matthew 10:5 concerns Christ instructing His disciples to go to the Lost Sheep of the House of Israel, not to the Gentiles. This chapter will show the historical evidence of how this mission was carried out, especially to the group considered the Lost Sheep of the House of Israel.

JOSEPH OF ARIMATHEA

In the previous chapters, we introduced you to Joseph of Arimathea, the uncle of Mary, the mother of Christ. The scripture records that it was Joseph of Arimathea who took Christ's body and buried it in his own tomb. However, this was not to be the end of his work and service, but only the beginning.

Soon after Christ's ascension, as mentioned in Acts 1, there was great persecution of His followers in the area around Jerusalem. The Bible clearly records the death of the church's first martyr, Stephen.

> Then they cried out with a loud voice, and stopped their ears, and ran upon him with one accord, And cast him out of the city, and stoned him: and the witnesses laid down their clothes at a young man's feet, whose name was Saul. And they stoned Stephen, calling upon God, and saying, Lord Jesus, receive my spirit. And he kneeled down, and cried with a loud voice, Lord, lay not this sin to their charge. And when he had said this, he fell asleep. And Saul was consenting unto his death. And at that time there was a great persecution against the church which was at Jerusalem; and they were all scattered abroad throughout the regions of Judaea and Samaria, except the apostles. (Acts 7:54–8:1)

James was killed and Peter was put in prison. Acts 12:2–3, "And he killed James the brother of John with the sword. And because he saw it pleased the Jews, he proceeded further to take Peter also. (Then were the days of unleavened bread.)"

An early church leader, Clement stated that James, the brother of John, was brought to the judgment seat along with his accuser and was sentenced to death. Clement states that James' accuser was much moved in his heart and conscience when he realized what he had done. As a result, his accuser confessed and desired for James to forgive him and also confessed that he too was a Christian. Clement reports that James made the following statement: "Peace be to thee, brother;" and kissed him and both of them were beheaded at the same time in 36 AD.

According to *Fox's Book of Martyrs*, James, the half-brother of Jesus, was killed by the scribes and Pharisees. James was leader of the New Christian church at Jerusalem and is the same one that is mentioned in Acts 15:13. James was a senior minister in the early church, making the final decision concerning how the Gentiles were to be treated by the Jews and leaders of the New Testament Church.

Apparently, James was achieving renown in Jerusalem and Jewish converts were flocking to him as their new Christian leader. As a result of the growth of his following, the scribes and Pharisees of the Jewish hierarchy sensed there was danger brewing for them if the Jews continued to look to Jesus as "the Christ." Therefore, they took counsel among themselves and decided to approach James and set a trap for his demise. They asked James to warn the people that they shouldn't be deceived about Jesus "the Messiah," while at the same time they flattered James saying they were willing to listen to him and obey whatever he said.

The Jewish leaders, therefore, recommended that James stand upon the pinnacle of the temple so that all might be able to see him and that his words would be easily heard by all the people. When James was above the crowd at the temple, the scribes and Pharisees cried out to him, "Thou just man, whom we all ought to obey, this people is going astray after Jesus which was crucified." James gave the following answer with a loud voice, "Why do you ask me of

Jesus, the son of man? He sitteth on the right hand of the most High, and shall come in the clouds of heaven."

Fox reports that, upon this testimony given by James, many of those who were there were persuaded and glorified God upon this witness of James.

When the scribes and Pharisees realized that James crossed them, they pressed up against him while he was standing on the high place and threw him down to the pavement among the onlookers. However, the fall did not kill James, but he raised up on his knees and it was said he made the following statement, "O, Lord God, Father, I beseech thee to forgive them for they know not what they do." This incited the scribes and Pharisees even further and they urged the crowd to stone James; "mob rule" won and they began to stone him. One of those present in the crowd saw the suffering James was going through and, according to Fox, he took a fuller's instrument which is used to beat cloth and struck James on the head until he died.

The disciple Thomas went to the scattered Israelites in the area of the Parthians, Medes and Persians, also to the Carmanians, Hyrcanians, Bactrians and Magians. According to Fox, Thomas was ultimately slain in Calamina, a city of India by an arrow or a dart. Andrew, the brother of Peter, preached to the Scythians (Israelites), Sogdins, to the Sacae (Israelites), and in a city called Sebastopolis. He was crucified by Aegaes, the governor of the Edessenes. This was the area where the northern tribes were first transported from Northern Israel. For more reading concerning the early martyrs, we recommend reading *Fox's Book of Martyrs,* prepared by W. Grinton Berry.

Christ was not about to allow the New Testament Church, which began on the Day of Pentecost, to be stamped out by the Jews or the pagan Roman Empire. To this end, many Biblical historians believe that Christ made a bold move to ensure that His Church and the New Christianity would be taken to the Lost Sheep of the House of Israel.

CAST OUT

Cardinal Seasar Baronius, (AD 1538–1609) a learned historian and librarian to the Vatican, spent 30 years compiling Ecclesiastical Annals ending in AD 1198. He identifies an incredible event involving Joseph of Arimathea and others who were very close to Jesus. Cardinal Baronius included documentations from a manuscript which was originally compiled by Rabanus Maurus, Archbishop of Mayence (AD 766–856) now housed in the Magdalene College Library at Oxford, England. In this work, Maurus, in chapter 37, lists the names of those who accompanied Joseph of Arimathea and describes a precarious voyage from Judea across the Mediterranean Sea.

"Leaving the shores of Asia and favored by an east wind, they went round about down the Tyrrhenian Sea [Mediterranean] between Europe and Africa, leaving the city of Rome and all the land of Italy to the right. Then, happily turning their course to the right, they came near to the city of Marseilles, in the Viennoise Province of Gaul, where the river Rhone is received by the sea. There, having called upon God, the King of all the world, they parted; each company going to the province where the Holy Spirit had directed them; presently preaching everywhere, 'the Lord working with them, and confirming the word with signs following.'" (chap. 37)

Another manuscript which is actually older also agrees with Maurus and they all agree on the essential facts. (M.S. Laud, 108) Other writings indicate that Joseph and his party were actually rounded up by irate Jewish leaders after James was killed and cast adrift in a small boat on the coast of Caesarea by the Jewish Sanhedrin. Their boat was without sails or oars. They were left to drift with the wind and currents, unharmed until they arrived at Cyrene, a port on the Mediterranean Sea. Upon arriving in that port, the castaways were able to obtain sails and oars and the little party of refugees followed the trade route of the Phoenician and Israelite merchant ships ending up as far west as Massilia

(Marseilles), France. According to Cardinal Baronius, the following people accompanied Joseph of Arimathea on the voyage, "The two Bethany sisters, Mary and Martha, their brother Lazarus, Eutropius, Salome, Cleon, Saturninus, Mary Magdalene, Marcella (the maid of the Bethany sisters), Maxim (or Maximin), Martial, Trophimus (Restitutus, the man who was born blind). Mary, the mother of Jesus, undoubtedly was not left behind." (Capt, 37)

Roger of Hovedon (AD 1174–1201), in the *English Chronicler,* further confirms the event, "Marseilles is an episcopal church [meaning the church was administered by bishops, not the name of a denomination] under the dominion of the King of Aragon. Here are the relics of Lazarus…who held the position of Bishop for seven years after Jesus had restored him from the dead." (51) The Catholic Church for over a thousand years has accepted the presence of these individuals in France before the time of the Catholic Church.

The *Chronicler* further agrees that some of the party of the refugees actually settled in France, while Joseph of Arimathea, Mary, the mother of Christ, and eleven other companions crossed France to the Atlantic coast of Britain. They were following the well-known Phoenician trade routes to Britain as described by Diodorus Siculus. This route would have taken them through the country of the Lemovices to the seacoast in Brittany at Vannes or Morlaix. From Morlaix, according to one story, the refugees sailed to Falmouth, England, before continuing on to their final destination in Cornwall, where modern-day Glastonbury is located.

Since Joseph of Arimathea was well acquainted with Glastonbury because of his previous years in the area, it was the logical place for him and his companions to choose as their final destination. When Joseph and his party arrived in Glastonbury, they were met by King Arviragus of the Silurian Dynasty of Britain. This king was the son of King Cunobelinus (the Cymbeline of William Shakespeare) and cousin to the renowned British warrior Caradoc, who became the first Christian king in Britain, whom the Romans called Caractacus. Undoubtedly King Arviragus and Joseph knew each other because of Joseph's business dealings as a metal merchant for the Romans in earlier years.

King Arviragus is recorded as having granted to Joseph and his followers "twelve hides" of land which is about 1900 acres "tax free" in "Ynis-witrin" described as a "marshy tract." We now know this has been identified as the "Isles of Avon." Confirmation of this royal charter is found in the official *Doomsday Book* of Britain written in AD 1086. In the *Doomsday Book*, the following statement is made, "The Domus Dei in the great monastery of Glastonbury called the secret of the Lord. This Glastonbury church possesses in its own villa "XII Hides of Land which have never paid tax." (*Doomsday Survey Folio,* 49b)

This notable act of King Arviragus gave these recipients many British concessions including the right of citizenship with its privilege to pass unmolested from one district to another in the time of war. The grant was given using the following terms, "To the Judean Refugees." It should be noted that 1086 AD is not the date the *Doomsday Book* was first written, but it represents the date on which the Norman King William had all the historic events recorded within the ancient book, rechecked and brought up to date to include his reign as King of England. The king's historians used the original source of information which was found in the *Anglo-Saxon Chronicles,* preserved today in the British Museum. Part of the *Anglo-Saxon Chronicles* overlap the period of the Doomsday Book.

Further confirmation of this Land Grant is found in the writings of William Malmesbury, the historian of Glastonbury noted for the accuracy of his works. He wrote this document in 1126 AD as an account of "The Writings of the Ancients," which he said was found in the Glastonbury Abbey, later destroyed in 1184 AD.

NEW SETTLEMENT IN GLASTONBURY

According to William Malmesbury, the records of the Abbey at Glastonbury make the following statement, "These holy men built a chapel of the form that had been shown them. The walls were of 'osiers' wattled together." This is a description of a building common for that day. The building was built using timbers and pillars for the framework. After the framework was constructed, the building was sealed in, both inside and out, with a combination of straw and clay, and the roof was thatched with reeds. Often these buildings were painted or white-washed with lime to improve their appearance and help them to withstand the most inclement weather. Even castles in those days were built of the same material. Giraldus Cambrenisis, while speaking of the Pembroke Castle, wrote, "Arnulphus De Montgomery, in the days of Henry I (1068–1135 AD), built a small castle of twigs and slight turf." (Capt, 43)

As a result of gaining legal title to the land in Glastonbury, granted them by King Arviragus, Joseph and his companions built huts for themselves and Mary who accompanied Joseph to Britain. This undoubtedly was the site of the first Christian church to be erected above ground, away from Judea. Further proof of the construction is shown by F. Bligh Bond, a member of the Somerset Archaeological Society and former director of excavations at Glastonbury Abbey. He confirms that the building and surrounding community were made of mud, twigs and beams of wood. His excavations indicate that the first community was circular in nature with twelve huts, one for each of the members of the party. Excavations prove that all the buildings were enclosed in a circular stockade, possibly to keep out wild animals. It is also believed by the Somerset archaeologists and historians that, in the center of the compound, was a building that may have actually been built by the hands of Christ Himself, perhaps in earlier years when He was there.

Testimony of this early church in Glastonbury is in a letter written by Augustine to Pope Gregory in 600 AD as follows, "In the western confines of Britain, there is a certain royal island of large extent, surrounded by water, abounding in all the beauties of nature and the necessities of life. In it, the first neophites of Catholic law, God beforehand acquainted them, before a church constructed by no human art, but by the hands of Christ Himself for the salvation of His people."

In this letter from Augustine, we are not absolutely sure whether his words "constructed by no human art" referred to a building erected by Jesus during His years in England before age 30, or to the fact that the Glastonbury Christian community was established on a "doctrinal foundation" laid by Christ Himself. However, at that point, the original wattle building would have been over 500 years old. If it still existed, this would be a remarkable age for such a structure of such material. The admission of this early origin of the British Church by the Roman Church is a remarkable testimony to the fact that it existed.

The English historian, Bede (672–735 AD), in his *Ecclesiastical History of the English Nation* gives this account of the faith of the British Church before the coming of Augustine: "For they did not keep Easter Sunday at the proper time, but from the fourteenth to the twentieth moon which computation is contained in a revolution of 84 years. Besides, they did several other things which were against the unity of the Church... After a long disputation, they did not comply with the entreaties, exhortations or rebukes of Augustine and his companion, but preferred their own traditions before all the churches in the world... They could not depart from the ancient customs without consent of their people."

In this statement by Bede, he is obviously referring to the Passover Season, which begins with the fourteenth and ends with the sunset on the twenty-first day of the month.

Easter was a perversion of Passover. Easter began to be observed in the Roman Church after the departure and death of the original apostles and disciples. It was in 325 AD at the direction of Constantine that the Roman Church could no longer celebrate Passover, but would only observe his pagan religious celebration, Easter, named after the pagan Chaldean goddess, "Ishtar."

According to the record of the Angles, the wattle church was called by them the "Ealde Churche" or "Old Church." According to the Angles, the church was encased with boards and covered with lead by St. Paulinus in 624–644 AD, who was the Archbishop of York and afterwards the Bishop of Rochester. Later, a stone church was erected over it and the old church was thus preserved intact inside. The wattle church became known as the "Culdee Church" or "Church of the Refugees."

The word "Christian" is a composite of the Greek and Hebrew word for "Christ," and is the Greek word meaning "consecrated" and "ian" is from the Hebrew word "ain" meaning a person or people. The settlers in Glastonbury were not called *Christians* because that word was unknown to those of Britain in the early ages.

In the ancient British triads, Joseph and his twelve companions were referred to as "Culdees" as were Paul, Peter, Lazarus, Simon Zelotes, Aristobulus and others. However, the name "Culdee" was not known outside of Britain; therefore, it could only have been assigned to those who had actually dwelt in the Celtic British area of Glastonbury. In later years, the name "Culdee" took even greater significance emphasizing the fact that the Culdee Christian Church was the first and original church of the Christian faith on the earth. This title rested upon the early British church for centuries and, even after the name died out in favor of the more popular name of Christian.

PREACHING THE GOSPEL

It is noteworthy to see how the early settlers in southwest Britain spread the message entrusted to them by Christ with great zeal. In fact, in the face of constant harassment and raids by the heathen Saxons, the true disciples carried out their mission with great zeal and vigor.

The first converts of the Culdees were the Druids of Britain who had no difficulty in reconciling the teachings of the Culdees with their own teaching of the Resurrection and Inheritance of Eternal Life. Many writers have noted the remarkable coincidence which existed between the two systems, Druidism and Christianity. Before the introduction of Christianity to Britain, the Druids made reference to the Supreme God as "Distributor, Governor, The Wonderful, The Ancient of Days," and terms of the Old Testament origins which had been handed down to them after the breakup of Israel in 720 BC.

Support for the movement of Joseph of Arimathea and his companions shortly after the Resurrection is found in several sources. Tertullian (155–222 AD) is the earliest of the writers and only possibly surpassed by Augustine concerning the church in the west. Tertullian makes the following statement, "The extremities of Spain, the various parts of Gaul, the regions of Britain which have never been penetrated by Roman arms have received the religion of Christ."

The great historian, Eusebius, (260–340 AD) who is considered the father of Ecclesiastical History, wrote the following, "The apostles passed beyond the oceans to the isles called the Britannic Isles." St. Hillary of Pottiers, another historian, (300–367 AD) wrote, "Afterwards the apostles built several tabernacles, and through all the parts of the earth wherever it was possible to go, even in the isles of the oceans, they built several habitations for God."

Another historian and religious leader in Gaul, Arnobius the Younger, about 400 AD wrote, "So swiftly runs the word of God that within the space of a few years, His word is concealed neither from the Indians in the east, nor from the Britons in the west." Chrysostom (347–407 AD) wrote in his *Sermo De Utilit*, "The British Isles which are beyond the sea and which lie in the ocean have received virtue of the word. Churches are there found and altars erected.... Though thou shouldst go to the ocean, to the British Isles, there thou shouldst hear all men everywhere discoursing matters out of the scriptures with another voice indeed, but not another faith, with a different tongue, but the same judgment."

Church historians essentially agree that the dates for the establishment of the church in England by Joseph of Arimathea was about 36–39 AD. They also agree that it was the first Christian Church to be built above ground and was done so in approximately 39–41 AD. The Roman Catholic hierarchy was not officially founded until circa 350 AD under the guidance of Constantine. The first Christian Church above ground in Rome is dated 56 AD when Paul dedicated the home of Palatium Britaanicus of the British Royal Princess Claudia and her husband Rufus Pudentius.

When Paul arrived in Rome, he ordained Linus, the brother of Claudia and the son of Caractacus, the British Monarch, to be the first bishop to the Christian Church in Rome. Peter affirms the fact in his The Apostolic Constitutions, "Concerning those bishops who have been ordained in our lifetime, we make known to you they are these: Of Antioch, Eudius, ordained by me, Peter; Linus, brother of Claudia, first ordained by Paul and after Linus' death, Clements the Second, ordained by Peter."

Confirmation of Linus becoming the first Bishop of Rome is found in two other sources: Irenaeus, Bishop of Lyons, 180 AD, who was personally acquainted with the first church in Rome wrote, "The apostles have founded and built the Church at Rome and committed the ministry of its supervision to Linus. This is the Linus mentioned by Paul in his Epistle to Timothy." The *Encyclopedia Britannica* names Linus as the first bishop of Rome. It is believed Linus was baptized and confirmed as a true Christian in Britain, possibly by Joseph of Arimathea, long before being taken hostage with Caractacus back to Rome (circa 51 AD). If so, then the Church of Rome had its roots in the Culdee Church of Britain.

One cannot escape the fact that so many historical records confirm that the first church building erected above ground was, in fact, the one in Glastonbury. From this seat of Christianity in the British Isles, the followers of Christ and the companions of Joseph of Arimathea began their assigned task of going to the lost sheep of Israel before it ever began to be spread among the Gentiles. From the very beginning, we can understand that Christ, as the head of His Church, made sure that it did not die at its infancy. Notice the statement He made to Peter and the Apostles in Matthew 16:18, "And I say also unto thee, That thou art Peter, and upon this rock I will build my church; and the gates of hell shall not prevail against it."

In spite of the fact that the anti-Christian Jews and their followers thought they were destroying this *new* Christian movement, they, in fact, facilitated the spreading of the true *gospel* to the *lost sheep of Israel*. The fact that the very first Christian Church to be erected above ground was founded in Britain is further proof of the British people being the modern-day descendants of the ancient Israelites. In Leviticus 26:11, God promised to put his tabernacle, or his church within the boundaries of Israel, "I will set my tabernacle among you and my soul shall not abhor you."

On the day Christ was crucified, the veil separating the holy of holies in the temple in Jerusalem was torn from top to bottom at the exact moment of His death. This tearing of the veil signified God withdrawing from the land of the Jews and the temple that stood in Jerusalem. The temple was soon destroyed after this in 70 AD by the Roman legions led by Titus.

God promised He would keep a tabernacle dwelling in Israel and sure enough a building was constructed in England near Glastonbury based on the same dimensions as the temple in Jerusalem. And as Israel (Ephraim and Manasseh) separated from each other to grow and prosper, they carried the message of Christ to the heathen world. Most of the evangelizing of the world emanates from the United States of America. God indeed did place His tabernacle among us, expecting us to teach the world God's way.

2520 YEARS

After God saved Israel from slavery in Egypt, He revealed to them through His servant Moses why He had saved them and what He had planned for their future.

As the Israelites departed Egypt on the fifteenth day of the first month, Passover, they came to an area called Mt. Sinai on the fifteenth day of the second month. (Exodus 16:1) Archaeologists have now discovered that Mount Sinai is in Saudi Arabia. So, indeed the children of Israel did cross the Red Sea, and not the Sea of Reeds, as we have been told by some trying to debunk the idea that God was strong enough to hold back the strong waters of the Red Sea. The crossing occurred near where the Gulf of Aqaba has a small jut-out leading to an undersea ledge that is about midway down the length of the Gulf of Aqaba. Books have been written and films have been made proving this such as *The Gold of Exodus* by Howard Blum and *The Exodus Case* by L. Moller. .

The Israelites remained camped near Mt. Sinai for an additional month and, in the third month, God told Moses to prepare the people to receive a proposal from God—an agreement between them and Himself. God revealed to Moses that the Israelites were a people He treasured above all other people on the earth. Notice the statement in Exodus 19:5, "Now therefore, if ye will obey my voice indeed, and keep my covenant, then ye shall be a peculiar treasure unto me above all people: for all the earth is mine:"

In verse 6, God reveals to the Israelites their destiny which He desired they should fulfill. "And ye shall be unto me a kingdom of priests, and an holy nation. These are the words which thou shalt speak unto the children of Israel." In this verse, God told the Israelites that He wanted them to be a people who would teach others how they should live according to the standards God set forth; He intended that the Israelites should live by these standards as an *example to the entire world.* When the people heard that God had chosen them and intended to bless them above all other peoples of the earth, they quickly answered that they were willing to do whatever God requested of them in Exodus 19:8, "And all the people answered together, and said, All that the LORD hath spoken we will do. And Moses returned the words of the people unto the LORD."

When God heard that the people were willing to enter into this agreement, or *covenant,* He told Moses that He would come down to the people in a great cloud and speak directly to them the words of the agreement. Exodus 19:10–11, "And the LORD said unto Moses, Go unto the people, and sanctify them to day and to morrow, and let them wash their clothes, And be ready against the third day: for the third day the LORD will come down in the sight of all the people upon mount Sinai."

On the third day, God began speaking to the Israelites.

And it came to pass on the third day in the morning, that there were thunders and lightnings, and a thick cloud upon the mount, and the voice of the trumpet exceeding loud; so that all the people that were in the camp trembled. And Moses brought forth the people out of the camp to meet with God; and they stood at the nether part of the mount. And mount Sinai was altogether on a smoke, because the LORD descended upon it in fire: and the smoke thereof ascended as the smoke of a furnace, and the whole mount quaked greatly. And when the voice of the trumpet sounded long, and waxed louder and louder, Moses spake, and God answered him by a voice. And the LORD came down upon mount Sinai, on the top of the mount: and the LORD called Moses up to the top of the mount; and Moses went up. (Exodus 19:16–20)

God revealed the *terms of the agreement* which are covered in Exodus 20:3–17. In these verses are the Ten Commandments; these commandments established a *rule of law* by which the Israelites were to live in order to fulfill their part of the covenant agreement between them and the Eternal God. After hearing the Ten Commandments directly from God, the people agreed to keep them as the national standard for all of their laws and their way of life. When the people heard God's voice, they became very afraid when the ground shook as God spoke to them out of the cloud. In fact, they begged Moses to become God's spokesman to pass on the information from God directly to them because of their great fear of God. God and Moses agreed to this request and God, from that point on, dealt directly with Moses who then conveyed God's Words to the people.

BLESSINGS AND CURSES

The Covenant God made with the Israelites included numerous physical and national blessings He would shower upon the Israelites for their obedience to the covenant agreement. Notice the blessings.

> If ye walk in my statutes, and keep my commandments, and do them; Then I will give you rain in due season, and the land shall yield her increase, and the trees of the field shall yield their fruit. And your threshing shall reach unto the vintage, and the vintage shall reach unto the sowing time: and ye shall eat your bread to the full, and dwell in your land safely. And I will give peace in the land, and ye shall lie down, and

none shall make you afraid: and I will rid evil beasts out of the land, neither shall the sword go through your land. And ye shall chase your enemies, and they shall fall before you by the sword. And five of you shall chase an hundred, and an hundred of you shall put ten thousand to flight: and your enemies shall fall before you by the sword. For I will have respect unto you, and make you fruitful, and multiply you, and establish my covenant with you. And ye shall eat old store, and bring forth the old because of the new. And I will set my tabernacle among you: and my soul shall not abhor you. And I will walk among you, and will be your God, and ye shall be my people. I am the LORD your God, which brought you forth out of the land of Egypt, that ye should not be their bondmen; and I have broken the bands of your yoke, and made you go upright. (Leviticus 26:3–13)

These blessings sum up every human need. If the people followed the Ten Commandments, they would have peace, prosperity and happiness. God intended to use the Israelites and their blessings as a *model* to entice the Gentile world to reject the ways of the world's religions and Satan. This is why God said that the Israelites were to be a kingdom of kings and priests to act as the guides to all people of the world to lead them to God; then all people would also enjoy the blessings of the Covenant.

These blessings are only physical blessings. God did not promise the Israelites eternal life by simply keeping the conditions of the original covenant. The covenant was expanded under the New Testament to receive the blessings of the original covenant and to include the ultimate blessing of *eternal life* as a king and priest in the Kingdom of God at Christ's Return.

These Covenant Blessings are available to anyone or any group of people who will follow to the best of their ability the laws as stated by the Ten Commandments

THE CURSE OF DISOBEDIENCE

It wasn't long until the Israelites began to break the conditions of the covenant between themselves and God. As a result of breaking the agreement (covenant), the Israelites faced the penalties. These penalties are described in Deuteronomy 28:15–68.

In Leviticus 26, we find essentially the same penalties mentioned in Deuteronomy 28, but there is a time frame attached to the length of God's Punishment. Just like a criminal who is convicted and receives a punishment for a number of years in prison, God warned the Israelites in the very beginning that, if they did not live up to the covenant agreement, not only would they be punished, but He would withhold the blessings for a particular number of years, after which they would once again be blessed.

> But if ye will not hearken unto me, and will not do all these commandments; And if ye shall despise my statutes, or if your soul abhor my judgments, so that ye will not do all my commandments, but that ye break my covenant: I also will do this unto you; I will even appoint over you terror, consumption, and the burning ague, that shall consume the eyes, and cause sorrow of heart: and ye shall sow your seed in vain, for your enemies shall eat it. And I will set my face against you, and ye shall be slain before your enemies: they that hate you shall reign over you; and ye shall flee when none pursueth you. (Leviticus 26:14–15)

These punishments, or curses, would come in stages or waves. God did not punish them just to hurt them; He did so in order for them to stop and realize they needed to change or repent. In the beginning, the punishments were relatively mild, but as the Israelites continued to break the agreement of the covenant, the punishments became more severe until finally, God removed them out of their own land. But, that is not the end of the story.

PUNISHMENT FOR A TIME

We have seen how Israel was punished and dispersed from their homeland, but God always knew where they were, even if they had forgotten. Leviticus 26 gave a specific number of years that God would punish Israel for their sins. Notice Leviticus 26:18, "And if ye will not yet for all this hearken unto me, then I will punish you seven times more for your sins."

"Seven times" is a prophetic utterance or a code God uses to identify a period of time. "Times" refers to years. This same use of the word *time* or *times* can be found in Daniel 12:7 referring to the length of the time that the end-time beast power will rule the world.

> And I heard the man clothed in linen, which was upon the waters of the river, when he held up his right hand and his left hand unto heaven, and sware by him that liveth for ever that it shall be for a time, times, and an half; and when he shall have accomplished to scatter the power of the holy people, all these things shall be finished. (Daniel 12:7)

In the phrase "Time, times and a half," *time* means one year, *times* means two years and *a half* means one-half year. This is God's way of expressing to those who have "an ear to hear" that the great beast power will rule for three and a half years. This is further proved in Revelation 12:14, when He promises that people living in our time who have agreed to live by the covenant of God will be protected for a time, times and a half time from the face of the serpent and the Beast Power. This equates to 3½ years. Revelation 13:5 identifies the time, times and a half time as also equated to forty-two months.

However, in Leviticus 26 the term "seven" times does not mean seven years of punishment. In this case, the seven times refers to *many days* and each day equals a year. In this prophecy, God says that the punishment will last seven years of prophetic years. A prophetic year has 360 days in it. This is exactly the same use of prophetic years as is used in Daniel 9:24, in determining the exact time of the crucifixion of Jesus Christ.

Seven prophetic years equate to 2520 days. In this case, we know that Israel was defeated, captured and removed from the land in the year 721–720 BC. We know from historical facts that the Israelites lost their identity and did not return on the scene after seven short years to begin anew to receive God's blessings. Therefore, by expanding our thought processes to allow a day to equal a year of the 2520 days expressed in the Seven Times Prophecy, we then arrive at 2520 years of punishment. God intended to punish the Northern Ten Tribes of Israel 2520 years before He would again bless their descendants in the manner listed in Leviticus 26 and Deuteronomy 28.

By subtracting 720 BC years, which represents the date the Israelites went into captivity, from 2520 years, we come to the period beginning the nineteenth century with the year 1800.

THE NINETEENTH CENTURY

History leads us to an inescapable fact. In the late 1700s and early 1800s, the British Empire enjoyed its greatest expansion and became the world's greatest empire since Rome. In fact, the Empire of Britain was far greater than the Roman Empire because it was said that the vast holdings of the British Empire extended to so many corners of the world that "the sun never set on the great British Empire." It was during the Nineteenth Century (the 1800s) that Britain and its naval forces ruled the seas of the world and continued to do so into the Twentieth Century (1900s) and into World War I.

During this period, Britain established colonies all over the world and became a financial powerhouse, which even to this day allows her to exercise much influence over world affairs. The British monarchy became the most powerful monarchy the world had ever seen, and the English people came into the Industrial Revolution of the Nineteenth Century far more advanced than all other nations. During the American Civil War of the 1800s, England continued to be the most powerful industrial nation on the face of the earth. England was able to supply much of the capital and equipment used by both sides in the American Civil War. The British navy was undisputed in its rule over the seas of the world.

The results of British rule can be seen in such faraway places as Japan. Have you ever wondered why the Japanese follow the same traffic rules as the British? The Japanese build their cars for their own consumption with the steering wheel on the right hand side just as the British. The fact is, during the Nineteenth Century, England was responsible for developing Japan into a great industrial nation, pulling her out of the Dark Ages which was so widespread in the Far East.

During the Nineteenth Century, Great Britain became the greatest power the world had ever seen.

The United States, even though insignificant as far as world power was concerned, also had a tremendous growth spurt with the purchase of the vast Mid-American territory known as the Louisiana Purchase in April 1803.

The authors of a recent college edition of American History, entitled *Nations of Nations*, Volume I to 1877, made the following observations.

> Thomas Jefferson was the president of the United States and he recognized the importance of the Mississippi River to western interests. The fact that Spain's New World Empire was disintegrating toward the end of the 1700's, he was confident that it would not be long before the New United States would gain control of Florida and the rest of the Mississippi area either through purchases or military occupation.
>
> Unfortunately, this comforting prospect was shattered when Spain secretly ceded Louisiana—the territory lying between the Mississippi River and the Rocky Mountains—to France. France had just

recently emerged from its own revolution in the late 1700's under a new young military commander by the name of Napoleon Bonaparte. Under his rule, France had become the most powerful nation on the European continent, with military might to protect its new colonies and stop the American expansion in the American continent to the West. American anxiety intensified when Spain, while in control of Louisiana, suddenly revoked America's rights to navigate the lower Mississippi River which was guaranteed by the Pinckney Treaty some years earlier. Western farmers who were suddenly denied access to the sea through the Mississippi angrily protested Spain's high-handed action. As if this were not enough, word came that Spanish officials dangling the bait of access to the Mississippi River were attempting to disrupt the New United States by attracting the western settlers into the Spanish dominated territory west of the Mississippi.

Thomas Jefferson, recognizing the potential problem facing the new nation, sent James Monroe to Paris to join Robert Livingston, an American minister, to negotiate the purchase of New Orleans and West Florida from the French. Jefferson made the following statement: "There is on the globe one single spot, the possession (i.e. possessor) of which is our natural and habitual enemy. It is New Orleans." Jefferson noted that should they fail to acquire the city, he instructed them to seek an alliance with Great Britain whose navy offered the only possible protection. "The Day that France takes New Orleans, we must marry ourselves to the British fleet and nation," he observed with a notable lack of enthusiasm.

In the meantime, Napoleon continued to have difficulty with Britain and other European nations and lost interest in Louisiana. With war looming in Europe, he desperately needed money, so in April 1803, he offered to sell not only New Orleans, but also all of Louisiana to the United States. The French offered to sell the Louisiana Territory to the Americans for the paltry sum of

$15,000,000. History records this proposal flabbergasted Livingston and Monroe. Their instructions said nothing about acquiring all of Louisiana and they certainly had not been authorized to spend what the French demanded. On the other hand, here was an unprecedented opportunity to dramatically expand the boundaries of the United States westward.

The millions of acres of fertile farmland, untold natural resources and control of the vital Mississippi River and its tributaries was one of the most extraordinary bargains in the history of the United States. In one fell swoop, the American negotiators had doubled the country's size, adding some 830,000 square miles. Livingston asserted, "The United States take their place among the powers of the first rank of nations." This unbelievable event came about at the end of the 2520 years of punishment God had declared the Israelites must complete before He would open His Hands and begin blessing the modern-day descendants of the ancient Israelites.

WHEN GOD MAKES A PROMISE, HE ALWAYS KEEPS IT!

To tie the blessings of God to Israel, we must first understand that God promised His blessings irrevocably to the Patriarchs, starting with Abraham before Israel actually became a nation. As we recall, in Genesis 22, Abraham proved to God, without a shadow of a doubt, His obedience and willingness to follow God no matter what! In return, God made an astounding promise He would not go back on.

Notice verse 16, after God stopped Abraham from killing his son, Isaac, the sworn statement of a promise God made to Abraham and his descendants.

> And said, By myself have I sworn, saith the LORD, for because thou hast done this thing, and hast not withheld thy son, thine only son: That in blessing I will bless thee, and in multiplying I will multiply thy seed as the stars of the heaven, and as the sand which is

upon the sea shore; and thy seed shall possess the gate
of his enemies; And in thy seed shall all the nations
of the earth be blessed; because thou hast obeyed my
voice. (Genesis 22:16–18)

At this point, the promise God made to Abraham was unconditional and He would accomplish it in spite of the fact that neither
Abraham nor his immediate descendants would live long enough
to receive it. The last part of verse 17 is especially interesting where
God promises that Abraham's descendants would ultimately control
the "gates of their enemies" in times of great trouble and warfare.

THE UNITED STATES OF AMERICA AND GREAT BRITAIN ARE BROTHERS

The Israelites come from Isaac through his son, Jacob. Remember,
Abraham also had another son, Ishmael, through a handmaiden
and one whom God would not recognize to carry on Abraham's
line for the special people God would call. Ishmael is the father of
the Arabs. Isaac, the other son, was the line through which Israel
and another group of people would emerge. Isaac also had two sons,
Esau and Jacob. Esau counted his birthright as nothing and sold
it to Jacob for a mere bowl of soup. Esau became the father of the
Biblical Edomites, the modern-day Palestinians. Genesis 25 identifies Esau as the father of Edom.

Jacob, on the other hand, is the patriarch from whom only the
Israelites came!

> Jacob's name was changed to *Israel*. And he said, Thy
> name shall be called no more Jacob, but Israel: for as a
> prince hast thou power with God and with men, and
> hast prevailed." His name meant "a prince from God,"
> which now established the new name by which his
> descendants would be called. (Genesis 32:28)

Jacob had twelve sons. His favorite son was next to the youngest, Joseph, who was Israel's firstborn son of his beloved wife,

Rachel. Rachel died giving birth to her second and Israel's last son, Benjamin, Joseph's brother. As Joseph grew, his brothers became very jealous of him and sold him into Egyptian slavery. He emerged some years later to rescue his aged father, Israel, and his brothers. Israel and Joseph were reunited in Egypt. After some years, it became obvious that Israel was about to die.

I have mentioned this earlier, but I want to emphasize just how important it is by again bringing it to your attention. Before Israel died, he requested that Joseph bring his two sons, Ephraim and Manasseh, to him. The events listed in Genesis 48 are overlooked by almost everyone in the world, including all of the great religions. The failure to understand these verses causes modern-day Israel to be unaware of its real identity. Genesis 48:5 gives the account of Israel adopting Joseph's two sons, Ephraim and Manasseh, and placing his name (Israel) upon them.

Notice, Joseph brought his two sons, Ephraim and Manasseh, to the elderly Israel and the events that followed.

> And Israel beheld Joseph's sons, and said, Who are these? And Joseph said unto his father, They are my sons, whom God hath given me in this place. And he said, Bring them, I pray thee, unto me, and I will bless them. Now the eyes of Israel were dim for age, so that he could not see. And he brought them near unto him; and he kissed them, and embraced them. And Israel said unto Joseph, I had not thought to see thy face: and, lo, God hath shewed me also thy seed. And Joseph brought them out from between his knees, and he bowed himself with his face to the earth. And Joseph took them both, Ephraim in his right hand toward Israel's left hand, and Manasseh in his left hand toward Israel's right hand, and brought them near unto him. And Israel stretched out his right hand, and laid it upon Ephraim's head, who was the younger, and his left hand upon Manasseh's head, guiding his hands wittingly; for Manasseh was the firstborn. And

he blessed Joseph, and said, God, before whom my fathers Abraham and Isaac did walk, the God which fed me all my life long unto this day, The Angel which redeemed me from all evil, bless the lads; and let my name be named on them, and the name of my fathers Abraham and Isaac; and let them grow into a multitude in the midst of the earth. (Genesis 48:8–16)

Notice, Israel said that his name would be the name which Ephraim and Manasseh would be called. He also mentioned that the other tribes would continue to follow the names of their fathers such as Judah, Levi, Simeon, Dan, and so forth, but not "Israel," even though they were part of Israel. The name of Israel was to be applied to the two sons of Joseph *only.*

Israel crossed his hands, placing his right hand on the younger son, Ephraim, and his left hand on the older son, Manasseh. The custom was that the birthright flowed through the right hand and it was always placed upon the head of the oldest. Joseph tried to prevent his father, Israel, from blessing Ephraim above Manasseh.

And when Joseph saw that his father laid his right hand upon the head of Ephraim, it displeased him: and he held up his father's hand, to remove it from Ephraim's head unto Manasseh's head. And Joseph said unto his father, Not so, my father: for this is the firstborn; put thy right hand upon his head. (Genesis 48:17–18)

But, Israel knew exactly what he was doing as he stated, "And his father refused, and said, 'I know it, my son, I know it: he (Manasseh) also shall become a people, and he also shall be *great:* but truly his younger brother (Ephraim) shall be greater than he, and his seed shall become a multitude of nations.'" (Verse 19)

This verse gives us the key to understand which two nations would be called "Israel;" just who would be the descendants of these two sons of Joseph? Notice Israel stated the younger would be far greater than the older, but that the older would also be "great." In fact, he goes on to say that the younger would become a multitude of nations, or states, while the older would become a single great nation. This is a major clue to understand who these two nations are in these modern days. Ephraim was to become a collection of many nation states, and yet he would be far greater than his older brother, who would also be a great nation. In the history of the world, since 1800, there have only been two nations in the world that fulfill this promise. There is the single great nation known as Great Britain and the other greater nation, which is made up of 50 nation-states known as the United States of America.

The United States of America was populated, in the very beginning, on the Eastern Seaboard by immigrants largely from Great Britain and the British isles. The British and the Americans enjoy the same language and many of the same customs. Many British family names are found in America today and especially those of the founding fathers. British Common Law is based upon the Ten Commandments and the Laws found in the Old Testament. Since America came out of Britain, she traces much of her laws and ideals back to her brother country, Manasseh.

In the Nineteenth Century, England was the most civilized country in the world and controlled more territories than any of the ancient empires, including Rome, Babylon and the Chinese dynasties. England was truly a worldwide empire; because England colonized much of the heathen world, many backward, uncivilized nations were introduced to the rule of law and morality based on the Ten Commandments.

ALL THE WORLD HAS BEEN PHYSICALLY BLESSED THROUGH EPHRAIM AND MANASSEH

As we have seen in previous chapters, Christianity was first introduced to England and from there much of Western Europe and the Western Hemisphere received the Truth of God in the form of Bibles.

The King James 1611 Bible continues to be the most popular Bible in the world today. The King James Bible has been the standard for all Bibles. It was England who was responsible for bringing civilization out of the Dark Ages with the publication of the English Bible using the common language of the Sixteenth Century up through the present day. The world was blessed financially and otherwise, just as God had indicated to Abraham would be the case in the latter years. Genesis 22:18, "And in thy seed shall all the nations of the earth be blessed; because thou hast obeyed my voice."

All nations have been blessed who have come in contact with England, even as they became colonies and were ruled over by the British Royal House. The English and Americans have always had a sense of fair play and concern for individual liberty and human rights, unlike the Gentile governments of the world. When you consider the most evil and beast-like leaders the world has ever known, you will not find them in British or American history. They can only be found in the nations of the Gentiles, such as Germany, Japan, China, Russia and many nations of the Middle East, Far East and Africa.

Those Gentile leaders, even today, have little respect for human life and murder more of their own people than most of their enemies have done. It has been said that during the Reign of Terror of Joseph Stalin, he murdered over 30,000,000 of his own Russian countrymen. Adding to that the beast-like qualities of Adolf Hitler in the Twentieth Century, there were lost over 40,000,000 lives due to the actions of these leaders. Never in the history of Britain and America was there ever such a wholesale slaughter of human beings as in the Gentile countries.

To the modern-day Israelites, America and England, human rights, personal liberty and individual freedom rules supreme in their nations and governments. This proclivity existed among the ancient Israelites because it was God that granted them liberty and taught them the need for good human relations through the Laws He gave the Nation of Israel.

Truly, England and America have been the recipients of the blessings God promised Abraham in Genesis 22. England is identified as Manasseh who was the older brother and Ephraim, the younger, is identified as the United States or collection of small nation states brought together under one banner as the Untied States of America. The histories of America and Britain clearly show that the Nineteenth Century belonged to Britain and the Twentieth Century belonged to the United States.

GATES OF THEIR ENEMIES

God's promise to Abraham and then repeated to Isaac's wife, Rebekah, in Genesis 24:60, "And they blessed Rebekah, and said unto her, Thou art our sister, be thou the mother of thousands of millions, and let thy seed possess the gate of those which hate them," was never fulfilled in ancient Israel before they went into captivity in 720 BC, nor in the Southern three tribes of Judah before they went into captivity in 586 BC. Actually, a better translation can be found in *Fenton's Translated Bible* and it reads: "And your race shall possess the gates (plural) of its enemies." As we have said before, the "gates" referred to "of our enemies" are strategic sea gates and/or passes which lead to the entrance and exit from most of those nations that hate us. The fact that actual wealth comes from the ground, prosperity and affluence on a national scale always have come as a result of industry and commerce. Commerce between nations has been transacted almost totally by sea lanes of the world by ship, or with overland transportation systems such as the railroads.

Together, America and Britain have been the recipients of the *promise* of "controlling the gates of their enemies" around the world. Those gates include the Rock of Gibraltar that the English took away from the Spanish in 1704. The Rock of Gibraltar at the mouth of the Mediterranean Sea, made it possible for England to control all traffic in and out of the Mediterranean Sea. On the other end of the Mediterranean, the British built and controlled the Suez Canal, which essentially bottled up its enemies during World War

II. The British had additional control in the Mediterranean Sea area controlling the island of Cyprus, Egypt, Palestine, and wherever the far-flung British Empire extended.

When you consider the need for efficient and fast transportation, one cannot overlook the tremendous invention by Robert Fulton, an American who operated the first steamboat in 1803. This is precisely the same time when Britain and America began to multiply their national wealth. It was also the 1800s that saw the development of railroads in England, and the connecting of the western and eastern seaboard of the United States was completed.

As we have stated before, the *birthright* pertains to the nations that control the gates of their enemies, and we have seen that these gates and passes, such as Gibraltar, Suez, Hong Kong, Singapore, and the Panama Canal belonged to two nations, England and America. Britain and the United States came into possession of every major gate in the world! History clearly reveals that modern-day Israel—the United States of America and Britain—were the controllers of these gates during World War II; these "gates" were not only strategic passes, but the world's greatest fortifications.

Britain did not begin to lose control of the "gates of her enemies" until after World War II when she began to withdraw from her worldwide empire. The latest control point that Britain gave up was the city of Hong Kong, which essentially controlled the finances of China and much of the Far East.

America reached its zenith soon after World War II and the latter years of the Twentieth Century. History clearly reveals how great and powerful and wealthy American and British people became in the Nineteenth and Twentieth Centuries. Most Americans take their wealth and power for granted and believe that it is as a result of only human endeavors and America's form of government. True, the American form of government has encouraged free enterprise and growth. However, other nations that have adopted the same pattern and Constitution have not been as blessed as the American people.

Very few Americans realize that it was God's direct intervention on our behalf that contributed to the great wealth and prosperity of the United States. There is another prophetic scripture in Genesis 39:2 concerning Joseph's descendants, Ephraim and Manasseh, "And the LORD was with Joseph, and he was a prosperous man; and he was in the house of his master the Egyptian." Notice that, while in slavery, Joseph prospered greatly. Notice also verse 23 concerning Joseph's prosperity, even though he was in prison, "The keeper of the prison looked not to any thing that was under his hand; because the LORD was with him, and that which he did, the LORD made it to prosper."

Consider also the prophecy delivered by Moses to the children of Israel concerning what would happen to the tribes in their latter days.

> And of Joseph he said, Blessed of the LORD be his land, for the precious things of heaven, for the dew, and for the deep that coucheth beneath, And for the precious fruits brought forth by the sun, and for the precious things put forth by the moon, And for the chief things of the ancient mountains, and for the precious things of the lasting hills, And for the precious things of the earth and fulness thereof, and for the good will of him that dwelt in the bush: let the blessing come upon the head of Joseph, and upon the top of the head of him that was separated from his brethren. His glory is like the firstling of his bullock, and his horns are like the horns of unicorns: with them he shall push the people together to the ends of the earth: and they are the ten thousands of Ephraim, and they are the thousands of Manasseh. (Deuteronomy 33:13–37)

America (Ephraim) and Britain (Manasseh) are the only two nations in all of history that have been in the possession of the earth's choicest agricultural, mineral deposits and other wealth—the great gold and silver mines, iron, coal and oil, timber and other natural resources. No other nations have fulfilled these prophecies except America and Great Britain!! More than half of all the tillable, usable farm land in the temperate zones of the earth came into production after 1800 and the two great powers of Britain and America controlled the vast majority of it! The rich agricultural lands of the Mississippi Valley and the vast wheat and grain fields of the western United States and Canada are unparalleled in the history of man. Canada, because of its close ties with Great Britain, is part of Manasseh.

The great forest lands of the American northwest and other parts of the American continent produce wood and paper products in a far greater abundance and with more efficiency than any other nation in the world. Paper products in America continue to be the most abundant and the best quality produced in the world today by the most efficient means. Only America has the water, power and forests to support such a huge papermaking enterprise. Paper/wood products continue to be one of America's major exports to all nations of the world. Even though countries like China and Russia and Third World countries have vast land areas with many untapped forests, they do not have all the essentials such as power and water to produce the quantity and quality of paper that the American paper industry is capable of producing. Nearly all of the great growth and wealth in America and Britain came after 1800.

AMERICAN INGENUITY

During the late Nineteenth Century and the early Twentieth Century, America produced more inventions that directly affected the health and well-being of man than any other place on the face of the earth. They were such inventive giants as Alexander Graham Bell, Thomas Edison, Orville and Wilbur Wright, Henry Ford, Harvey Firestone, and the list continues up through the Twentieth Century, including technological geniuses as Bill Gates with his Microsoft Corporation providing the operating systems for 99% of all personal computers produced in the world.

Americans today own more cars per family, bigger homes, more color television sets, computers, refrigerators, dishwashers and washing machines than all the other people in the world combined. America continues to consume more electricity and petroleum products than all the rest of the world put together. The American economy, through its ingenuity and its hard working people, since 1950, has outgrown and become bigger than the rest of the world put together. The state of California alone has an economy greater than most countries of the world. In fact, the economy of California is the sixth largest economy in the world today.

Is this all because we are smarter, more industrious people? Yes, but it was God who blessed us with great minds and uncommon abilities in order to fulfill the promise to Joseph's descendants.

HOW DID WE GET THIS WEALTH?

How did we come to possess all this vast wealth of the earth? Did we acquire it through our own human wisdom? Foresight? Ability to build and produce?

Abraham Lincoln provides us with the answer. "We find ourselves in the peaceful possession of the fairest portion of the earth, as regards fertility of soil, extent of territory and salubrity of climate. We find ourselves the legal inheritors of these fundamental blessings. We toiled not in the acquirement or the establishment of them."

In the dark days of the Civil War, in April of 1863, President Lincoln proclaimed a nation-wide Day of Fasting and Prayer and stated, "It is the duty of nations, as well as men, to owe their dependence upon the over-ruling power of God and to recognize the sublime truth announced in the Holy Scriptures and proven by all History that those nations only are blessed whose God is their LORD.... We have been the recipients of the choicest blessings of heaven, we have been preserved these many years in peace and prosperity. We have grown in numbers, wealth and power as no other nation ever has grown; but we have forgotten God! We have forgotten the gracious hand which preserved us in peace and multiplied and enriched and strengthened us; and we have vainly imagined in the deceitfulness of our hearts, that these blessings were produced by some superior wisdom and virtue of our own."

The location of Britain, surrounded by water, proved to aid her greatly in her defense against enemy intrusions through the Nineteenth Century. The two great oceans that surround America also provided a formidable wall against the Japanese and German empires in World War II in their quest to conquer and rule the world. The Germans and the Japanese, in their diabolical plan, intended to split America at the Mississippi River, with Germany controlling all of the territory east of the Mississippi and Japan controlling all of the territory west of the Mississippi. The two great oceans acted as insurmountable walls protecting the continental United States against German and Japanese invasions.

The historical evidence concerning the massive blessings that America and Britain received in the Nineteenth and Twentieth Centuries further provides irrefutable evidence that we are the two nations who benefited from the blessings God proclaimed to Abraham and his descendants coming through Isaac, Jacob, Joseph and his two sons, Ephraim and Manasseh.

LOCATION OF EPHRAIM AND MANASSEH

Some might argue that Ephraim is England and Manasseh is the United States. However, God has planted Ephraim and Manasseh in the same relationship today as they were in ancient Israel. Manasseh, being the older of the two brothers, was split into two divisions—Manasseh had part of its land mass East of Ephraim and North of Ephraim when settling in the Promised Land. Ephraim also remained as a single tribe just south of the western portion of Manasseh. Today, the two remaining major components of Manasseh are split exactly the same way; Great Britain and Canada, split into two parts and divided by the Atlantic Ocean. The United States however, remains as a single land mass with the

48 states; Alaska and Hawaii were added in the last half of the Twentieth Century.

Manasseh was the older of the two brothers as England is the older of the two nations. England, at no time, has ever equaled the massive political, economic and military power the United States has enjoyed since 1950. The American political and economic power is more far-reaching than the British commonwealth of nations was ever able to achieve. America is a far more numerous people than all of the English-speaking peoples that made up the British Empire, which were Britain, Canada, Australia and New Zealand and the British West Indies. Today the combined numbers of Britain, Canada, Australia and New Zealand are less than half of the number of people living in the 48 contiguous states of the United States of America.

NATIONAL EMBLEMS OF THE BRITISH ROYAL HOUSE

The emblem of the British Royal House also provides more evidence as to the origin of the British Monarchy and the British people. The emblem of the royal house includes the *lion*, the *harp* and the *unicorn*.

The lion finds its origin in the fact that the British Royal House descended from the tribe of Judah and Judah's Emblem was the lion. This is also pointed out in the prophecies of Israel when he spoke regarding each of his sons.

> Judah is a lion's whelp: from the prey, my son, thou art gone up: he stooped down, he couched as a lion, and as an old lion; who shall rouse him up? The sceptre shall not depart from Judah, nor a lawgiver from between his feet, until Shiloh come; and unto him shall the gathering of the people be. (Genesis 49:9–10)

A common phrase used when speaking of Jewish kings in ancient Jerusalem was the *lion of Judah*. The Lion symbolized the ruling house. In fact, the Lion is used to depict royalty in many of the crests of the Royal families of Europe. This verse indicated that Judah would always have a descendant in a position of royalty, exercising authority over Israel as the chief lawgiver and ruler until Shiloh comes. Shiloh, in this case, is referring to Christ Himself when He comes back and occupies the throne of David (Tribe of Judah) at the establishment of God's kingdom on this earth.

The *unicorn* has its original derivative from the bull or oxen which was the emblem (ensign) for the tribe of Ephraim, Manasseh and Benjamin.

The *harp* comes from the fact that the Irish believe that Jeremiah brought the Harp of David as well as the Stone of Destiny when he rescued the daughters of King Zedekiah and brought Tea Tephi to Ireland. The Harp in the Crest represents David's Harp.

Even the Archbishop of Canterbury and the British Royal family are reminded of their Israelite heritage in the coronation prayer which is accompanied with the coronation of every British monarch. The prayer follows:

> The Coronation Prayer:
> O Lord,
> Who by anointing with oil
> Didst of old make and consecrate kings, priests
> and prophets
> To teach and govern the people of Israel,
> Bless and sanctify thy chosen Servant,
> Who by office and ministry is now to be
> Anointed with this oil and Consecrated King
> (or Queen) of this realm.

This prayer has been handed down for untold ages and the origin can only be from the Kings who were crowned over the House of Judah, predating 586 BC.

UNITED STATES EMBLEMS

United States emblems also provide evidence as to our real origins. The Official Seal of the United States is an *eagle* with a cloud above its head, displaying 13 stars. Again, the fact that Joseph was divided into two tribes (Ephraim and Manasseh) accounts for the 13 tribes of the nation of Israel. The great seal indicates the 13 stars for the 13 original colonies, and also America was, in a sense, the thirteenth tribe.

The *cloud* with the stars in it is a representation of the cloud in which God resided as He led the Israelites out of Egypt and through the wilderness for 40 years.

RACIAL CONSIDERATIONS

Many will argue that America is a melting pot of many people and not just Angle-Saxon ancestry. This is true, but one must also consider that ancient Israel was never made up of a single race of people.

Throughout the history of Israel, many strangers came to dwell in the land and they could become naturalized citizens of Israel by following the directives listed in Exodus 12. Israel was never a pure breed of people because of their intermarrying with non-Israelites and a mixing of the peoples who ultimately made up Israel. Just as ancient Israel had other races living among them, today America and Britain represent much of the same mixture that the nation of Israel did before it was taken into captivity circa 720 BC.

However, the original thirteen colonies were primarily settled by people of Anglo-Saxon derivatives.

PROPHECY FOR ISRAEL

Most of the prophecies of the Old Testament are directed toward Israel. In most cases, the only time other nations are mentioned in the Old Testament is when they come in contact with the Israelites. When you read the prophecies of the Old Testament, you can't help but notice the prophecies for Israel are dealing with the two modern-day descendants of the Tribes of Ephraim and Manasseh. As we have shown in previous chapters, Israel placed his family name only on his two grandsons, Ephraim and Manasseh.

> And now thy two sons, Ephraim and Manasseh, which were born unto thee in the land of Egypt before I came unto thee into Egypt, are mine; as Reuben and Simeon, they shall be mine. (Verse 16) ...bless the lads; and *let my name be named on them,* and the name of my fathers Abraham and Isaac; and let them grow into a multitude in the midst of the earth. (Genesis 48:5, 16)

In the preceding chapters, we have proved with the preponderance of evidence that Great Britain and America essentially are composed of Caucasian Anglo-Saxon people who are the modern-day tribes of Ephraim and Manasseh, or as the Bible calls them—Israel!!!

UNDERSTANDING PROPHECY

Unless a student of Bible prophecy can accept the fact that Great Britain and America are truly the modern-day Israelites, prophecy cannot be understood. The reason the religious world misunderstands prophecy is because they have ignored the overwhelming facts that America and Britain make up the modern-day Israelites. Granted, the majority of the other tribes now reside in Western Europe, while many of the Jews (Judah) have returned to the Middle East, calling themselves "Israel."

We go on record as of the publishing of this book that America, Britain and several of her commonwealth states such as Canada do represent the modern-day Israelites prophetically spoken of in the pages of Old Testament prophecies. This knowledge, of course, begs the question as to the remaining tribes of Israel and where they are presently located.

THE OTHER TRIBES

The whole House of Israel was actually composed of thirteen tribes because Joseph received a double portion of the inheritance in that Ephraim and Manasseh were adopted by Jacob (Israel).

The location of the modern-day settlements of the remaining eleven tribes have also been located, based on the unique proclivities of those peoples identified by Jacob in Genesis 49. Notice, Jacob indicated that these people would display certain traits in the last days, which could be used to identify them just before the Return of Jesus Christ. Genesis 49:1, "And Jacob called unto his sons, and said, Gather yourselves together, that I may tell you that which shall befall you *in the last days*."

Extensive research was conducted in the Mid-twentieth Century by church historian, Dr. Herman Hoeh, in his two-volume book, *The Compendium,* using the proclivities as described in Genesis 49. A brief summary of Dr. Hoeh's findings concerning the location of the remaining eleven tribes will be included in the light of Genesis 49.

REUBEN

Genesis 49:3–4, "Reuben, thou art my firstborn, my might, and the beginning of my strength, the excellency of dignity, and the excellency of power: Unstable as water, thou shalt not excel; because thou wentest up to thy father's bed; then defiledst thou it: he went up to my couch."

Reuben was the eldest son of Jacob and much was said about him in Genesis 37:12–35. These scriptures describe the events that took place when Jacob's other sons made the decision to kill Joseph. It was Reuben who intervened to prevent Joseph's death. The Bible also shows that Reuben was not party to the selling of Joseph into slavery and that he intended to rescue Joseph and return him to his father, Israel.

The Biblical account indicates Reuben had good intentions, but it also shows one of his major weak points. The fact that Reuben's goal was to rescue Joseph was good, but he lacked the follow-through to implement Joseph's rescue. The proclivity of Reuben to wander away from the urgent crisis which required his full attention gives us a clue to his modern-day descendants. Even though Reuben, being the oldest, was not willing to participate in the plot against Joseph, he did join his brothers in deceiving Jacob about how Joseph supposedly was killed.

Many years later, guilt spread among the brothers because of what they had done to Joseph. According to Genesis 42:18–23, Reuben essentially told his brothers, "I told you so." They had guilty feelings. This account confirms that, while Reuben still recalled his good intentions, he never had the determination to act on them. These accounts of Reuben's inability to stand up for what was right proved that he was willing to cave in when pressured or intimidated by his peers. It shows that Reuben preferred to grudgingly coexist with something he opposed instead of confronting the evil at hand.

Genesis 35:22 indicates that Reuben had great physical appetites and had difficulty in controlling his sexual urges. Reuben had sexual relations with Bilhah, his father's concubine, the mother of Reuben's own half-brothers, Dan and Naphtali.

Reuben was the firstborn and he ordinarily would have received the birthright blessing, but because of his uncontrolled sexual appetites, God inspired Israel to pass the birthright promise to Joseph, firstborn of the wife of his first love, Rachel.

The Reubenites lived in Gilead with Gad and half of the tribe of Manasseh, east of the Jordan River. They were carried away in the Assyrian captivity years before the fall of Samaria circa 721 BC. When the Assyrian Empire fell, many of the liberated Israelites who were still part of the Assyrian Empire migrated northward into southern Russia. However, not all of the Reubenites migrated into southern Russia, but many remained with their brothers, Manasseh, and migrated with them northwesterly across Europe, ending up where they reside today. Genesis 49:4 indicates that Reuben's descendants would be as unstable as water in all things and that they would have great sexual appetites.

There is only one nation in Western Europe that fits the mold of those identified as Reubenites and that is the nation of France. France is the only nation in modern Europe that has substantial power and is very volatile and emotional and is also known for its physical and sexual appetites.

Many modern encyclopedias, when they describe the French, use the same term "instability" as Genesis 49 uses to describe Reuben in the latter days. The word "French" has become synonymous with passion and physical sexual appetites. "French" is a common adjective for nouns associated with sexuality and eroticism (French perfume, French kisses, French films, French-cut fashions).

The French, or Reubenites are a people associated with satisfying the physical appetites for food and drink, as well as sexual desires. Gourmet food and drink have long been associated with the French chefs and French cuisine includes the world famous French wines. France greatly displayed her Reubenite trait in World War II. When pressured by Hitler's armies, they quickly yielded and chose to coexist with the Nazi government rather than continue to oppose it. In fact, they even fought sea battles against the United States in the Mediterranean Sea when the American ships were trying to land in North Africa. Many of you saw the movie *Casablanca*, which showed how the French were in bed with Germany, trying to appease both sides. Just as their forefather Reuben yielded to his brothers' pressures to lie to their father about Joseph's fate, instead of opposing what he knew to be wrong, the French fully cooperated with the Nazis rather than continue to oppose what they knew to be wrong.

SIMEON AND LEVI

Genesis 49:5–7, "Simeon and Levi are brethren; instruments of cruelty are in their habitations. O my soul, come not thou into their secret; unto their assembly, mine honour, be not thou united: for in their anger they slew a man, and in their selfwill they digged down a wall. Cursed be their anger, for it was fierce; and their wrath, for it was cruel: I will divide them in Jacob, and scatter them in Israel."

The tribes of Levi and Simeon will not have their own nation in the last days. Notice that God said that He would divide them in Jacob and scatter them in Israel. The Levites were not given a land to possess because God intended to use them as the teachers and religious leaders of the nation. Their inheritance was to be the 10% tithe from all the other tribes for their service to Israel.

> And the LORD spake unto Aaron, Thou shalt have no inheritance in their land, neither shalt thou have any part among them: I am thy part and thine inheritance among the children of Israel. And, behold, I have given the children of Levi all the tenth in Israel for an inheritance, for their service which they serve, even the

service of the tabernacle of the congregation. Neither must the children of Israel henceforth come nigh the tabernacle of the congregation, lest they bear sin, and die. But the Levites shall do the service of the tabernacle of the congregation, and they shall bear their iniquity: it shall be a statute for ever throughout your generations, that among the children of Israel they have no inheritance. But the tithes of the children of Israel, which they offer as an heave offering unto the LORD, I have given to the Levites to inherit: therefore I have said unto them, Among the children of Israel they shall have no inheritance. (Numbers 18:20–24)

Therefore, the Levites were scattered throughout all the tribes of Israel as the priests and teachers of the people. With the dividing of Israel into two separate countries during the reign of Solomon's son, Rehoboam, most of the Levites migrated back into Judah and remained there with the Jews and the Benjaminites. These three tribes made up the population of the Kingdom of Judah prior to its fall circa 586 BC.

The ultimate fall of the nation of Judah (Judea) came many years later in 70 AD when the Roman general Titus was victorious over the nation of Judea, composed of Jews, Levites and Benjaminites. Notice, Paul tells us in Romans 11:1 that he was of the tribe of Benjamin. At that time, the Jews, the Levites and the Benjaminites still occupied the area of Judea. With the conquest of Judea, the Jews and the Levites were dispersed into many areas bordering the Mediterranean Sea. History records that large enclaves of Jews were established in Spain and remained prominent in their society until 1492 when they were cast out of Spain; most of those who remained became Catholics, rejecting their Jewish heritage.

Simeon, like Levi, was also dispersed throughout the land of Israel. However, most of the Simeonites remained with the Ten Northern Tribes and they were taken into captivity and cast out of the land with the fall of Samaria in 720 BC. The Simeonites traveled in conjunction with their other brother Israelites and they portrayed a proclivity for violence and fighting. Notice these verses in the Moffat translation: Verse 5–7, "Simeon and Levi are a pair: their plots are ruthless stabs. Their plans, my soul, never shares; heart of mine join not their counsel! For men they murder in their ire and wantonly disable oxen. A curse on their ire so fierce! A curse on their rage so cruel! I will disperse them throughout Jacob and scatter them over Israel."

A reference in the *Living Bible* indicates that Levi and Simeon maimed oxen just for fun. This prophecy in Genesis 49 clearly shows that God would not allow these two tribes to become sovereign nations in the last days because of their wasteful and ruthless ways. God said their descendants would be scattered among all the other tribes of Israel and their inclination to warfare would surely draw many of them into the military services of the nations of Israel. Today, many Simeonites and Levites populate the mountainous regions of the United States, because the lay of the land is so much like it was in Scotland and Ireland, from where they came.

JUDAH

Genesis 49:8–10, "Judah, thou art he whom thy brethren shall praise: thy hand shall be in the neck of thine enemies; thy father's children shall bow down before thee. Judah is a lion's whelp: from the prey, my son, thou art gone up: he stooped down, he couched as a lion, and as an old lion; who shall rouse him up? The sceptre shall not depart from Judah, nor a lawgiver from between his feet, until Shiloh come; and unto him shall the gathering of the people be."

The Jews were also scattered throughout the world as a result of the loss of their homeland in 70 AD. However, since 1947, many Jews have returned to their Middle Eastern home and have labeled their small country "Israel." While the Jews were part of Israel, they should more properly be called Judah or Judea as it was in the time of Christ.

Another striking point about Judah is that it is like the power of a lion as noted in verse 9, and his symbol was to be the lion. The so-called "star of David" is not the proper symbol for the nation of the Jews. The "star of David" actually found its way into the modern Jewish culture as a result of the fall of the Khazar Empire circa 965 AD. The Khazars embraced Judaism when they found themselves a buffer state between the expansion of Islam and the established European nations of Christianity. In order to survive, they chose to embrace Judaism as their official religion rather than the religion of Mohammed or the Christians. In the Twelfth Century, a Khazar patriot by the name of Solomon Ben Duji claimed that he was the Messiah and he assumed the name of David al-Roy and his sign was the six-pointed star that adorns the modern Israeli (Jewish) flag. This six-pointed Star of David al-Roy was attributed to King David in the mystic and ethereal German writings from the Thirteenth Century and appeared on the Jewish flag in Prague in 1527 AD. (Coestler 136–137)

Genesis 49:10 also indicates that the descendants of Judah would be ruling kings until Shiloh returns, referring to the return of Jesus Christ. As we have pointed out before, the ruling house of England traces its lineage back to King David and their official emblem includes the *lion!* The ruling houses of Europe were all related and they were Jews. (Allen)

ZEBULUN

Genesis 49:13, "Zebulun shall dwell at the haven of the sea; and he shall be for a haven of ships; and his border shall be unto Zidon."

This verse plainly indicates that Zebulun will be living next to the sea and will rely heavily on ships for its survival. The Dutch were terrific sailors and set up the Dutch East India Company to bring spices to Europe from India and the East Indies. A dictionary definition for the word *haven* includes the alternate meanings of "any shelter, safe place; refuge and a port or harbor." Any student of European history will realize that the nation of Holland or the Netherlands is one that has been created from the ocean by moving earth to create livable land. The Netherlands is literally sheltered from the sea by its huge dike system which allows the people to live on the land without the fear of excessive flooding.

In modern times, the Dutch port of Rotterdam has been the busiest seaport in the world. According to the *Encyclopedia Americana*, "Its port in volume of freight handled is the busiest in the world ... In addition to foreign trade, the port handles the huge barge traffic that is carried on the Rhine River and associated waterways ... The port now extends continuously from Rotterdam to the sea." Many of the early American settlers from central Europe came up the Rhine River to Rotterdam to book passage to the new lands because the period of the Thirty Years' War created such havoc in their homeland of central Europe. There was war, pillaging, raping, pestilence, famine, and religious persecution. To escape this, many of the central European, Germanic peoples, some of whom were Israelites, made their way to these United States, Israel.

Rotterdam has now become a gateway by the sea to Europe through its system of connecting canals into the European mainland. The Netherlands perfectly fulfills the Biblical prophecy about the modern seacoast that is sheltered from the sea and is a major seaport for all of Europe.

ISSACHAR

Genesis 49:14, "Issachar is a strong ass couching down between two burdens: And he saw that rest was good, and the land that it was pleasant; and bowed his shoulder to bear, and became a servant unto tribute."

Issachar was Jacob's son by his first wife Leah. With the fall of Israel in 720 BC, the tribe of Issachar migrated north up through Russia and ultimately came to their final resting place which is between two world powers of the West and the East. The people of Finland are the modern-day descendants of Issachar and they have long been a buffer zone between stronger and competing sections of the world. In the 1700 and 1800s, Finland was caught between Russia and Sweden who fought for control over Finland. During the Twentieth Century, Finland's sovereignty was regularly compromised by Russian domination over Finnish officials. The Russian language was forced upon the Finns. They were ultimately under the control of the Tsar who required an annual tribute to be paid to Russia. Finland has long been known as a buffer zone between the Western and Eastern bloc as indicated in the prophecy that she would be a strong donkey crouching down between two great burdens.

DAN

Genesis 49:16–17, "Dan shall judge his people, as one of the tribes of Israel. Dan shall be a serpent by the way, an adder in the path, that biteth the horse heels, so that his rider shall fall backward."

The Tribe of Dan is the easiest of all the Israelites to identify because of their proclivity to name all of the places where they have traveled or lived by the name of their forefather, Dan. Verse 17 indicates that Dan will be like a serpent going through the sand, leaving his trail as he moves. The Danites certainly have accomplished this which is a major proof as to where the rest of his Israelite brothers settled.

Dan, like Judah, Levi and Simeon, also was scattered throughout the Israelites. However, there is one country in the world which actually goes by the name Dan and that is Dan Mark, or as we call it in the English, Denmark. Danites are also found in Ireland and their descendants in America. Many Danites become judges and policemen.

GAD

Genesis 49:19, "Gad, a troop shall overcome him: but he shall overcome at the last."

According to this scripture, it would seem that Gad is the only Israelite tribe prophesied to be severely injured during the latter days. The Hebrew word for troop also means "an invading force." To find the location of Gad, we must look for a European nation which "during the latter days" is able to survive in spite of enemies surrounding it. The only way for that nation to have survived in the face of all of her enemies meant that she had to become neutral. This leaves us with the nation of Switzerland which is made up of people from many different nations such as Germany, France, and Italy. These people have been able to come together in this small mountainous nation and forge out a country that escapes battles, but has actually been settled by many of these ethnic groups who were, in fact, descendants of Gad dispersed into other nations.

ASHER

Genesis 49:20, "Out of Asher his bread shall be fat, and he shall yield royal dainties."

When you first read this prophecy, it seems to be disjointed and without any real meaning. However, the phrase "his bread shall be fat" indicates prosperity. But, there are many nations in the world that have prosperity; therefore, we must do some additional searching. The real clue lies in the statement "royal dainties." The word "royal" is based on the Hebrew word "melek" which means literally "a king." The word "yield" comes from a Hebrew word literally meaning "to give" and the Hebrew word translated "dainties" also means "delight or delightful."

The tribe of Asher is actually split between two Western European countries, Belgium and Luxemburg. These two European countries are noted for their delightful pastries that have been enjoyed by kings and their courts throughout Europe.

NAPHTALI

Genesis 49:21, "Naphtali is a hind let loose: he giveth goodly words."

History records the tribe of Naphtali as the people of Ephthalite or Nephthalite, Huns and they were also known as "white Huns" because they were members of the fair-skinned Caucasian race. The striking similarity between Israelite Naphtalites and the Asian Ephthalites is obvious. The fact that Naphtali went into captivity as a whole unit, rather than piece-meal, likely explains why they continued to be known by their Israelite tribal name as late as the Sixth Century AD. The prophesy about Naphtali "hind let loose" refers to a female deer known as a hind. The words "let loose" implies a condition of being liberated or active in the wild. Female deer are most active in the wild during the mating season and this prophecy seems to imply that the females of Naphtali will be identified by their sexual sensuality in the latter days. Sweden has the reputation of being a sexually open country with the women liberated from sexual bonds. Blonde, Swedish women have a reputation for beauty and have been "made" prominent sex goddesses in the movie industry, contributing to the image that "blondes have more fun." The term "fair young maiden" in ancient prose meant a "blonde girl." Fair meant fair skin and fair hair, and the Swedes certainly have been considered the most beautiful in the world.

Sweden is also the country that sponsors the Nobel Prizes which are given for many outstanding achievements in various fields. The prize is presented with a very pleasing pronouncement of "goodly words" to the recipient.

BENJAMIN

Genesis 49:27, "Benjamin shall ravin as a wolf: in the morning he shall devour the prey, and at night he shall divide the spoil."

Benjamin was the youngest son of Jacob and Rachel and the only full brother of Joseph. The Benjaminites were almost totally exterminated because of their foolhardy war-like activities against the other tribes. A civil war that just about destroyed them is discussed in Judges 19:21.

Benjamin was a tribe of fierce fighters, and did not hesitate to attack those who were superior to them militarily. The Benjaminites also became a seafaring people and were fierce attackers of their neighboring countries using specially designed boats for speed and maneuverability. The scripture refers to Benjamin being like a ravenous wolf, devouring its prey. Wolves are most commonly found in northern climates indicating that Benjamin's latter-day territory would be in the northern latitudes. The only European nation in a northern latitude not yet identified as one of the tribes of Israel is Norway. Therefore, Norway was the Viking home of the Benjaminites after they came to their final settling place after the fall of both Israel and Judah. The Vikings attacked and settled colonies among the other Israelite tribes in Ireland; York, England; and Normandy, France. In fact, William the Conqueror was of Viking descent because some of his Viking ancestors from Norway settled earlier in Normandy, France.

This brief discussion identifies all of the thirteen tribes of the nation of Israel and their present-day location. As we have previously stated, for one to truly comprehend prophecy, it is necessary to know who the people are that the prophecy is addressing. The prophecies directed only toward Israel are essentially prophecies directed at Great Britain and the United States. The prophecies directed toward Judah are those intended for the Jews who live in the Middle East in the small Jewish nation called Israel. The prophecies that include the whole house of Israel are for all thirteen tribes of the Israelites.

PROPHECY CONCERNING AMERICA AND GREAT BRITAIN

As we have stated before, God imposed a punishment of 2520 years against the Northern Kingdom of Israel, which began when Samaria fell circa 720 BC. The 2520-year punishment directly relating to America and Britain ended circa 1800 AD. The last 200 years attest to the fact that God restored His Blessings upon Ephraim and Manasseh, as proclaimed by Israel in Genesis 48–49. God blessed our two nations in spite of the fact that we have been ignorant regarding our identity, and have continued in the sin of idolatry begun by King Jeroboam shortly after the split-up of the nation of Israel upon the death of King Solomon.

Most people make a very wrong assumption regarding how God views sins. Too many times people assume that God is overlooking their sins because He does not immediately react. The Bible plainly says that God is slow to anger and willing to give us plenty of time to repent. However, God does have limits. When it becomes indisputably obvious that the nation will not repent, God has few alternatives except to punish the nation, which will ultimately cause a general repentance among the survivors. The immediate future of America and Britain, according to Biblical prophecies, provides a foreboding picture of bad news and terrible calamities to be brought upon our people.

ACTUAL STATISTICS

When you look at the actual statistics of wealth in the United States and Britain, compared to the rest of the world, it becomes clearly obvious that God has blessed the descendants of Joseph practically beyond all measure. But, it is also clear those blessings are dwindling. Back in 1921, it was obvious to many American industrialists such as Charles M. Schwab, in his speech before the Massachusetts Bankers Association, "Our United States has been endowed by God with everything to make it and keep it the foremost industrial and commercial nation of the world."

When you consider the world's petroleum output in the Mid-twentieth Century, around 1950, there were almost 3,800,000,000 barrels of oil being produced at that time. Of this total, the United States alone produced more than half of the total output. Together the United States and Britain and her colonies produced 60% of the crude petroleum for the world's consumption. However, by the year 1966, the year the British Colonial office in London closed its doors, marking the official death of the British Empire, that 60% had been reduced to 32%.

The United States and Britain mined one and one-half times as much coal as all of the other nations combined, but by 1966 the United States portion had shrunk to less than one third of the world's production, down to 30.9%.

The countries that composed the British Commonwealth and America produced in 1950 three-fourths of the world's steel. The United States alone produced almost 60% of the world's steel production in 1951. We produced one and one-third times as much pig iron as all the other nations combined. By 1966, U.S. steel production had dropped to 33% and pig iron had dropped to 17.8%.

America, Britain and especially Canada produced 95% of the world's nickel supply, 80% of the world's aluminum and 75% of the zinc products, which are absolutely essential in an industrial society. However, after 1966, the United States, Great Britain and Canada produced only about 3.6% of the world's nickel, 40.2% of its aluminum and 12.4% of its zinc.

In 1950, when Britain was in control and dominated the area of South Africa, they completely controlled all of the chromium mined and produced in the world. Together Britain and America produced two-thirds of the world's rubber and dominated the world's copper, lead, tin and other precious metal outputs. By the end of 1966 and the latter part of the Twentieth Century, combined, they only produced 2.3% of the world's chromium, 23.4% of its copper, 9.9% of its lead, no tin, and 6.3% of its bauxite.

Britain and its Commonwealth produced two-thirds of the world's gold up until about 1950. The United States had three times as much gold reserves as the total of the rest of the world. By 1966 and the latter part of the Twentieth Century, the U.S. gold supply had been drained so much that the dollar standard was changed, taking away gold and silver for its backing.

The United States produces and utilizes two-thirds of the world's output of electricity. Britain and Canada, even though they are much smaller in population, outstripped Russia, Germany and France combined in producing and utilizing electricity!

Up until the 1970s, Great Britain and the United States possessed well over half of the world's merchant marine fleet tonnage. By 1980, that figure was well below 30%! Prior to 1970, the British Isles constructed more vessels for the sea than any other place on the earth. By the year 2000, at least two Gentile nations have out-stripped Britain and America in ship building.

In 1950, the United States possessed over half of the world's railroad mileage. Today, as we have seen the American railroads decline dramatically, they now account for less than 25% of the world's total rail mileage.

Prior to 1970, the United States alone produced 73% of all the automobiles in the world. By the beginning of the Twenty-first Century, Japan, Germany, France and Italy have made such huge gains until the Big Three only include two manufacturers from the United States. GM and Ford are the only two auto giants left. Some economic forecasters believe that the Japanese auto industry will ultimately buy out Ford and possibly GM.

THE GREAT TRIBULATION

America and Britain and, yes, a good portion of Western Europe, are going to face a Tribulation so severe that, unless God steps in and intervenes, all flesh on the face of the earth will be destroyed. Christ spoke of this Tribulation in Matthew 24:21–22, "For then shall be great tribulation, such as was not since the beginning of the world to this time, no, nor ever shall be. And except those days should be shortened, there should no flesh be saved: but for the elect's sake those days shall be shortened."

The message Christ brought was a message about the establishment of the Kingdom of God and the restoration of the nation of Israel as a great nation, even surpassing Israel during the time of King David and King Solomon. However, before the Restoration of Israel as that single great nation by which God will lead all people to Himself, Israel is first going to be severely punished almost to the point of extinction before they finally come to their senses and repent.

AMERICA AND BRITAIN DESTROYED

Believe it or not, the Bible clearly states that God intends to allow an almost total destruction of the modern-day Israelites, namely Great Britain and the United States. The prophecies foretell the beginning of a Great Tribulation which will see America and Britain punished drastically for three and one-half years. A description of this prophecy can be found in Hosea 4 where God plainly shows the reasons why we, the Americans and the British people, are going to face the wrath of God. Notice Chapter 4:1 and replace "Israel" with America and Britain.

THE ASSYRIANS

The Assyrians are prophesied to play a big part in the punishment of Israel just as they did in 720 BC. We have been able to discover the modern-day location of the Israelites; we can also find the modern-day location of the Assyrians.

The Assyrians moved the Israelites out of their land and repopulated Israel's land with some of their people and other Gentiles from the countries surrounding the Ten Northern Tribes. The Assyrian Empire continued to flourish until about 710 BC, when it was defeated and driven out of their land, just as they had driven the Israelites from their homeland.

Like the Israelites, they followed the same migration their conquered foes had followed when they were dispersed out of their land in 720 BC. The Assyrians and the Israelites migrated north and westward across Europe. The Assyrians did not continue their westward march, but remained a thorn in the side of the Israelites, forcing them to move farther west. The Assyrians were, in fact, the Germanic Teutonic tribes that settled in Germany, Austria, parts of Switzerland, and central Europe. Today, the modern-day Germanic tribes of Germany and Austria are the descendants of the ancient Assyrian Empire.

Since that time, God has used Assyria as His "rod of anger"

to punish Israel in World War I and World War II, led by the European Germanic people in these two great wars. Unfortunately for America and Britain, these two world wars, which inflicted great punishment, especially on Britain and to a lesser degree on America, did not cause our people to reject the idolatry and false teachings that we cling to so dearly. There will be yet a World War III in which Germany and her allies, the New World Order, will be victorious over the tribes of Israel, including the Jews now located in a small country by the name of Israel.

THE PUNISHMENT WILL INTENSIFY

We have seen in the Twentieth and now the Twenty-first Century that Ephraim (America) and Manasseh (Great Britain) continue to refuse to turn to God in complete obedience.

Before the September 11, 2001, attack on the United States, people did not believe America was vulnerable to an outside attack. But now, people are beginning to realize that we too can suffer devastation as the nations of Europe and Britain did during World War II.

Open your eyes to the fact that Britain's sun has already set and now *America's sun is on the horizon near the time for its setting*. God promised in Leviticus 26 a terrible destruction will be upon us because of our rebellion and disobedience to His Laws and Statues.

Notice what He says.

> But if ye will not hearken unto me, and will not do all these commandments; And if ye shall despise my statutes, or if your soul abhor my judgments, so that ye will not do all my commandments, but that ye break my covenant: I also will do this unto you; I will even appoint over you terror, consumption, and the burning ague, that shall consume the eyes, and cause sorrow of heart: and ye shall sow your seed in vain, for your enemies shall eat it. And I will set my face against you,

and ye shall be slain before your enemies: they that hate you shall reign over you; and ye shall flee when none pursueth you. And if ye will not yet for all this hearken unto me, then I will punish you seven times more for your sins. (Leviticus 26:14–18)

God is going to intensify His Punishment upon us so greatly that He will bring a sword upon our land that will literally bring our nation to its knees and kill one-third of our population. Notice Leviticus 26:25, "And I will bring a sword upon you, that shall avenge the quarrel of my covenant: and when ye are gathered together within your cities, I will send the pestilence among you; and ye shall be delivered into the hand of the enemy."

In addition to the sword, He is also going to bring famine and pestilence to ensure that the remaining two-thirds who survive the enemy attack will be punished and die because of continued stiff-necked, stubborn ways. Verse 26 is referring to famine. "And when I have broken the staff of your bread, ten women shall bake your bread in one oven, and they shall deliver you your bread again by weight: and ye shall eat, and not be satisfied."

Also notice that cannibalism will result because of the great famine we are going to face. Verse 29, "And ye shall eat the flesh of your sons, and the flesh of your daughters shall ye eat."

Finally, those who do survive will be taken captive and scattered throughout the world as slaves. Leviticus 26:32–33, "And I will bring the land into desolation: and your enemies which dwell therein shall be astonished at it. And I will scatter you among the heathen, and will draw out a sword after you: and your land shall be desolate, and your cities waste."

WHO WILL BE RESPONSIBLE?

The Bible plainly shows that a new, world-ruling government with a single leader at its head will be responsible for these terrible acts of devastation brought upon America, Britain, and many other parts of the world. Notice Revelation 13:1, "And I stood upon the sand of the sea, and saw a beast rise up out of the sea, having seven heads and ten horns, and upon his horns ten crowns, and upon his heads the name of blasphemy."

This individual is described also in Daniel 8:11–12, "Yea, he magnified himself even to the prince of the host, and by him the daily sacrifice was taken away, and the place of his sanctuary was cast down. And an host was given him against the daily sacrifice by reason of transgression, and it cast down the truth to the ground; and it practised, and prospered."

The prince spoken of here will be the one the Bible calls the Beast; his reign will last for a period of forty-two months. Notice Revelation 13:5, "And there was given unto him a mouth speaking great things and blasphemies; and power was given unto him to continue forty and two months."

The concept of ten world rulers is also discussed in Daniel 7:7, "After this I saw in the night visions, and behold a fourth beast, dreadful and terrible, and strong exceedingly; and it had great iron teeth: it devoured and brake in pieces, and stamped the residue with the feet of it: and it was diverse from all the beasts that were before it; and it had ten horns." The ten horns are defined in Verse 24, "And the ten horns out of this kingdom are ten kings that shall arise:"

This great new world government will turn out to be the greatest curse man has ever known. This is a government sponsored in secret by Satan himself as a last-ditch effort to destroy God's Chosen People. Notice Matthew 24:22 in which Christ plainly shows that He will intervene in order to protect those whom He has called out, the few chosen ones.

CHRIST WILL RETURN AS A CONQUERING HERO

Christ will return during the sounding of the Seventh Trumpet by the Angel mentioned in Revelation 11, which coincides with the Resurrection of the saints to become part of God's returning army led by Jesus Christ Himself. Revelation 19 describes this great and powerful army of God returning to deal with this new world Assyrian leader, known as the Beast, and his powerful army in what is commonly referred to as the Battle of Armageddon.

> And I saw the beast, and the kings of the earth, and their armies, gathered together to make war against him that sat on the horse, and against his army. And the beast was taken, and with him the false prophet that wrought miracles before him, with which he deceived them that had received the mark of the beast, and them that worshipped his image. These both were cast alive into a lake of fire burning with brimstone. And the remnant were slain with the sword of him that sat upon the horse, which sword proceeded out of his mouth: and all the fowls were filled with their flesh. (Revelation 19:19–21)

This battle will bring an end to man's government and his ability to wage war against his fellow man. This event is the beginning of the Kingdom of God and the Millennial Rule of Christ on this earth for 1000 years. King David will be, once again, on the throne over a United Israel as the leading nation under the Kingdom of God. This time, Israel will fulfill her original mission she completely failed to accomplish under the Old Covenant. At this time, Israel will set the example for human living and will be the guide to the Gentiles for proper living under God's Laws.

THE GOOD NEWS

Israel will be saved at last! After the battle and the destruction of the Beast, the Bible says God will set about a second time to recover Israel and restore her to a greatness as never before. Notice this promise.

> Therefore, behold, the days come, saith the LORD, that it shall no more be said, The LORD liveth, that

brought up the children of Israel out of the land of Egypt; But, The LORD liveth, that brought up the children of Israel from the land of the north, and from all the lands whither he had driven them: and I will bring them again into their land that I gave unto their fathers. (Jeremiah 16:14–15)

God shows where His people have been taken as captives in Isaiah 11:11, but God will bring the small remnant of Israel back to its original land in the Middle East to begin building a great nation. At this time, the stiff-necked Israelites will have been so humbled that now they are willing and ready to follow the God of Israel and be obedient.

And in that day thou shalt say, O LORD, I will praise thee: though thou wast angry with me, thine anger is turned away, and thou comfortedst me. Behold, God is my salvation; I will trust, and not be afraid: for the LORD Jehovah is my strength and my song; he also is become my salvation. Therefore with joy shall ye draw water out of the wells of salvation. And in that day shall ye say, Praise the LORD, call upon his name, declare his doings among the people, make mention that his name is exalted. Sing unto the LORD; for he hath done excellent things: this is known in all the earth. Cry out and shout, thou inhabitant of Zion: for great is the Holy One of Israel in the midst of thee. (Isaiah 12:1–6)

Truly God is going to spare His people to the amazement of the rest of the world, and for a thousand years He will have His eyes upon the Israelite nation working to bring them prosperity and to make them truly His sons, as Jesus Christ is now His Son.

CONCLUSION

For thousands of years, the true Israelites have believed that they were Gentiles and that only Jews were Israelites. What a pity that we have missed out on many blessings from God because we did not know who we were or where we came from. Now, at last, *our true national identity* has been revealed.

BIBLIOGRAPHY

Allen, J.H. 1902. *Judah's Sceptre and Joseph's Birthright* 19*th* Ed. Destiny, Merrimac, MA.

Bede. *Ecclesiastical History of the English Nation.*

Berry, W.G. 1978. *Foxes Book of Martyrs.* Baker Book House, Grand Rapids.

Boyd, Moody. 1945. *Israel.* Louisville.

Capt, E. Raymond. 1983. *The Traditions of Glastonbury.* Artisan, CA. 1983.

Canon, A.B.R. Rev. *Traditions of Ireland.*

Castle. *History of England.*

Chartwell Books Inc. 1977. *Early Civilization.* Great Britain.

Coestler, Arthur. 1976. *The Thirteenth Tribe.* Random House, NY.

Colles, Ramsay. 1919. *The History of Ulster.* Greshaam Publishers, London.

Collier, William F. 1707. *Ecclesiastical History of Great Britain, Vol.* 1.

Curtis, Edmund. 1936. *A Hstory of Ireland.* Routledge, London.

Doomsday Survey Folio.

Doubleday 1987. *Great Events of Bible Times.*

Encyclopedia Britannica (11ᵗʰ Ed.).

Fell, Barry. 1986. *America* BC. Pocket Books, NY.

Fletcher, Ivor C. 1984. *The Incredible History of God's True Church.* Triumph Publishing Co. Altadema, CA.

Fuller. *The London Edition.* 1837, Vol. 1, Book 1, Sect. 13.

Gratten. *History of the Netherlands.*

Gibbs, R. 1988. *The Legendary* 12 *Hides of Glastonbury.* Llanerch Enterprises, Wales.

Herne's Edition. *King Arthur,* Vol.1.

Herodotus. *The Histories. Vol.* 1.

Hine, Edward.1874. *The British Nation Identified with the Lost Ten Tribes of Israel.* S.W. Partridge & Co. Manchester.

Hovedon, Roger. *English Chronicler,* Vol. 3.

King James Bible 1611. Cambridge Publishers, Cambridge.

Latham, R.G. *Ethnology of the British Isles.*

Laud, M.S. *The Bodleinn.*

Lawless, Emily. *Ireland.*

Lewis, L.S. 1922. *St. Joseph of Arimathea at Glastonbury.* James Clarke & Co., Ltd. Cambridge.

MacAlister, R.A.S. 1931. *Tara.* Chas. Scriber's Sons, NY.

MacKendrick, W.G. Lt. Col. 1925. *The Destiny of the British Empire and the USA*. Covenant Publishing.

Marx, G.O. *The Coronation Stone at Westminster*. Royal Research.

Milton, John. *History of Britain*.

Moller, L. 2002. *The Exodus Case*. Scandinavia Publishing House, Slovadia.

Moore, Thomas. 1835. *The History of Ireland*. Cabinet Cyclopaedia.

O'Flaherty, Roderick. *Ogyeia or a Chronological Account of Irish Events*.

Poole, Rev. W.H. 1921. *Fifty Reasons Why the Anglo-Saxons are Israelites*. Covenant Publishing Co. Ltd. London.

Pinnock, William. *Improved Edition of Dr. Goldsmith's History of Rome*.

Pryce, Dr. William. 1790. *Archaeologia Cornu-Britannica*. England.

Smith, Geo. LLD. 1863. *The Cassiterides*. Wm. Nichols, London.

Stanley, Dean, D.D. *Historical Memorials of Westminster Abbey*.

Staples, George F. Jowett. 1961. *The Drama of the Lost Disciples*. England.

Turner, Sharon. 1799. *The Story of the Anglo-Saxons*. England.

Wilson, J. 1851. *Lectures on Ancient Israel*. Daniels & Smith, Philadelphia.

Wood, Leon. 1970. *A Survey of Israel's History*. Zondervan Publishing, Grand Rapids.

INDEX

"God save the king"–110, 293–294
"queen of heaven" - 277
"seven times"–80, 179, 183, 221, 344–345, 381

A

C

D

I

J

K

Q

R

S

T

Z